Published by
Saurabh Publishing House

Advanced Educational Psychology

ADVANCED EDUCATIONAL PSYCHOLOGY

D. S. Gill

Saurabh
Publishing House
4263/3, Ansari Road,
Darya Ganj, New Delhi-110002

Published by :
SAURABH PUBLISHING HOUSE

Distributed by :
LOTUS PRESS
4263/3, Ansari Road, Darya Ganj, New Delhi-110002
Ph : 32903912, 23280047 • E-Mail : lotus_press@sify.com

Saurabh Publishing is an imprint of
Lotus Press

Advanced Educational Psychology

ISBN : 978-81-89005-40-5 (H/B)

Printed in India by Saras Graphics, Delhi

Preface

Educational psychology is the application of psychological findings in the field of education. Educational psychology is the systematic study in development of the individual within the educational setting. It helps the teacher to foster harmonious development of the student into a responsible and participating citizen, a sensitive and reflective human being, a productive and creative person.

Educational psychology is an applied discipline which combines the two different fields of education and psychology. It is the scientific study of human behaviour by which it can be understood, predicted and directed by education to achieve goals of life.

It is concerned primarily with learners and how they respond to various conditions they meet in school and life situations. It selects from the total field of psychology those facts and principles that have direct bearing upon the growth, learning and adjustment of children. More specifically, educational psychology is a study of human behaviour as it bears upon learning and teaching activities. It is an application of principles of general psychology to the problems of education.

This book deals with the topics of—*Introduction to Psychology of Education; Nature and Scope of Educational Psychology; Learning of Skills; Psychology of Creative*

Thinking; Intelligence Tests; Psychology of Growth and Development; Psychology of Achievement Tests; Personality; Child Behaviour and Treatment; Psychology of Learning; Individual Differences; Socialization and Its Role; etc.

I hope that students and those in the education field will find it useful for academic and competitive examinations. I owe a deep sense of gratitude to my publisher for materialising my present endeavour.

D. S. Gill

Contents

1

Introduction to Psychology of Education

The term psychology has come into common use. One hears the word used at the store counter, in the office, at the baseball game, and around the bridge table. Almost everyone familiar with the term considers himself an amateur psychologist. When the instructor reports the findings of some study, students frequently react with the expression, "Why, that's just plain common sense." A twenty-year-old college student reacted to a discussion of some problems connected with habit formation, "Why, I have known that all my life." This is, perhaps, to be expected. The subject matter of psychology is human behaviour, and everyone has observed human behaviour in many situations. Surely these personal observations are in a very large percentage of cases verifiable through experimental studies. However, the reason a formal science of psychology relying on experiments and a special vocabulary is necessary, that everyday observations are frequently colored by subjective states, such as feelings and emotions, likes and dislikes. Only through careful observations scientifically conducted can we determine whether an everyday observation is dependable.

Science and Common Sense

There are those who would rely on what is termed *common sense.* We should be concerned with the source of what we refer to as *common sense.* Concerning this Barnett has stated: "But as Einstein has pointed out, common sense is actually nothing more than a deposit of prejudices laid down in the mind prior to the age of eighteen. Every new idea one encounters in later years must combat this accretion of 'self evident' concepts."

Teachers have always had common-sense rules and principles to guide them in their activities, which they were sure were correct. We see this in the early reading primers and in the methods used in teaching reading. For example, common sense indicated that a child must first learn letters before he could learn words. Then, he must proceed to acquire a large word-reading vocabulary before he could be introduced to sentences. This was quite generally accepted as the correct and logical procedure to follow. In the *New England Primer* the alphabet was taught first, followed by letter combinations, such as *ab, ac, ad,* etc. This common-sense method of teaching reading continued until the reading process was scientifically studied. Careful observations showed that good readers do not notice each of the letters and syllables that make up a word, but take in whole words at a glance. The child, likewise, learns to use cues such as outline, pattern, beginnings and size to recognize words.

The Role of Psychology in Education

Education is possible because humans can learn. The plasticity of the growing child makes it possible to begin an instructional program during the early years of life. However, it is evident to observers of human learning that much learning takes place outside of school. Mary and Henry have already acquired a culture, which they bring with them, when they enter school. It is not, however, the function of educational psychology to determine why Mary and Henry should be required to go to school and what the goals of the school should be. This responsibility lies with the social and educational philosophers of the present age. Once these goals are determined, the contributions educational psychology can make are numerous.

Psychology and Educational Theory

A careful reading of the history of education in the United States shows that educational psychology has continuously made significant contributions to the theory and practice of education. Before the turn of the century William James had published his *Talks to Teachers.* The importance of psychology is vividly presented as follows:

Everywhere teaching must *agree* with the psychology, but need not necessarily be the only kind of teaching that would so agree; for many diverse methods of teaching may equally well agree with psychological laws....

But, if the use of psychological principles thus be negative rather than positive, it does not follow that it may not be a great use, all the same. It certainly narrows the path for experiments and trials. We know in advance, if we are psychologists, that certain methods will be wrong, so our psychology saves us from mistakes. It makes us, moreover, more clear as to what we are about.

John Dewey, American philosopher and educator, is also closely associated with American educational theory in this century, and E.L. Thorndike, another American, is also widely noted for his pioneer studies in educational psychology. The contributions educational psychologists have made to teaching have been instrumental in furnishing a sounder foundation for educational theory and practice.

Educational Psychology and Contemporary Practices

The vast amount of research conducted by educational psychologists and others continues to initiate important changes in the school curriculum and in instructional methods.

Frequently, however, a considerable gap exists between theory and practice. Therefore, an important function of educational psychology is to help bring educational practice more clearly into line with the results obtained from educational research. Many educational practices today definitely result from the applications of the methods and findings of general and educational psychology to educational problems. These may be noted as follows:

1. The development of the psychology of learning has furnished a guide for evaluating methods of teaching.
2. Developments in motivation have made teachers more sensitive to the need for motivating classroom learning.
3. Developments in child growth have made teachers sensitive to the problems children encounter at different stages in their growth. These developments have also caused teachers to focus their attention on all aspects of the child's development.
4. The increased understanding of transfer of training and mental discipline has continued to produce significant changes in the school curriculum and in methods of teaching.
5. The development and use of a wide variety of measuring instruments have brought into focus individual differences. This has led to an increased interest in individualizing the educational program.
6. The development and widespread use of educational statistics have led to more accurate interpretations of test data as well as of other data bearing on problems in education. This has led to a refinement of educational practices and to continued educational progress.

7. Developments in personality adjustment and mental hygiene have led to a reevaluation of classroom control and discipline. Teachers are now more sensitive to the needs and the personal-social-emotional problems of the children they encounter in the classroom and on the playground. These developments have also shown the crucial role of constructive interpersonal relationships between teacher and children to creating good personal adjustment.

Educational Psychology and Teaching

Three questions may be considered by the student of educational psychology. The first concerns the child or learner who is to be educated. The second deals with the educative process, while the third concerns man's need for specialized schooling in addition to the education he gets from everyday experiences.

The school as an institution exists to guide children in the development of skills, subject matter, attitudes, and behaviour patterns essential for effective living in a particular society. The teacher, therefore, has two major tasks: to help children learn as efficiently as possible the subject matter being studied, and to help them acquire those desirable personal and social behaviour patterns. Where religious education is part of the curriculum, the teacher's function is to nurture the child in the proper relationship to God. Since children need the teacher's guidance to learn, and since teaching may be defined as a set of actions directed to pupils, an important aim of educational psychology is to help teachers acquire understandings needed to guide children in their educational development.

Teaching is based upon the concept that children can learn. Although many studies dealing with the learning ability of children at different maturational stages have been conducted, considerable theoretical differences exist about the relative importance of heredity and environment in learning. Despite numerous studies this problem is still unresolved. The viewpoint presented throughout this book, however, is that the child is a product of the interaction of the human organism and various environmental forces and conditions. This viewpoint emphasizes the role of both heredity and environment—not one to the exclusion of the other. Certain principles have emerged from this viewpoint, an understanding of which is essential for a successful educational program. They are summarized here:

1. Heredity provides the broad basic pattern and sets the limit in the development of the various traits, characteristics, and abilities of the human organism.
2. Within the limits and broad pattern set by heredity, the human organism develops.
3. The human organism is remarkably plastic, making it possible for individuals very similar in their native endowment to develop in diverse ways.
4. Although the human organism is remarkably plastic, it is dependent upon the experiences provided for its development.
5. The optimum development of the human organism can only be attained under favorable environmental conditions existing from the beginning of life.

Educational Psychology and the Needs of Teachers

A study of the teacher's task reveals something of his needs. Teachers cannot safely imitate others or depend upon trial-and-error in their teaching. It was pointed out two decades ago that, "Good teachers will know how to select subject matter suitable to the children with whom they work, and how to present it in ways that will make it likely that it will be genuinely absorbed."

A great many studies have been made dealing with the problems for the teachers encounter. One author summarized the results of thirty-one studies involving thousands of teachers-male and female, experienced and inexperienced, rural and urban-who listed their most pressing problems. They show that problems of individual differences, teaching methods, discipline, motivation, directed study, organization of materials, classroom procedures and many miscellaneous difficulties in the teaching-learning-testing process, rather than knowledge of additional subject matter were their main concern. An earlier study by Davis showed that motivation, testing and evaluation, diagnosing and correcting difficulties, modes of presentation, and individual differences ranked among the five most frequently mentioned difficulties at the elementary, junior-high, and senior-high school levels.

Teachers everywhere are confronted with tasks and problems having a common psychological basis. Some of these will be considered in the following discussions. We need to understand clearly how children learn and what the school, particularly the teacher, can do to foster these learnings. Every teacher should have a conscious, consistent set of principles and beliefs about how children learn.

In addition to understanding how children learn, teachers need knowledge and information about growth and the characteristics of children at different age levels. Closely related to this second need, to which educational psychology contributes, is the need for knowledge and skills involved in studying children. Varied techniques have been developed and made usable for studying school-age children. Through the use of these techniques teachers gain a better understanding of particular children.

A fourth need of teachers for which educational psychology attempts to provide assistance is to evaluate the outcomes of different learning procedures and programs.

Teachers should be able to develop particular tools for their needs as well as make use of tools already available for studying the changes that have taken place in learners and for determining whether these changes are sufficient in amount and quality for each learner involved.

These needs require that students of education and teachers have an extensive working knowledge of the experimental findings and contributions of psychology to growth, learning, motivation, and adjustment of school-age individuals. Such knowledge furnishes the teacher with a basis for evaluating and trying out different techniques in learning situations. A method of teaching out of harmony with proved learning principles is unsound, a waste of time to the teacher, and unfair to the learner.

Psychology and Educational Research

The science of psychology has not yet reached the stage of maturity whereby it can present a unified, coherent, and generally acceptable set of principles of learning, motivation, and adjustment. However, scientific studies have furnished useful information to teachers and others concerned with guiding and motivating pupils in learning situations. Educational psychology has furnished teachers and students of education with the informational background and scientific methods for studying pupils and evaluating different educational practices.

This book incorporates recent research on problems dealing with children and adolescents in learning situations. Such research will provide us with additional information and encourage keener insight into many educational problems.

Problems and exercises are presented at the end of each chapter. They will require further reading, reflective thinking, and in some cases, a limited amount of research on your part.

As students of educational psychology you should be alert to the problems presented and discussed in the text. They should furnish you not only with useful information, but should also help you to develop scientific attitudes and methods of solving educational and psychological problems. Successful teachers are always trying out new materials and techniques in their classroom activities in an effort to improve their teaching, and thus further the learning and adjustment of their pupils. They are participating increasingly in research projects as part of their educational activities.

PSYCHOLOGY AND THE EDUCATIVE PROCESS

The sciences concerned with human behaviour, learning, and adjustment have advanced sufficiently to be of real service to those concerned with the educative process. The human organism, unlike other organisms, is equipped by nature to acquire cultural patterns of behaviour and to modify the existing culture in harmony with his needs. The function of the educative process is to promote or facilitate desirable changes in the organism. These changes are necessary if the individual is to function effectively in his environment. The emerging personality of the child, discussed in Part V of this text, is to a marked degree a product of varying educational influences, although the student of educational psychology should realize at all times that educational influences are limited by what the child inherits.

The student of educational psychology is faced with the task of applying the materials and methods of psychology to the education of individuals in the classroom and elsewhere. It is the purpose of this chapter to furnish the student with an understanding of *(1)* the relationship between the organism and his environment, *(2)* the learner in relation to the educative process, *(3)* forces influencing the educative process, and *(4)* the role of the teacher in the educative process.

Organism and His Environment

Since every child is born into a culture or perhaps, in a more exact sense, into multiple cultures, it is important to study the two forces and conditions affecting his growth and learning. The first deals with heredity. What does the child bring genetically into the world? The second deals with the influences of his environment upon his development. Considerable controversy still exists over the influence of heredity and environment upon the growing child. Brief descriptions of the roles of heredity and environmental conditions upon the individual should give the student of educational psychology a better understanding of the developmental processes operating on the school-age child.

Genetic Factors in Development

The development of the individual begins with the fertilization of the egg cell. In this process of development the original fertilized ovum divides and subdivides until thousands of cells have been produced. From the moment of the fertilization of the egg cell, the new life is influenced by various environmental stimuli, which help to mold the potentialities for growth and learning which are inherited from the parents. Regardless of how heredity is defined, psychologists agree that the genes play an important role in development. Geneticists have found that coded instructions for growth and development are inherited through the nuclei of egg and sperm when they unite to begin the history of the living organism. These instructions are then perpetuated throughout the organism's lifetime when cells divide and specialize. Thus, it may be said that the infant is patterned by both hereditary and environmental influences from the moment of birth. His inherited gene structure is an important determinant of the kind of biological potential with which he starts life. This inheritance will be important in determining the extent to which his abilities and characteristics emerge later in interaction with his environment.

Considerable research has been carried on in an effort to ascertain the relative importance of heredity and environment. Much of this research has employed the co-twin method—an attempt to control the influence of heredity by selecting identical twins for study. Since heredity is thus assumed to be constant, the environment becomes the variable and any differences appearing in the twins are ascribed to environmental influences. In other studies, particularly those with animals, the physical and physiological environments are held as constant as possible, and the effects of differences due to heredity are observed. A number of studies have utilized siblings and identical twins who were reared apart to determine the effect of environmental forces. Although such studies have furnished useful information about the roles heredity and environment play in the individual's development, they have oversimplified the operation of these forces and have implied that they operate independently in the child's development.

The Influence of Heredity. Although authorities fail to agree on the relative amount of influence the biological inheritance exerts on the development of a given individual, it is commonly agreed that the individual's inheritance sets limits within which he can achieve his potential. The influence of heredity may be noted in the baby's general characteristics. He is born tall or short, with a narrow or broad body build, small or large ears, and blue-gray or dark eyes. The different combination of genes from his parents determine, in the main, his general physical appearance at birth.

We do not expect the child who is mentally or physically handicapped to perform like the child who is not handicapped. We do not expect many children with musical talent to develop into Beethovens, but simply, to develop within their limits.

This does not mean that the child with average musical talent cannot learn to participate in musical activities; he can develop within the limits set by his heredity. Exploiting his full potentiality would enable him to take part in a wide range of musical activities.

Interaction of Heredity and Environment. Environment has sometimes been regarded as a passive place in which an individual's behaviour and growth occurs. Such a view regards the environment as a setting for behaviour and growth, rather than as an active stimulating agent. The child enters into a world of people, things, ideas, attitudes, and values. He grows and develops according to certain fundamental principles. The type of adult he becomes will depend upon the interaction of various environmental influences upon him as a living and maturing organism. Although American culture offers children born into it both differences and similarities in opportunities, family life, neighbourhoods, religious beliefs, discipline, social strata, attitudes, and values, an identical background for two children is not found even in the same family with identical twins. Each individual's environment is as unique as his individual self because he not only responds selectively to the forces within him and about him, but he also gives those constantly selected elements a particular interpretation coloured by his past experiences, his organic make-up, his specific needs, and the level of his maturational development.

The most widely recognized principle involving the operation of heredity and environment upon the individual is that there is a continuous interaction between the two factors. The tendency of early investigators to ascribe a certain percent of the individual's development to heredity and a certain percent to environment met with many difficulties. It became apparent to many researchers concerned with such problems that the two forces are so closely related that behaviour and growth could not be separated or exclusively classified under either one of the two categories. Functional development is an outgrowth of the interaction of the organism with its environment. The hereditary "determiners" of the genes cannot function unless environmental forces are able to play their roles. Kallmann states, "Environment influences are vital, and after conception they gain coequality with those arising from heredity. However, only within the limits set by the genetic constitution of the organism can external factors have an effect on the dynamics of physiologic functions and interactions. Beyond these limits no power plant exists for generating behavioural potentials."

The failure of a typical first-grade child in the United States to identify a television set from a simple descriptive definition is likely to be an indication of mental inferiority, while such a failure among typical six-year-old from the villages of India would indicate their lack of opportunities to learn about television sets. One's selection of elements in his environment and his reaction to them will be affected by varying conditions of either heredity or environment. The hard-of-hearing child will fail to respond to the differentiation of tonal qualities present in certain pieces of music, while the child with a very limited rural background will reveal a very superficial understanding of farm crops.

The Early, Sociocultural Environment. The child is born into a home where specific forms of social behaviour are practiced and where certain cultural behaviour patterns are manifested. Socialization and cultural behaviour patterns, then, may be said to begin at birth. It is worthwhile for the teacher to realize that the child acquires ways of responding in social situations as a result of his experience. His readiness for school and the learnings introduced at school will depend in large measure upon his earlier sociocultural experiences.

Children in every society must learn to behave according to certain expectations. They must learn what to say and when to say it; what to wear on different occasions; what to believe; and how to respond to the actions of others. Eventually society determines which characteristics and behaviour are to be positively reinforced, which to be shunned or avoided, and which to be merely tolerated. The typical child learns to operate physically, psychologically, and socially within the culture into which he is born and reared. Learning the accepted ways of behaving makes the child a functioning member of his society. This learning process begins at birth and continues throughout one's life. Members of a group tend to adopt similar cultural patterns, giving them a national or religious character. Those who have visited different cultures and studied how the socialization of children is accomplished are often amazed at some of the child-rearing practices they see. Some of these practices may seem cruel to the outsider. Yet, like those in our own society, they must be judged in terms of the total environmental setting and the general objectives and philosophy of that society.

The Expanding Physical Environment. During infancy, childhood, and adolescence the individual's physical environment continuously expands as he gains strength and agility, knowledge, and meaningful complex skills. Similarly his social environment expands as he moves from the home to school and other formal and informal community agencies and institutions. The most obvious expansion of the child's environment is in his range of physical stimulation. Environment for the newborn child is limited to his crib and other places where those caring for him take him. As he learns to walk and talk he is able to move around, thus expanding his physical environment to many areas in and around the home. At the kindergarten and on the playground he comes into contact with a larger environment, providing him with a wider range of stimulation. Entrance into kindergarten is a significant stage in his personal and social development, since it carries him beyond the home and the supervision of his parents.

Until the child enters school he is largely concerned with people, objects, and activities around the home. Entrance into school brings him into contact with different adult figures and many other children of his own age. Induction into school also furnishes him with opportunities for learning skills and acquiring information, which increase his span of interests and activities. He is now called upon to learn to read, to write, to recite events, and to deal with a variety of numerical problems.

The Expanding Social Environment. The normal infant is endowed with potentialities for development. He comes equipped in such a way that he could develop anyone of a number of personalities. Of the environmental factors affecting the developing personality, the most influential are the social and cultural forces that surround him from birth. The social factors include the types of relationship he forms from repeated association with people. The significant cultural factors consist of the values and judgments people have applied to conditions and behaviour.

For most children the home furnishes the main stream of their social activities before they enter school. Entrance into school brings the child into contact with a new adult, the teacher, who plays an important role in his development. The importance of the teacher-pupil relationship is given special consideration in chapter. The child also comes into contact with children from varied backgrounds. As he develops further he will most likely become involved in other groups—Sunday school, Scouts, clubs, and neighborhood gangs. Each of these groups affects, for better or worse, the socialization of the child. Materials bearing on the influences of these groups on the socialization of the individual child are presented in subsequent chapters.

Maturation and Learning

The development of the individual results partly from an intrinsic maturing of abilities, characteristics, and structures, and partly from experience. The term *maturation* has been used by geneticists for many years to designate the stage of development during which a germ cell becomes mature. The term was borrowed and made popular in psychology largely through the efforts of Gesell. He states: "Maturation may be defined as the net sum of the gene effects operating in a self-limited life cycle. Here lies an important key to his constitutional individuality."

Any behavioural change resulting from experiences may be regarded as the product of learning. Many of the characteristics we identify as *human* stem from learning, and all facets of development are affected by learning. The complexity of the human organism and the integrated patterns of behaviour which characterize the individual at all stages in his development make it difficult if not impossible to evaluate the exact influence of learning. An example illustrating this may be useful. Child psychologists constantly encounter difficulty in differentiating those changes in the behaviour of the young child primarily due to maturation and those due to learning. Parents, for instance, frequently speak of the child who "learns to walk." Although the phrase "learning to walk" is commonly used to describe the development of motor skills involving locomotion, it is likely that maturation plays a more important role than learning. It is equally true, however, that learning plays some part in the child's early attempts to master this skill. We encounter similar difficulties in describing the mastery of such tasks as talking, throwing, handwriting, and other similar activities.

The Nature of Learning

The question may be raised: What is learning? Unfortunately, many definitions may give the reader oversimplified concepts. Like the problem of defining electricity, it may be more fruitful at this stage of our thinking to describe the concept rather than to define it. The child is born equipped with the potential to mature, to grasp, and to learn at different age levels, the language ways of behaving, attitudes, and values of his culture. We should also realize that he is born with potentials for reorganizing and remolding many aspects of his culture in harmony with changed conditions and needs. Any view of the child as a product of culture must also consider him as the product of biology. We must remember that through the years, it is the biological man that has developed the culture into which the child is born.

Many individuals and agencies contribute to teaching the child the cultural patterns of his social group. Through maturation and learning the child is capable of acquiring a culture. The term *enculturation* is used to describe the process whereby the child is taught the cultural ways society expects him to follow. The process of enculturation requires the child to adjust his innate biological characteristics to the prevailing cultural practices in his society. *Homo-sapiens* are the only biological group that have developed a culture requiring each newborn member to modify his biological characteristics according to rather highly specialized cultural ways. It is through the educative process that the individual organism is molded to fit into a particular culture and to function effectively as a member of that culture.

The Significance of Maturation. Learning and maturation are closely interwoven in all aspects of the child's development. This may be noted in the development of language, motor, and social skills. The co-twin method was used by Gesell and Thompson in studying the influence of early practice or exercise on motor development during childhood. This method makes use of identical twins, one of whom becomes the control subject while the other becomes the experimental subject.

In this study, beginning at the age of forty-six weeks, one twin (twin T) was given training in stair-climbing, while the other twin (twin C) was given no such training. After six weeks of training, twin T climbed the stair case in twenty-six seconds. At the beginning of the fifty-third week, twin C was given training in stair-climbing. At this time she climbed the stair case in forty-five seconds, but after two weeks of training she was able to climb it in ten seconds. Thus, twin C rapidly reached an achievement level as high as that attained by twin T, primarily because of her advanced maturation when she began the stair-climbing.

Similar results have been obtained with infants in studies dealing with manipulating cubes, cutting with scissors, language development, memorization, and the like. In an experiment reported by Hilgard two groups of fifteen children each were matched by chronological and mental age, sex, and initial ability in three skills-buttoning, cutting with scissors, and climbling. One group, the practice group, trained for twelve weeks; a second group, the control group, received no training during the twelve-week period, but was given four days of training immediately following the twelve-week period. Tests were given both groups at the beginning and end of the twelve-week period, and at the end of the four-day period immediately following the twelve-week training period. These curves indicate that both groups improved throughout the twelve-week period, even though the control group was not practicing. The control group showed marked improvement during the four-day practice period following the twelve-week period.

These studies show that progress in learning depends upon the maturation of the learner, as well as the kinds of experiences he has had. Readiness for learning motor skills, like readiness for other learnings, depends upon maturation and experience, among other factors. The effects of training in the learning of a motor skill will be most beneficial when it is introduced at the time the learner has reached a sufficient level of development enabling him to profit from such training.

FORCES INFLUENCING THE EDUCATION OF A HUMAN BEING

In the life-long process of education the individual develops or changes according to his needs or according to the nature and level of his choices. The influences in an individual's environment may be consciously planned and formulated, or may be subconsciously pressuring and informal. The community in which he lives offers many informal agencies of education, like social organizations, clubs, camping groups, jobs, religious organizations, the movies, and television. As we have pointed out, these influences may be positive and enabling or negative, inhibiting, and crippling.

In our American culture the most important formal agencies of education are the home, the church, and the school. There is an increased awareness of the need for every agency of education, formal and informal, to cooperate in educating the personal, social, intellectual and moral aspects of the student so that he will be better equipped to participate as a useful and effective citizen in a democratic society.

The Home

The family is a social unit existing for the procreation, guidance, and education of the newborn child in his growth toward maturity. A favorable home environment that guides the growing child in an atmosphere of love and affection is well equipped for this task. How the child integrates into the family unit, the emotional climate, attitudes, values, aspirations, and emotional maturity of the family members, especially the parents, are strong influences in the child's education. These influences begin even before birth and continue beyond the period of the child's maturity. By the time the child is of school age he has acquired important attitudes, values, and habits that have a bearing on his adjustments at school and elsewhere. Although the school should not attempt to supplant the home, it is frequently called upon to supply many elements essential to the healthy growth of children that are not supplied in certain homes. Some children will need special attention and consideration; some will need affection and acceptance; others will require successful experiences; still others will need friends of their own age. All these needs will be met, to some extent at least, in a good school situation.

The most important social, political, or educational organization is the family. Lessons are acquired in the home during the early years, which affect the whole individual throughout his life. Every competent and experienced teacher realizes the important role parents play. The convictions presented by Stella Center, arising from her experiences in her Reading Center, are shared by most experienced educators.

Early ... it becomes unmistakably clear that I had to know the parents as well as I knew the students. I could, except in very rare instances, count on the parents' affection for their children and an earnest desire to promote the children's welfare. Convinced of my sincere interest in the boys and girls, parents were willing to listen to reports on diagnoses and analyses of children's difficulties that were often as disturbing as a surgeon's report must at times be.

The School

In more complex societies like ours, children need to learn more complex skills and need to acquire a greater amount and variety of knowledge than would normally be required through the informal activities at home and in the community. However, children in our society still rely upon their parents and family for much of their learning, particularly emotional habits of childhood, good personal relations, attitudes toward conditions, objects, and persons in their immediate environment, and ways of behaving.

In the United States the education of the child is a joint responsibility of the family and the school. Entrance into school plays an important role in the child's conception of himself as well as of the world about him. It further implies that he has matured sufficiently to benefit by the program of instruction at school. Before one can determine the role of the school in the educative process, he must first consider the function of the school in modern society. Its primary task is to assist children and adolescents by providing experiences, guidance, instruction, and discipline in learning facts, skills, attitudes, and habits essential for them to function effectively as members of the society in which they live.

In America the schools transmit the cultural heritage through the language arts, the curriculum, teaching, and such mass media as books, radio, and television. The discovery of this heritage and experiences in it are means and aids to personal fulfillment and enrichment, and to social and civic effectiveness. The school is concerned essentially with each learner, the whole child, accepting him with his individual endowments, personal experiences, unique reactions, and particular rate of development. In cooperating with other agencies and institutions it guides him in his growth toward maturity so that he will be able to function more effectively and attain greater satisfaction from daily living.

The Church

To be effective in his relations with others, a mature person with an integrated personality needs to have his knowledge and understanding, emotional habits, attitudes and values, ideals, and moral concepts unified into a consistent philosophy of life, which will then be reflected in his self-concept, self-realization, self-expression, self-restraint, and in his relationship with the universe, his neighbor, and his God. The American way of life and American democracy is built on the Judaeo-Christian tradition and religious values, which have been the fundamental principles of Western civilization for peoples of many different cultures and traditions for nearly twenty centuries.

In a sense, therefore, the church can be considered an important agency in the educative process. While growing and learning, the child may have been instructed in basic religious beliefs and may have been trained in the formation of behaviour patterns consistent with these beliefs. But as he matures, he must make, and should be guided in making, objective judgments and choices in incorporating beliefs, ideals, and values into his own life patterns and guiding philosophy. In the process of developing, each person must also develop his own conscience, moral values, and habits of action. He needs guidance and practice in appraising his own conduct, and he needs opportunities for making rational choices between alternate courses of action. From infantile automatic responses, the first real choices may be tentative, but conscious control will become habitual and confirmed through successful practice.

THE TEACHER AND THE EDUCATIVE PROCESS

We have already pointed out that many agencies are concerned, either directly or indirectly, with the educative process. The school as an institution exists to guide children in the development of skills, subject matter, attitudes, and behaviour patterns essential for effective living in a particular society. The school situation involves *(1)* pupils, *(2)* teachers, *(3)* teacher-pupil relationships, and *(4)* ideas or problems. Teaching may be defined as a system of actions directed toward pupils, the learners.

The Teacher and Educational Objectives

If the learner is central in the educative act, educational objectives can best be thought of in terms of the changes we would like to see take place to him. Therefore, what the educative act will accomplish depends on the teacher's objectives. He may wish to cover so much subject matter, or he may require his students to write so many term papers. On the other hand, he may work for certain kinds of changes or learnings in his pupils. Educational objectives should be formulated in terms of the behaviour changes desired, and the educational approaches by which these objectives will most effectively be achieved. Materials and methods should be chosen with these objectives in view. Without clear, comprehensive, and fairly specific statements of objectives, the teacher will overlook some important educational goals.

The Teacher and Learning Experiences

Teachers need to remember that the heart of all education is learning, and that their role is to guide and stimulate pupils. The teacher needs to know the conditions, which make for effective learning, and must be able to apply these conditions in the classroom. He must have an understanding of the characteristics of children and adolescents, and of the principles of learning. The successful teacher is able to bring to bear his understanding of the principles of learning to a specific classroom situation.

From a psychological point of view it might be stated that the function of the teacher in the learning environment is to *(1)* elicit the desired behaviours or responses, *(2)* reinforce these responses, *(3)* help the learner to integrate these into previous learnings, and *(4)* overcome or eliminate undesirable forms of behaviour or responses. There is no mechanical device or magic formula for achieving these aims. Educational psychology is not concerned with providing the teacher with magic tricks or gadgets for helping him with his teaching.

Each child in the classroom has had a variety of experiences, and on the basis of his concepts, attitudes, and previous learnings, he interprets his environment and new experiences encountered at school and elsewhere. The function of the learning experience in the classroom is to help the child broaden his existing concepts, develop new skills, acquire changed or new attitudes, and reorganize his existing behaviour. The teacher can do this best when he guides the child in his learning through the process of *realization* so that he integrates new learnings into existing patterns of behaviour.

Teacher Evaluation of Results

Evaluation is an important aspect of the educative act. Without it the teacher will be unable to determine the extent to which his objectives are being reached. The process of evaluation is complex, since it is very difficult to evaluate the results of learning experiences involving, as they must, personality changes and character formation. Considerable research has been completed and much more is now in progress dealing with various aspects of this problem. Teachers should constantly keep in mind objectives that have been set forth and use a variety of means for evaluating behavioural changes.

The errors teachers most frequen ly make may be listed as follows: *(1)* relying wholly on some simple evaluating device; *(2)* failing to make continuous evaluations, but waiting until the end of the school term for one lengthy measurement; *(3)* evaluating behaviour changes which have little or no reference to the objectives set forth; and *(4)* failing to evaluate the behavioural changes that have been listed as the desired ones and for which learning experiences have been provided.

Interpersonal Relations

Experienced teachers are aware that the quality of the interpersonal relations in the classroom markedly affects the learning and behaviour of their pupils. Much teaching takes place somewhat silently across a bridge of feelings embedded in favorable interpersonal relations between teacher and pupils. One of the most frequent complaints young teachers make is that they failed to learn how to deal with such problems as discipline during their professional training programs. No teacher-training program can adequately anticipate the variety of behaviour problems that will appear during the course of a year in a typical classroom. Emphasis, instead, will be given in subsequent chapters to understanding child behaviour, problems of motivation and learning, the importance of understanding the individual child, and the importance of a favorable emotional climate in the classroom.

Learning is much more than a matter of books and school subjects. Children and adolescents are likely to see it in terms of how well they get along with teachers. Accordingly, learning depends upon the relationship teachers build with their classes. When discussing a subject, pupils express, what they think of the teacher. A good teacher makes a subject interesting; a poor one makes it dull or disliked.

2

Nature and Scope of Educational Psychology

The word Psychology is derived from two Greek words, 'Psyche' and 'Logos', "Psyche' means soul and 'Logos' means science. Hence the original or etymological meaning of Psychology is the science of soul. In due course the meanings of psychology have undergone many changes. From Science of Soul, it became 'Science of Mind', 'Science of Consciousness' and 'Science of Behaviour' which is its modern concept.

1. Psychology as a Science of Mind. Philosophers in the middle ages considered psychology as the science of mind. They used to distinguish between the mental and spiritual life of the individual. These philosophers, however, failed to give the exact nature and, force of the mind o' the individual. Hence psychology the science of mind could not progress.

2. Psychology as a Science of Soul. The earliest definition of psychology was 'a Science of Soul'. Philosophers like Plato, Aristotle and Descartes interpreted psychology, according to this concept. In the 16th century this meaning of psychology was rejected.

3. Psychology as a Science of Behaviour. The latest and modern concept of Psychology is in times of behaviour. Behaviour is the resultant manifestation of both conscious and unconscious urges. Behaviour can be observed objectively and is a more suitable method of studying Psychology.

4. Psychology as a Science of Consciousness. In the 19th century psychologists like William James, William Wondt and others considered psychology as a science of consciousness. By consciousness the psychologists meant awareness or wakefulness. They, however, had different interpretations of the term wakefulness. As this definition of psychology had a very limited approach, it was not universally accepted.

Modern Definitions of Psychology. Let us now acquaint ourselves with some of the definitions of Psychology:

1. 'Psychology is the study of human nature'. (Boring Lang Feld).
2. 'Psychology is the science of behaviour and experience'. (Skinner).
3. 'Psychology is the study of human behaviour and human relationships'. (Crow and Crow).
4. Psychology undertakes to make a scientific study of the individual considered as a unit as he really is in his dealings with other individuals and with the world.' (Woodworth).

The most acceptable Meaning and Definition of Psychology. It is in terms of behaviour. A lot of work has been done by psychologists in this field. Detailed experiments have been conducted on human behaviour. William Wondt established the first Psychological Laboratory at Leipzig in 1879.

Human behaviour is highly complex. All human beings do not behave in the same manner. They differ in abilities, likes-dislikes, interests, attitudes, emotions and sentiments.

Why is it so? The science that answers such questions and studies human behaviour is called Psychology:

Classification of Psychology. Psychology can be divided into eleven branches:

1. ***General Psychology.*** It studies the behaviour of human organism in general. Its scope is very large but generally it studies normal organisms. It is the mother of all other branches of Psychology.

2. ***Abnormal Psychology.*** The scope of Abnormal Psychology is limited to the study of abnormal individual only.

3. ***Adult Psychology.*** It studies the behaviour of adult humans. An adult is a mature person and his emotional, social and intellectual behaviour is not like the behaviour of a child. So it is totally a separate branch of Psychology.

4. ***Child Psychology.*** It deals with the development of behaviour of the child. The child is an adult in the making. He differs from the adults very much. "His life urges, his emotions, his sentiments, his intelligence and his aspirations all differ from those of the adult individuals. Therefore, Child Psychology is a fullfledged science in itself.

5. ***Individual Psychology.*** It deals with the variation in human beings. No two persons are alike. They always differ in their behaviour according to their intelligence, race and sex. They also differ in behaviour in other factors such as interest, philosophy and education.

6. ***Social or Group Psychology.*** This branch of Psychology deals with the behaviour of individual as member of a group or mob does not act in the same way as a majority of the individual members would act individually.

7. ***Educational Psychology.*** It is the most important branch of applied Psychology. It is the study of the

psychological aspects of educational situations. It is the study of educational problems with reference to psychological facts. Psychology is science of behaviour and Education aims at modifying the behaviour in the most desirable way. But modification of behaviour depends on some fundamental psychological laws and limitations. Educational psychology studies those facts and limitations. It covers the development of the child from early childhood to maturity, general facts of psychology which may have any relation with the modification of the behaviour of the child, psychologised methods of learning, measurement of capacities, attitudes and interests and other problems of applied Psychology related to education.

8. *Industrial Psychology.* This is also a branch of applied Psychology. It is in fact Social Psychology with reference to work, individual as well as collective. Industrial work may be made more attractive and interesting and output of industry may be increased and improved if we exploit the finding of Industrial Psychology.

9. *Experimental Psychology.* It studies mental processes and behaviour in laboratories with the help of experiments.

10. *Para-Psychology.* This is the latest development in the field of psychology. It deals with the problems of what happens to an individual after death.

NATURE OF EDUCATIONAL PSYCHOLOGY

Nature of educational psychology is scientific, as it uses scientific methods. Following are the essential elements of science:

1. **Scientific Method.** A science makes use of the scientific method.
2. **Universality.** Scientific laws are universal.
3. **Factuality.** Science is the study of facts, the search for true facts.

4. **Validity.** Scientific laws are also valid. They are valid at all times and in all places. They are found to be invariably true. They are open to examination at all times.

5. **Discovery of Cause and Effect Relationship.** Science studies cause and effect relationship, it searches for cause and effect relationship in its material. On the basis of such relationships it creates universal and valid laws.

6. **Prediction.** Science makes predictions.

On the basis of above criteria of science we find that educational psychology is a science as it possesses all the characteristics of being a science.

The nature of educational psychology is scientific as it employs scientific method in the study of behaviour of the learner in an educational environment. Educational psychology makes use of scientific techniques such as observation, experimentation, case history, interview and projective techniques. Thus, educational psychology as a science is systematic as its procedures are orderly.

Educational Psychology is Empirical and Factual

— It is a body of facts or information that has resulted from observations and investigations. Its conclusions are objective and unperjudiced.

— It has developed a methodology by which investigations are made, information is discovered hypothesis tested and theories are derived.

— It is one of the applied branches of psychology. It studies the behaviour of the learner in relation to learning situation.

— It is a positive science of human behaviour. Its function is to describe, control and predict human behaviour. Human behaviour is quite dynamic and unpredictable.

— It defines cause and effect relationship and on the basis of this knowledge it analyses behaviour of the learner.

— After establishing cause and effect relationships concerning the behaviour of learners it becomes possible for the educational psychologist to predict the behaviour of other learners. He can predict the development of learners in future.

It is clear that educational psychology is an applied and positive science of behaviour of the learner. Its subject matter is subtle, complex and varied. As the human behaviour is unpredictable, more variable and less reliable, viewing this concept, we can say that educational psychology is not a perfect science. Educational Psychology cannot claim the same degree of validity, accuracy, objectivity and exactness as claimed by natural science.

Aims of Educational Psychology

Aims of educational psychology are parallel with aims of education. Various views have been expressed by different thinkers about these aims as given below:

According to **Kuppuswamy,** "The aim of educational psychology is to use psychological principles for good teaching and learning."

According to **Garrison,** "The aim of educational psychology is to know the behaviour of the child and to predict and control it."

According to **W.A. Kelly,** the following are the aims often subject to:

(1) To give an insight with teacher about the nature of child.

(2) Enlightening the teacher with the growth and development of the child.

(3) Imparting knowledge about the principle and methods of learning.

(4) Giving knowledge about the character formation of the child.

(5) Helping the teacher in finding out ways and means of social adjustment for the child.

(6) A study of the techniques of evaluation of various school subjects.

(7) Studying about the control of emotions and their educational importance.

(8) A study of the psychological methods of investigation used in the field of educational psychology.

Charles Skinner has classified the aims of educational psychology as general and particular:

The gerneral aim is to provide a body of organised facts and generalisations that will enable the teacher to realise increasingly both cultural and professional objective:

The particular aims are as follows:

(1) Creating confidence in the teacher to plan harmonious development of the child.

(2) Understanding the social problems of children and planning for their total social adjustment.

(3) Approaching the problems of children in a sympathetic and impartial manner.

(4) Imparting knowledge to the teacher about the latest developments in the field of child psychology and various methods of teaching.

(5) Planning education of children according to their age, ability and aptitude.

(6) Helping the teacher in solving the problems that may arise in the classroom.

(7) Enabling the teacher to evaluate himself and his methods of teaching.

(8) Helping the teacher to understand and analyse the behaviour of children.

In other words we can say that the general aim of educational psychology is to provide a body of facts and principles which will enable the teacher to enhance and enrich his own life and which will help him to bring about improvement in the quality of instruction, thus, equipping him adequately, both culturally and professionally and the specific aims are following:

(a) To explain the nature and characteristics of the learner.

(b) To describe the nature of learning processes.

(c) To explain the manner in which these processes may be facilitated by the teacher, and in the light of these, to explain, how he or she should teach.

(d) "To assist in defining and setting up educational objectives and standards in terms of desirable behaviour (conduct, attitudes etc.) that ought to be the goals of all teaching efforts. If the teacher knows what the desired outcomes should be, he can set-up appropriate situations (curricular materials, teaching procedures etc.) for bringing about the wanted changes." (Skinner)

(e) To assist the teacher in the better adjustment of children and in the prevention of maladjustments.

(f) To help the teacher in defining and planning suitable guidance programmes, and functional forms of organisation and administration.

(g) To aid in developing a scientific problem solving attitude toward the problems of learning and teaching.

(h) To help in the evaluation of the outcome of the educational process.

Relation Between Psychology and Education

(1) Education determines aims and ideals, and psychology decides which aims can be attained.

(2) Psychology deals with facts as they are. Education determines the standards to be achieved. Psychology tells the way of attaining these standards.

(3) Psychology helps the teacher to know the child and plan for the maximum development of the child, which is the ultimate goal of education.

Importance of Educational Psychology to the Teachers

1. Psychology Helps the Teacher in the Realisation of the Aims of Education. The main aim of education is the harmonious and all-round development of the educand. Development comes from within and the inner potentialities must be understood and approached for the desired modification in the development of the child. The knowledge of Psychology helps the teacher to understand the inner potentialities which underlie the behaviour of the child. He can direct and modify the development of the educand quite efficiently if he knows Psychology.

2. Character Development. Educational psychology helps a lot to the formation and development of character. The teacher comes to know the methods he should adopt in inculcating character traits, and moral principles among the children.

3. Educational Psychology Proves Useful in the Methods of Teaching. Psychology has discovered many secrets about mental forces. Recent researches made in the field of psychology gives us valuable suggestions for the better methods of teaching and memorizing, for making desirable habits and eradicating anti-social tendencies. Psychology tells us how significant play and recreation are for the children and how play-way-methods turn the work of learning into an interesting play.

4. The Knowledge about the Child is as Necessary as that of the Subject. The educator will have to consider the mental processes of the child and not only the quality of knowledge which he is going to be put into the living mind. Psychology helps him in understanding 'John'. The teacher may be a great scholar but he will not succeed in teaching if he has no knowledge of the mental forces of the child.

5. Educational Psychology and Nervous System. The entire education depends on the function of the brain and nervous system. It becomes essential to teacher to study the nervous system which controls human behaviour. He must have the knowledge of sensory organs which are the gates of knowledge.

6. Psychological Measurements are Very Useful for the Teacher. Psychology has developed many reliable tests and instruments of mental measurement. These are providing to be extremely useful in the field of education. We can quite easily measure mental capacities, basic intelligence, temperamental attitudes and special inclinations of children and base their educational programmes on these findings. These measurements show that all the children differ in their eventual capacities and that every child is a unique being. The teacher can know that children with I.Q. below 90 cannot do well in medical, engineering, administrative or other similar vocations. But he knows that such young ones are not doomed if they cannot do well in intellectual callings. He can easily explore some other fields where such children can also flourish.

7. Knowledge of Educational Psychology will Give a Scientific Attitude to the Teachers. The knowledge of psychology will make an educator more scientific in his educational practices and consequently he will be more and more objective and methodical in his work.

8. Educational Psychology can Change the Outlook and Attitude of the Teacher towards his Pupils. The knowledge of psychology will change the outlook and attitude of the teacher towards children. He will no more denounce his pupils on account of their undesirable behaviour. He will not hate the juvenile delinquent. Instead of being fed-up with the backward child the teacher will be more interested in him. The problem child will no more be a problem for him but he will be simply a child with problems and the teacher will be ever-ready to help him in the solution of his problems.

9. Educational Psychology Helps the Teacher in His own Mental Adjustment. A maladjusted personality can never be a good model for hundreds of developing personalities. He cannot solve his own problems and therefore he cannot help the children in this aspect. The study of psychology may help the teacher to readjust himself. He will know his own weaknesses and merits and will overcome his complexes.

10. Educational Psychology and Process of Learning. Teaching and learning go side by side. All education depends upon the learning of new responses and the capacity of a human child to learn new responses. Educational Psychology discusses the nature of learning theories and types of learning for different age levels and situations. It tells that learning is not possible if the child does not cooperate in the learning process. Therefore, knowledge of Psychology becomes essential to a teacher to study all these problems.

11. Individual Differences. No two persons are exactly alike. There is individual difference. Pupils always differ in their level of intelligence, aptitudes, likes and dislikes and in other propensities and potentialities. Different minds are to be trained by the teacher. There are gifted, backward, retarded, talented and handicapped children. All of them should not be treated in the same manner. So, the teacher should know their Psychology to satisfy them.

12. Educational Psychology and Play. Play is a natural tendency having great educational quality. Psychology helps in playgrounds also. Child finds outlet for pent-up feelings and energy through play. It also gives joy and pleasure to the pupils. Hence there is a great importance of play-way in education.

To sum-up, Educational Psychology has revolutionised education. It has made education child-centred. It is only with the knowledge of Educational Psychology that it is possible for the teachers to render proper guidance, arrange the learning situations and plan the instructional programmes and other activities for the all-round development of children.

PSYCHOLOGY ITS RELATIONSHIP WITH EDUCATION

Psychology has assumed an extraordinary importance in the life of an individual. Infact, every action of life, may it be home, school, neighbourhood or social gathering, is influenced by it. All communications between the teacher and students are based on the knowledge of psychology. Theories of intelligence, creativity and personality have been responsible for shaping and designing the educational system according to individual needs.

Psychology is the Science of Soul. The word 'psychology' comes from Greek words 'Psyche' and 'logos' where psyche means soul and logos means science. Thus, literally psychology means a science of soul. But this is not acceptable because of following criticisms:

(i) Nature, origin and place of soul is not known. It has no physical existence. It cannot be seen and heard. It has no weight and volume. It is a metaphysical cancept.

(ii) It makes psychology more of religion than of science because it is a theological concept and implies certain theories of religion and relationship to God.

(iii) Soul makes science speculative as it is not open to observation and experimentation and therefore not given to verification. So this definition of psychology is unscientific and hence this is discarded.

Psychology is Science of Mind. Alternatively philosophers evolved another definition of psychology as science of mind. Mind is a combination of sum total of mental processes and it stands for personal internal experiences of man, *e.g.*, pleasures and pains, hopes and wishes, dreams and desires. But this is also criticised on following grounds:

(i) It is subjective. We can know our own mind and not the mind of others. So it is half true.

(ii) Mind implies continuity and unity but it is lacking in abnormals, insanes and animals etc.

Psychology as a Science of Consciousness. Failing to define the nature of soul and mind, the psychologists defined psychology as a science of consciousness. The definition was considered too narrow as this did not include the unconscious and preconscious activities of mind. Freud in his psycho analytical theory described that mind consists of

3 states—preconscious, unconscious and conscious. About 9/10th part of behaviour is determined by unconscious and preconscious mind whereas only 1/10th part is determined by conscious mind. But in Freud's terminology, unconscious mind plays a major role in the development of personality of an individual. This definition was also discarded.

Psychology as a Science of Behaviour. Psychology was finally defined as the science of behaviour where the term behaviour carries a very wide meaning. According to **Woodworth,** "Any manifestation of life is activity" and behaviour is a collective name of all such activities. It includes all types of activities such as cognitive, affective and conative. So behaviour refers to entire life activities and experiences of all living organisms.

According to **Skinner,** "Psychology deals with responses to any and every kind of situation that life presents by adjustment activities."

According to **Crow and Crow,** "Psychology is the study of human behaviour and human relationship."

According to **Munns,** "Psychology today concerns itself with the scientific investigation of behaviour."

According to **Garrison,** "Psychology is concerned with observable human behaviour."

Thus, it can be concluded that psychology is a behavioural science which helps us to describe, understand, predict and control behaviour.

PROBLEMS OF EDUCATIONAL PSYCHOLOGY

1. Development of a Balanced Personality. The main problem that engages the attention of educational psychology is the development of a balanced personality in the child. And, generally speaking, a balanced personality is one in whom the intellectual, emotional, ethical and moral aspects are properly blended and synthesised, functioning properly.

2. Motivation. Often enough, the problems that are at the root of various adjustment defects are problems of motivation.

3. Increase in Understanding and Meaning. Another factor at the root of the motivation problem is sometimes a deficient understanding and an inability to comprehend the implications of the problems existing. It is to this end that the material chosen in teaching nowadays is such as is drawn from an environment with which the child is reasonably familiar and with which he is conversant enough not to be embarrassed by it. A simple example would be the creation of a model government within the class in order to explain the working of the actual government of the country to the student. In democratic societies the students usually understand the functioning of a democratic system in their student groups.

4. Individual Importance of Heredity and Environment in Individual Differences. The aim of education is the development of the child. Hence, one of the important problems facing the educational psychologist is the determination of the relative importance of heredity and environment in the child's development and in causing individual differences among children. Can education change the inherited qualities? Can children reach an adequate stage of development on their inherited qualities alone if they are placed in a common environment? Is it possible to make a child into anything on the basis of education irrespective of his heredity? These are questions of this nature that encourage and inspire the educational psychologist to make a comparative study of hereditary and environmental factors. For example, one important question is the extent to which intelligence can be developed through education regarding which educational psychologists have discovered numerous facts after much investigation.

5. Measurement and Development of Intelligence and Attainment. Education develops intelligence and attainment. Educational psychologists search for and discover methods and measures whereby one can know how this development can be achieved and once it has been achieved, to know how much development in the child has taken place.

6. Methods for Maximum Progress in Learning. Fundamentally, the process of education advances with learning. The most prominent question that interests the educational psychologist in this regard in what methods of learning can most facilitate learning and achieve the maximum progress? One such question could be—is there any conflict between imitation and creation? Should education pay more attention to the collection of factual details or concentrate on creative activities? Psychology has made considerable experiments with such methods as imitation, conditioned response, trail and error and insight, and has tried to discover the conditions that are best attend to the application of these methods, the coordination between the condition and method being productive of the best results.

7. Education of Emotions. The proper and adequate development of personality demands the proper and complete development of emotions. An absence of such education of emotions results in many mental diseases such as indiscipline, split personality, etc.

8. Individual Differences. Practical psychology is based on the fact of individual differences. Educational psychology, a knowledge that makes practical use of psychology in the field of education, finds out why and in what respects individual beings differ from each other. These differences are so obtrusive and well defined that the skilled teacher cannot function properly unless he can understand them. For example, the mental level of some individuals is so low that they can be taught even fundamental activities such as wearing clothes and eating only with the greatest of difficulty, while some children, precocious ones, are so intelligent and quick-minded that the normal teaching and study level of the class is not enough to occupy them so that they soon tire of it. Hence, the educational psychologist attempts to discover the limits, if any, of these individual differences, and even evolves methods for their measurement in exceptional children. The modern teacher discovers these individual differences and then makes efforts to help the children progress individually.

9. Problems Relating to Learning. Many of the problems of educational psychology are concerned with learning. The main among them are:

(a) nature of the process of learning,

(b) relation between level of maturity and learning,

(c) modes of evaluating the progress of learning,

(d) importance of individual differences to the speed of learning and limits of learning,

(e) relative importance of the formal and informal methods of the education or learning,

(f) internal changes taking place within the process of learning,

(g) psychological effect of social conditions upon the learner.

(h) relation between the methods of teaching and the results of learning.

10. Practical Problems. Educational psychology is no less a practical science than it is a therORetical one. Hence, in it one comes across many problems that arise before the teacher when he is teaching normally. Such problems would be:

(i) knowledge of the nature of every student and of the possibilities of his development,

(ii) individual and social adaptation necessary for adjustment in modern culture,

(iii) search for the fundamental psychological causes at the root of the processes of the learning and teaching.

As Educational psychology progresses, it comes face to face with newer problems. In modern democratic societies, educational psychology is engaged in adapting education to democracy. And it has the services of psychology on the one hand and many other social sciences on the other at its disposal in the solving of any problems that it come across in such an effort. And it is on the solution of these problems that the future of democratic societies depends.

SCOPE OF EDUCATIONAL PSYCHOLOGY

Scope refers to the fields of operations, applications, topics, and subject matter with which it deals. Since educational psychology is an emerging and growing subject, its scope has never been fixed or static. It has always been changing its boundaries. As a result of new findings in the field, educational psychology has always been adding new dimensions to its areas of activity.

According to **Crow and Crow,** "Educational psychology is concerned with the conditions that affect learning."

According to **Douglas and Holland,** "The subject-matter of educational psychology is the nature, mental life, and the behaviour of the individual undergoing the process of education."

It has been correctly said by **Garrison** and others that "The subject matter of educational psychology is designed to enhance and enrich the lives of the learners and to furnish teachers with the knowledge and understanding that will help them to bring improvements in the quality of instruction.

The following areas can be included in the scope of educational psychology:

Study of Stages of Child Development. Educational psychology studies the nature of growth and development and general characteristics of physical, mental, emotional and social development at the various stages, *i.e.*, at the stage of infancy, late childhood and adolescence.

Study of Heredity and Environment. Educational psychology studies the impact of heredity and environment on the student.

Study of Psychological Basis of Behaviour. It studies the psychological as well as the physiological behaviour of the learner. Psychological basis of behaviour are instincts, emotions, sentiments, suggestion, sympathy, imitation and play etc. Physiological basis of behaviour are nervous system and glands etc.

Study of Development of Various Aspects of Child. Educational psychology enquires how various modifications can be brought about in the behaviour of the child, how and when do physical, social, emotional and language development occur in children, and how do various instincts make their appearance.

Study of Motivation. Educational psychology studies the nature, principles and techniques of motivation in educational field.

Study of Learning Process. Educational psychology also studies nature and process of learning, laws and methods of learning as well as factors of learning. Interest, attention, motivation, memory, habits and transfer of training play very significant role in leraning.

Study of Individual Differences. Educational psychology studies individual differences and suggests ways and means to provide education to all types of pupils. No two individuals are alike. Individuals differ physically and psychologically. Individual differences are mainly caused by heredity and environment.

Study of Intelligence and Personality. Educational psychology also studies nature, development and assessment of personality and intelligence.

Study of Measurement and Evaluation. Educational psychology is helpful in giving newer and newer techniques and tests for measuring intelligence, personality, aptitudes, interests and achievements etc. It is educational statistics which helps us in measurement and evaluation.

Study of Exceptional Children. Educational psychology studies about exceptional children. It studies about backward, retarded, gifted and creative children and their adjustment problems with home, family and school.

Study of Guidance and Counselling. Child is like a book whose every page has to be studied by the teacher. The teacher has to guide and counsel the students at every stage. Educational psychology studies the nature and process of guidance and counselling.

Study of Group Dynamics. Educational psychology studies group dynamics and group behaviour in classroom teaching and learning. It studies importance and effect of group on the individual. It also considers how an individual can modify the group life. It emphasises the role of groups in the education of children.

Study of Statistics. Educational psychology studies mean, median, mode graph, rank difference and co-relation.

A careful analysis of the subject matter of educational psychology reveals that it has three important centres:

1. *The Learner.* In this area, educational psychology examines the following:

(a) The study of the child, his abilities, aptitudes and aspects of motivation.

(b) Individual differences among children.

(c) Various stages of growth and development.

(d) Influence of various social agencies like home, school, neighbourhood etc., on the child's presonality.

2. *The Learning Process.* In this area, the following aspects are examined:

(a) Nature of learning and how it takes place.

(b) Theories of learning and how maximum learning in the minimum time period can be achieved.

3. *The Learning Situation.* Under the aspect educational psychology examines the following:

(a) Nature of classroom management and discipline.

(b) New techniques of evaluation and their effective use.

(c) Use of techniques and aids which facilitate learning.

(d) Methods of teaching children with individual differences.

(e) Knowledge about educational and vocational guidance to be given by the teacher to the child.

Thus, it is evident that the subject-matter of educational psychology is designed to enhance and enrich the learners and to furnish teachers with the knowledge and understanding so as to help them bring improvements in their quality of instruction.

STEPS IN THE PSYCHOLOGICAL EXPERIMENT

Broadly speaking the following steps are involved in a psychological experiment:

1. **Defining the Problem.** First of all the field of study is defined. The experimenter knows clearly which factors to control, which factors to change, what changes to observe and with the help of which material.
2. Selecting the subject or the individual on whom the experiment is to be performed.
3. Setting the material for observation.
4. Observing the responses of the subject.
5. Instructing the subject or telling him his functions during the experiment.
6. Getting introspective report of the subject. In psychological experiment we have to deal with living human beings and while stating the result of an experiment we must mention the reaction of the subject towards the experiment and his mental state during the experiment.
7. Anlaysis of the data obtained and interpretation of the data.

Problems Tackled. The following problems have been tackled in Experimental Psychology:

1. Sensation, sense training and preception.
2. Attention, its span and duration.
3. Memory and methods of memorising.
4. Habits.

5. Laws of learning and transfer of training.
6. Work and fatigue.
7. Thinking and reasoning.
8. Imagery and association of ideas.
9. Intelligence and its measurement.

Criticism. 1. Further, Experimental method has serious limitations when it is applied to Educational Psychology. While dealing with human beings it cannot be as objective as it is claimed by its advocates, because human behaviour cannot be controlled to that extent as is possible in the case of physical and chemical phenomena.

2. Secondly, human behaviour under controlled conditions is different from spontaneous behaviour. Therefore, the experimental findings should be cautiously applied to the spontaneous behaviour of human beings under normal and free conditions.

Concluding Remarks. It is not always possible for every teacher to experiment scientifically because of no special training in doing so and of lack of facilities for experimentation in schools. Yet he can adopt new teaching methods with better results.

1. New teaching methods suggested by Psychology should be tried.
2. Experimental Psychology helps the teacher in dealing satisfactorily with the backward, the deficient, the emotionally deranged and the delinquent child.
3. Experiments can also be carried on in the development of character and leadership. Schemes of self-government and of giving responsibility to students can be tactfully introduced in schools.

IMPORTANCE AND UTILITY OF EDUCATIONAL PSYCHOLOGY

The contribution of educational psychology to the theory and practice of education is rich and varied. The knowledge of educational psychology is important as it provides teachers with some basic skills and guidelines to solve the problems of teaching-learning process.

Teaching is not everybody's cup of tea *i.e.,* everyone cannot teach.

According to **John Adams,** "Teacher should know John as well as Latin". It means teacher should know child and subject-matter. A teacher should know the nature, capacities, likings and aptitudes and attitudes of the child. Child is like a book, teacher should know each and every page of it."

Skinner's view, "The teacher needs psychology to bridge the lives of the young and the aims of education in our democratic society."

Kuppuswamy's view, "Psychology contributes to the development of the teacher by providing him with a set of concepts and principles."

Teaching is an art. Knowledge of educational psychology is very useful and indispensable for the teacher because it gives knowledge to the teacher.

Knowledge of Innate Nature. The child has got natural urges instincts, potentialities and propensities. These innate qualities are the "Prime movers" of his behaviour. The teacher who knows psychology can make his teaching very sucessful while keeping in view innate nature of the child.

Knowledge of Behaviour. Educational psychology assists the teacher in knowing the behaviour of the child at different stages of development. It also helps the teacher in understanding the physiological and psychological basis of behaviour, *i.e.*, nervous system, glands, instincts, emotions, sentiments, motives, play, intelligence, heredity and environment etc.

Knowledge of Unconscious Mind. It helps the teacher in knowing the unconscious mind of the students and plays very important role in the development of the personality of the individual.

Knowledge of Guidance. It helps the teacher in giving guidance to the pupils by having an understanding of interests, abilities, aptitudes, achievements, problems, educational and vocational plans of the pupils.

Understand Development Characteristics. Children pass through different stages of development as infancy, childhood and adolescence. These developmental stages have their own characteristics. If the prospective teacher knows the characteristics emerging at different stages of development, he can utilise these characteristics in imparting instruction and moulding their behaviour according to the specified goals of education.

Knowledge about Himself. It helps the teacher to know about himself. He learns the psychology of being a teacher and acquaints himself with the traits of a successful teacher.

Understand the Nature of Classroom Learning. The knowledge of educational psychology provides a teacher the knowledge of learning process in general and problems of classroom learning in particular. The teacher by the knowledge of educational psychology can understand the principles of learning and various approaches to learning process, problems of learning and their remedial measures and also about factors affecting and guidance for effective learning.

Understand the Individual Differences. No two individuals are alike. The teacher with the knowledge of the kind of individual differences may adjust his teaching to the needs and requirements of the class and thus may be helpful in creating conducive environment in the schools where the students can develop their inherent potentialities to the maximum.

Understand the Problems of Childern. By studying educational psychology a teacher may understand the causes of the problems of the children which occur at different age levels and can successfully solve them.

Knowledge of Mental Health. By studying educational psychology teacher can know various factors which are responsible for mental ill health and maladjustment and can successfully help in mental hygiene.

Understand Effective Teaching Methods. Educational psychology gives us the knowledge of appropriate teaching methods. It helps in developing new strategies of teaching. It also provides us with the knowledge of different approaches evolved to tackle the problems of teaching at different age levels.

Measurement of Learning Outcome. Psychological tools help the teacher to assess the learning outcome of the students and also to evaluate his teaching methods for required modification.

Curriculum Construction. Psychological principles are also used in formulating curriculum for different stages. Needs of the students, their developmental characteristics, learning patterns and needs of the society all are to be included in curriculum construction.

Research. Eductional psychology helps in developing tools and devices for the measurment of various variables which influence the behaviour and performance of students.

Understanding of Group Dynamics. Educational psychology helps the teacher to recognise the importance of social behaviour and group dynamics in classroom teaching learning.

Helps to Develop Positive Attitude. The teacher training programme aims to develop positive attitude towards teaching profession and provides the prospective teachers with the necessary competencies to meet the classroom challenges. Training colleges provide the knowledge of organising the subject matter in a sequential order to suit the needs of the class. The trainees are also aquainted with the techniques of motivating children for learning.

Problem of Discipline. With the knowledge of educational psychology teacher utilises the importance of indirect discipline rather than corporal punishment. It tells the teacher that discipline should be self-discipline, dynamic, positive and constructive through participation in purposeful activity. Pleasure and pain, reward and punishment, praise etc., should be judiciously used. If the teacher is unaware of the principles of educational psychology he may be unable to solve the problems of his students and thereby fail to induce order and discipline among them.

Use of Audio-Visual Aids. Educational psychology has helped the teachers to make use of various types of audio-visual aids in classroom teaching so as to make the concept more clear, definite and learning to last longer.

School and Class Administration. Former autocratic method of administration in school and class has been charged by democratic way of life where in the teachers and administrators are more democratic, co-operative and sympathetic and problems of administration solved by mutual discussion.

Time-Table. The knowledge of psychology is helpful to the teacher in preparing time-table. He should keep in mind the relative importance and toughness of different subjects and level and index of fatigue of the students.

Use of Innovations. Activity-centred teaching, discussion method, micro-teaching etc., are some innovative ideas adpoted to improve the teaching learning process.

Co-curricular Activities. Activities like debate, drama, games are given due importance alongwith theoretical subjects for the harmonious development of the personality of children.

Production of Text-books. Educational psychology has helped in planning of text-books according to the intellectual development of children, their needs and interests at different age levels.

Undoubtedly the study of educational psychology may be very helpful to equip our prospective teachers with necessary skills to deal with classroom teaching learning problems.

REVOLUTION IN EDUCATION INDUCED BY PSYCHOLOGY

The extent to which psychology has produced into the field of teaching and learning education is so impressive that only the term revolution can be applied to it with any accuracy. In pointing to the changes in education caused by psychology. Ryan has written, "In many schools of today one finds an atmosphere of friendliness and happy activity. Much of the traditional formality, the forced silence, the tension, the marching is gone. Childern's voices are heard in the halls and classrooms. The younger children come gaily down the stairways, naturally and relatively unrestrained, the older boys and girls through the corridor or outside walk making their way to school rooms, shops, studios, libraries, laboratories and playing fields to tasks that mean something to them, that make demands upon their energies and their imagination, that often invoive hard, difficult work, but work that they recognise as creative. Beauty of surroundings is considered a first, requirement in these schools—there are flowers about, brightly coloured murals painted by the children, attractive informal work rooms for the various groups....Art and music have begun to play the role that belongs to them as fundamental in education and life."

1. Child-Centred Education. In early times the teachers were mainly engaged in imparting various kinds of information to the children. In those times children were less the centre to attention, the school claimed more of their time. Today, it is the child who is the centre of attention in education. Every child is individually considered and treated. Efforts are always made to adapt the curriculum of study to the needs of the child with the result that the brilliant and dull witted children do not study the same subjects. Applied psychology has directed attention to the differing abilities and capacities of people. Such an attitude has made it possible for the teacher to gauge the special abilities of his wards and to make the best arrangements for the guidance of individual children. The teacher of today not only must be acquainted with teaching but also with his students since his profession is now centred about the child and not about the subject or teacher. The consequence of this kind of reasoning is that what matters isn't the beauty, knowledge or ability of the teacher but the extent to which he succeeds in developing the personality of his students.

2. Process of Education. Previously, education was believed to be a comprehensive process that trained the individual, provided him with a moral character and made him more cultured. In psychology as it is understood today, the conception of mind has completely changed. Analysis has led to the discovery that many kinds of forces and mental activities take place within the human being so that for the development of the child it is necessary to provide him with different kinds of programmes and subjects so that he may succeed in properly developing all his mental faculties and abilities. At present, variety is believed to be essential not only in education itself but it is equally held to be true that the education of one individual subject includes many different activities and functions. The teacher should be aware of all these functions. It is only than that he can understand the difficulties of the children in understanding the subject. If a child fails to memorise some one lesson, it can hardly be taken to indicate only a lack of effort on his part and no other cause. It is equally probable that he has a weak memory, or is not intelligent, or has no interest in the subject or that he is suffering from ill health. Learning is a complex activity and it is only through a complete knowledge of its various parts that one can diagnose the difficulty of a particular child in memorising or learning a lesson. The teacher has no alternative but to attend to the activity of learning.

3. Reform in Curriculum. Psychology has also managed to bring about important variations and reforms in educational curricula. Now it is the mental age and not the chronological age of the child that helps to determine the course of study to which he is to be subjected. Intelligence tests reveal the mental age of the child. Different courses are devised for brilliant and deficient children. After the eighth or delta class, the curriculum is sub-divided into various parts such as literary, scientific, agricultural or art class. The child then has the opportunity of selecting his subject according to his interest and aptitude. Various extra-curricular activities are organised for the emotional and sentimental development of the child. These include picnics, dramatic societies, etc. Other programmes are organised in order to develop the qualities of leadership, public speaking, etc., in the child. But no course of study or programme is foisted upon the child against his inclination. Inspiration is awakened in him according to his interests and his tastes. Education has now been made more interesting and appealing with the use of audio-visual aids such as television, film projection, etc. Many schools are also equipped with radio sets that provide both entertainment and information to the child. The use of analogies to penetrate the defences of the child is an inportant method in education.

Childern who choose to study history are also taken to visit historical places. And even a glance at the curriculum of basic education makes clear the extent to which psychology has revolutionised education.

4. Discipline. Discipline has an important place in education. One of the aims of education is to instil respect for discipline in the child. But the recent discoveries of psychology have changed the ways and means in which discipline is taught. Previously physical punishment was one of the chief methods of teaching and imparting discipline in the children. The main motive behind the discipline was fear of physical violence and injury. But instead of injuring the body of the child it injured his personality by making it distorted. Psychologists attracted the attention of enlightened people to the injurious effects of physical punishment and also suggested alternative means of making children disciplined. One suggestive example is here described. The inmates of a hostel were given to indiscipline during lunch time. They threw morsels of food at each other and wasted much more. The warden made every effort to stop this nuisance used every means of arousing fear in the children but without success. He never discovered the name of the mischief makers and neither did the boys give up their behaviour. Some time later he was replaced by a new warden who resorted to psychological methods for solving this menace. He made an announcement to the effect that the best behaved table with the most seemly boys would win a flag that would entitle them to twice the normal ration of the most succulent food. The strategy took immediate effect and the indiscipline promptly ceased. The children seated at various tables were now busily engaged in trying to look more disciplined and seemly than all the others so that they now even prevented the more hardened and incorrigible boys among them from mischief. In this way, the warden took advantage of the psychology of children to effortlessly perform a task that had completely foiled all the efforts of the earlier warden with his shock and fear tactics. Nowadays it has become customary in schools to allow the children to adopt discipline rather than foist it upon them. At the college level it is from among the students that the prefects are chosen to create and maintain discipline among their fellow mates and to help the proctor in maintaining order within the college. Very recently there was a high level debate on the spreading indiscipline among university students in India and almost all speakers put forward psychological solutions because the problem of indiscipline is fundamentally and basically a psychological one. It need hardly be pointed out that the more a teacher knows of child psychology, the easier will it be for him to create discipline in the motley group with which he is faced in the class.

5. Individual Differences. In days gone by, the same curriculum was prescribed for all stduents in the class. The development of applied psychology led to the fact that different individuals differ from each other in respect of their interests, intelligence, ability, capabilities, etc. This knowledge of individual differences proved a variable source of revolution for education. Now-a-days the essential pre-requisite to guidance of an educational nature is a knowledge of the subject's ability and interests. Choice of his curriculum and other extra-curricular activities is definitely governed by these individual differences.

6. Education on Personality. The modern methods of education place great emphasis upon the education of personality. Education is now understood to mean something more than mere reading or writing, it is also understood to involve the development of personality. Many schools have resident psychologists who solve problems related to personality of the students and give advice to teachers and parents in this regard. At places there are also child guidance clinics, that make special efforts toward the correction and normal rehabilitation of problem children or juvenile delinquents. A study of psychology is an essential part of the curriculum of teacher's training. In addition to these individual efforts most states and districts have a bureau of psychology whose functions are to solve all problems of students relating to their personality, to give personal guidance and to give advice to their parents and teachers regarding them. The truth of the matter is that the psychologist has become a link for the child's adjustment between the home and the school since such an adjustment helps to improve his personality. In the role of specialist his contirbution to the school has become indispensable.

7. Process of Learning. The experiments that psychology has carried on in connection with the process of learning have led to the discovery of many laws that economise of time and yet produce good results in terms of material learned. One example would be Thorndike's laws. It is the psychologist who has stressed the importance of reward and punishment in learning. Research in psychology has aimed at discovering the efficacy and inefficacy of the various methods of learning. The employment of the various methods of learning is improved and made more scientific by a knowledge of their qualities and drawbacks.

8. Teaching Method. In the manner already described psychology has changed teaching methods lock stock and barrel. All new research aims at evolving teaching methods that induce the child to learn for himself and thus himself achieve his development. The means of a changed teaching method are radio, cinema, cultural programmes, debates and other competitions, picnics, visits to historical places, games, election contests, students' unions, etc. It is psychology that has contributed the Kindergarden and Montessori methods of teaching. Speical learning and teaching methods have been evolved for the use of blind, dumb and deaf children and mentally backward or handicapped children.

9. Mental Testing and Guidance. Mental testing and guidance are important factors in applied psychology. Psychologists have evolved scientific tests to measure intelligence and other abilities. Students can be guided in educational and vocational matters with the help of these tests. Now, education aims both at the complete development of the individual as well as his best possible adjustment to his vocation and of his vocation to his natural abilities. Teachers need the help of psychologists in either of these two matters. Psychologists solve the problems of students through personal guidance and inform them of the job they are best suited to through vocational guidance. In this way, the co-operation and co-ordination between the teacher and the psychologist in the field of education is on the increase.

10. Reform of Problem Children. One of the most notable contributions of psychology to education is the improvement and reform of juvenile delinquents, absconding children, morons, backward children, unsocial and problem children, and advice to their parents regarding them. To this end the state and district psychological bureau assist the educational institutions.

11. Extra Curricular Activities. The aim of education is the complete development of the child so that mere book knowledge is insufficient to gain this end. In this connection many other programmes are included in the curriculum on the suggestion of psychologists apart from the normal theoretical knowledge.

In this manner, educational psychology provides the teacher with the means to attaining knowledge of the student's nature, capacity, characteristics, needs and motive. This knowledge is the equipment for him to modify his teaching methods sufficiently to attain the goal for education.

***

3

Learning of Skills

The refinement or perfection of an ability to do or perform something is a skill. Skills do not develop singly or in isolation but as integral parts of the individual's total development. The acquisition of motor skills begins in an elementary form so early in the child's life that it is identified as an integral part of the total growth process. Furthermore, such skills are at all times interrelated with all other aspects of growth. And, although we speak of different kinds of learning and growth, it should be emphasized that all growth and learning tend to follow certain general principles. Some of these principles, however, may be more readily observed in some kinds of learning. The importance of maturation, experience, motivation, and related habits and experiences may be observed in the acquisition of motor skills and meanings.

Nature and Characteristics of Human Skills

Skills of doing or performing are apparent in all aspects of the school program, although they are usually more in evidence in extra-curricular and vocational activities. Ragsdale groups motor activities and skills into three broad categories: object-motor activities, language motor activities, and feeling-motor activities.

A skill is a facile and automatic form of response to a stimulus or cue. Skilled performance, thus, involves the effective differentiation of cues and the continual correction of errors through feedback. As learning progresses, fewer cues are required and feedback becomes smoother and better integrated.

Patterns of Action Skills

Motor skills have form, internal organization, rhythm, precision, force, and coordination. The particular pattern developed by an individual will depend upon a number of factors, such as *(1)* maturation, *(2)* body build, *(3)* past experiences, *(4)* constitutional characteristics, *(5)* readiness, which includes motivation and the will to learn, and *(6)* exercise and guidance. Thus, skills are not fixed for an individual; neither are they similar in pattern for all individuals. Each person has his own particular rhythm and form. We see this with children jumping rope. One child may assume a posture almost completely upright while another child remains stopped. There may also be variations in the movements of different parts of their bodies. To perform best each individual will develop the form most appropriate for his ability and constitutional characteristics, although there are general features, which may be regarded as good form, while others may be regarded as bad form. Since all children are, however, biophysical organisms, there will be limits within which each child will tend to operate.

The task of the teacher is to determine the essentials of good form. Certainly there are some techniques of moving the lips and tongue, which have been found best for producing distinct sounds. There are methods of movement and co-ordinations, which are useful to the person in learning to bat a ball. Furthermore, certain motor co-ordinations are dependent upon previous learnings. The child who has not learned to skip will find it difficult, if not impossible, to acquire certain dance skills. Such a learner may have to practice essential movements before he can progress in the particular dance he wishes to perform. These preliminary, basic skills essential to the development of the new skills are aspects of readiness to learn a skill.

Object-motor Activities or Manipulative Skills

This category of motor activities includes the use of tools in household and industrial pursuits, manipulation of materials like wood, metal, and fabrics, the use of measuring and recording devices, and the manipulation of objects used in sports and recreation like balls, fishing materials, and swings. Most of these activities call for judgement, understanding, and a period of learning. The extent to which they require these components varies with the nature and complexity of the particular activity.

The development of manual-tool skills will depend upon a number of factors, among which may be listed *(1)* the maturity of the learner, *(2)* the organisation of the units of work, *(3)* the complexity of the learning task, *(4)* the learner's motivation, and *(5)* the kind of instruction and guidance. Manual-tool activities should be an important part of the elementary-school program and should be closely related to other aspects of the school programme. They should also be closely correlated with work in the fine arts. Good design should be carried over in the making of a baby crib or a home for a pet rabbit. Tools and procedures should be carefully chosen with regard to their functional use and the maturity and experience of the pupils.

Language-motor Activities and Communication Skills

The language-motor activities include movements of the speech organs, movements of the eyes in reading, and the movements in handwriting, telegraphy, commercial arts, and mechanical drawing. Special consideration will be given here to the vocal skills, writing skills, and reading skills.

Vocal Skills. A consideration of problems involved in speech, oral reading, and singing reveal that there are certain common elements. The child's speech begins with babbling sounds some of which are early understood by the mother. Growth in comprehensible speech continues until by the age of three approximately 90 percent of the child's remarks are understandable. The ability to articulate the words correctly, however, lags far behind. Even at the beginning of first grade, a rather large number of words are incorrectly pronounced. Most children will outgrow this faulty pronunciation, which is called baby talk. Too much attention, indeed, may aggravate the speech difficulty rather than correct it. With children who persist in lisping or stuttering, the teacher should seek the help of a specialist who, besides considering treatments, may suggest special exercises the teacher can administer.

Oral reading is recognized today as an important part of a well-balanced program in the elementary school. In addition to the values obtained in auditory acuity and discrimination, work in oral reading may be developed to provide for individual motivation, benefits that can accrue from group dynamics, and desirable personal and social development. Needless to say, correct articulation is essential for successful oral reading. This ability alone, however, is not sufficient. The child must also have mastered the fundamental skills requisite to reading and must have carefully guided experience in oral reading. It is important for the teacher to realize that successful oral reading does not just happen, but proceeds from developmental learnings in a whole complex of motor, cognitive, and affective skills and abilities.

Observers have noted that children spontaneously produce melodic fragments at an early age. These are marked by a lack of semitone steps, and appear with all kinds of rhythmic formations. One study on the effects of systematic training on the singing ability of children who were severely lacking in pitch-discrimination ability indicated that such a disability can be corrected significantly by training. The nature of this training, however, must harmonize with maturational level of the child. Specialized instrumental training at too early an age will only produce meager results, and may condition the child against such musical experiences. The same amount of time and effort given at an early age to the singing of folk songs, songs involving games, and the like, produces better results, since such training makes use of childhood interests and involves simpler muscular skills.

Writing Skills. The skills developed in learning to write are based on previously acquired movements and abilities. Readiness in writing is determined in part by the extent to which these movements and abilities are developed, and in part to the motivation of the subject. Thus, maturation, practice, and motivation are factors, which contribute to readiness for writing instruction as they do to the learning of any skill. In a study reported by Ames the spontaneous pencil and paper behaviour of approximately fifty children was observed at each six-month age period from three through six years of age. This behaviour was carefully analyzed to determine the normal course in the development of writing. Most of the subjects were enrolled in some sort of preschool program, which might have influenced the results.

Much the same developmental sequence occurs in all subjects. This had been earlier noted by Hildreth in a study in which she presented a detailed gradient of stages in writing from three through five years of age. The development at age three, for instance, shows a tendency toward horizontal lines with some systematic up-and-down writing through five years when the first name is often printed (although with occasional reversals and letter malformations).

Eye-movements in Reading. The early activities involved in learning to read furnish a splendid illustration of the close relationship between motor and verbal learning or between ocular and interpretive factors. During the early stages of reading the child must develop the habit of focusing the eyes on the left side of the page and work from left to right as he swings them back to the left side of the page after each line is completed.

As the person reads, his eyes progress along the line in a series of eye stops *(fixations)* and quick movements (called *saccadic movements).* Seeing occurs only during the fixations which last a fraction of a second each. Most people have reverse eye movements. *(regressions)* interspersed with their forward movements.

Studies have shown that beginning readers make more fixations per line, more regressions per line, have longer durations of fixation, and evidence less organisation in their characteristic patterns of eye movements than do mature readers. As the average pupil advances academically, his pattern of eye movements shows fewer fixations per line, indicating a broadening of the span of recognition. In general, with advancing grade level, the pattern becomes more regular and uniform, reflecting an increase in overall organisation.

Faulty habits in basic reading skills are often related to the psychomotor aspect of the reading skills. Although the first five or six grades are considered crucial for the development of desirable eye-movements and good reading skills, recent studies and expert opinion have identified constellations of skills that can be developed only at higher levels of maturity and as clusters built upon the basic skills of the elementary grades. Teachers, therefore, must understand the complexity of the skills they teach, like reading, if they are to see the need for sequence in the development and if they are to realize the importance of well-developed preliminary skills for more mature performance.

Feeling-motor Activities or Affective Abilities

The feeling-motor activities have also been referred to as manual-esthetic coordinations. These activities should not be thought of as functioning apart from vocal skills, manual-tool coordinations, and other perceptual-motor learnings. We have already suggested that manual-tool coordinations should be closely related to certain fine-arts activities. For example, creative dancing and the playing of musical instruments-regarded as manual-esthetic coordinations-involve the attitudes and feelings of the individual who practices them. The purpose of such activities is not primarily to communicate ideas and thoughts, but to express one's feelings, ideas, and values. Furthermore, through musical activities, the learner is able to express either his mood and feelings or the mood and feelings of the composer.

Teaching children to sing simple songs in unison should be the beginning of music instruction, and should continue to be a large part of the music programme. Music reading may be successfully introduced in the early elementary grades if such experiences are connected with music games and songs the children have already learned together. Some types of songs that have been suggested for children are festival songs, Mother Goose songs, lullabies, songs about animals and birds, Christmas carols and hymns, and songs about children in other lands. Besides singing, many schools are making good use of radio programmes, television instruction, and phonograph records to develop appreciation of rhythm and music. Rhythm bands, dancing, dancing and skipping to music, and special school programmes furnish means for developing motor-esthetic coordinations and motivating the work in music.

There is little systematic knowledge pointing to just when the average child is ready to learn to *sight-read* or to play a musical instrument. This type of readiness will be influenced by such factors as intelligence, musical aptitude, musical background, and motivation. Individual differences exist, but they are probably no greater than in other areas of education. However, inadequate cultural environment and exposure to substandard quality of performance and expression or to low-caliber programmes may prevent an individual from developing the proper readiness. Worse still, they may create undesirable tastes and faulty appreciations and insights, which will need unlearning before adequate development of skills, appreciation, and motivation can actually take place. Today children can be exposed to the undesirable and the unrefined almost constantly, even in the home.

Easy-to-play instruments afford opportunity for enjoyment and may be useful in the development of esthetic-motor coordinations and a greater appreciation of music. The use of rhythm instruments at school need not be restricted to the lower elementary grades. It has been observed that such Latin American instruments as the claves, maracas, and bongo drums appeal to the interests of teenagers. Such instruments can be made by the students and can be used in a variety of learning situations to develop an increased understanding of music, to further enjoyment, and to develop esthetic-motor skills.

Through art activities children may develop a greater appreciation of the world about them and increased esthetic-motor coordinations. The elementary-school art program usually includes the graphic and industrial arts. This is an integral part of the elementary-school programme. Through art activities the child is given the opportunity to explore the world about him and to relate this to his inner world of feelings, wishes, and understandings. If he is permitted to explore without too much adult interference and without the harsh imposition of adult standards, he will show an intense interest in art and will grow in self-expression, motor-esthetic coordination, and in increased appreciation of his surroundings at home, at school, and in his community. In all the variety of complex skills, which confront boys and girls in the educative process, the teacher or director is fundamental. She guides them, through wholesome experience and practice, to insightful learning and positive growth.

Higher-level Skills. Although we may characterise some skills as higher-level skills, it should be pointed out that most people with good ability do many things only moderately well chiefly because they lack motivation. Consider Ralph, a ninth-grade pupil with above average ability but with a low motivational index for school activities. Ralph is satisfied with a passing grade and manages to study sufficiently to make such a grade. Buswell and Kersh studied how 499 high school and college students solved six types of problem in practical arithmetic. The students were instructed to think aloud and their recorded remarks were carefully studied. It was found that frequently, capable students failed to solve the practical arithmetic problems for several reasons. Apparently, their failure to discriminate relevant materials, their poor planning procedures, and their confusion were among the factors responsible.

Similar evidence of inefficiency was noted in an earlier study by Symonds in which the problem-solving processes of teachers was studied. He concludes from his study that "teachers are not able to clearly formulate their problems, nor are they able to work out clearly thought through solutions to them. It would be more correct to speak of the process as one of emotional adjustment to personal difficulties than of problem solving."

Factors Affecting the Learning of Skills

The relationship between maturation and learning is clearly evident in the acquisition of motor skills. Through the influence of maturation the child is brought to the most favourable time to learn, and through his motor-learning experiences, properly timed with maturation, he is able to achieve the optimum degree of efficiency in motor skills.

Learning as Integration of Skills. In the development of motor skills there is progress not only from more generalized to more specialized forms of activity, but also from specialized to more inclusive activities that serve to integrate other operations. Thus, it is to the child's advantage to learn the basic motor skills as early as possible. In many performances, children will concentrate for a time on establishing a simple level of skill, then move on to a higher level. At various stages of their progress they will combine such skills with others, which were practiced independently at an earlier stage. When mastery of the new larger skill is achieved, the different operations involved may be subordinated to the more complex task. Development proceeds both from wholes to parts and from parts to larger wholes, just as the act of running is combined with the act of catching a ball when a child makes a "running catch" in softball.

Many motor tasks not only require complex motor coordination, but also involve increased attention span or difficult mental processes, which increase the learning difficulty. This augments the necessity for spaced practice among elementary school children.

Growth in Motor Ability. The sequence of increasingly complex skills mastered by a child is part of a larger, continuing process of motor development. Walking, running, sliding, climbing, hopping, and more intricate skills develop as a result of maturation and practice.

A study of the motor development of nearly 2,000 children from two to seven years of age showed that climbing stairs, low inclined planks, packing boxes, jungle gyms, and the like were well established as skills at three years of age in half of the children. After this age there was a steady increase in climbing ability. During the early stages it was noticed that climbing up was somewhat easier than climbing down. No difference was observed in the case of accomplishing these tasks after they were once mastered.

Skill in hopping on one foot, skipping, and jumping may be developed during the preschool years if children have the opportunity to practice these skills. Gutteridge reports that 42 percent of her group of three-year-olds rated well at jumping, while 72 percent were rated skillful at four and a half years of age. Skipping is a skill that few children can do at four years of age. At five a relatively large percentage are able to skip, while by the age of six most children are able to do so. The ability to hop on one foot develops more slowly, although the majority of children are able to hop by the time they are six years of age. Even at this age the range of ability to hop is very wide.

As the body develops and changes, new motor learnings are needed. The change in the amount and distribution of weight makes it necessary for the growing boy and girl to make new adjustments in maintaining balance. Furthermore, the development of motor coordination does not keep pace with the rapid growth of the limbs of the body. Thus, by age twelve, a girl's arms and legs have about reached the length they will have at maturity. Consequently, she finds herself breaking dishes and displaying awkwardness in many situations. This clumsiness in motor activities, in light of the fact that she has previously developed considerable confidence in her ability to perform certain motor skills, is most disconcerting, especially if adults laugh at her.

The *Lincoln-Oseretsky Motor Development Scale,* consisting of 36 items, was developed and standardized by William Sloane. This scale represents an extensive revision of Oseretsky's original scale, designed to measure motor development of school-age boys and girls. Its normative data, obtained from over 700 children between ages 6 to 14, show a continuous increase in motor ability with age.

It appears that gross motor skills develop largely as a result of maturation while complex motor skills depend upon practice, especially after the child has reached the elementary-school age.

Sex Differences. A comparison of the scores of boys and girls on the *Lincoln-Oseretsky Motor Development Scale* shows no consistent sex difference favouring either sex. A study by Jenkins of the motor achievement of children of ages five through seven in running, jumping, hopping, and accuracy of throwing yielded results favoring boys, who were slightly larger during this period of growth. On the other hand, Carpenter has presented data on the ability of children six to nine years of age to accurately hop on a hopscotch pattern. The results of this study favor the girls. Carpenter attributes this to the greater amount of practice girls have in this particular skill.

Physical Growth and Motor Performance. The first-grade teacher is concerned with gross motor performances of the children. A knowledge of the sequence of development in gross motor performances and the relationship of this phase of the child's development to physical growth will be useful to her in guiding the child during the early school years. A study reported by Seils deals with the relationship between the physical growth and maturity of primary school children and their proficiency in performing certain gross motor activities. An analysis of the data in terms of each grade level showed that the mean performance for both boys and girls becomes higher at each grade level, although the correlations between the gross motor skill performances and age, height, and weight were low. A positive relationship was found between gross motor skill performance and the results of a measure of maturity. When one considers the varied factors, which influence motor skill performances, this relationship between skeletal maturity and gross motor performances, although not great, appears more significant.

Certain skills were selected by Lachtaw as basic to performance in many motor activities for grades four, five, and six. These skills were running, jumping, throwing and catching, striking, and kicking. Selected tests to measure these skills were given to a group of 67 boys and girls in grades four through six. The results of the study tended to corroborate those of Seil's. The relationship between age, height, weight, and performance as measured by these tests was relatively low. Height and weight factors in general showed a lower relationship to performance than did the age factor for both boys and girls. It appears from this study that experience and maturation are significant factors in the development of more complex skills.

Importance of Maturation. Experiments with music training show that preschool children can profit from certain types of training. Studies conducted at the University of Iowa show the effectiveness of early training upon the development of singing ability and interest in music. Groups of nursery-school children were given intensive help in the use of the singing voice for an average of ten minutes daily for forty periods. The control group was given no intensive training, but did participate in the music activities of the nursery school programme. There was an accelerated development at all age levels in the singing ability of the children given the intensive training. This accelerated development was paralleled by an increased interest and desire to participate in musical training. The results of the study indicate quite clearly that singing ability and musical interest can be stimulated and accelerated through a training programme that emphasizes individual as well as group performance and gives special attention to children who need voice and ear training.

An important question about perceptual-motor development is, How early can we begin to teach a child a skill and expect to see improvement beyond that which would result from maturation and general practice? Dusenberry studied this problem with 56 children as subjects, ranging in age from three to seven years. Two groups of twenty-eight children each were carefully equated. One of these groups was given practice and instruction in ball-throwing twice a week over a period of three weeks, while the other group was used as a control group.

The children were found to vary greatly in the way they threw the ball. In general the boys made better use of their bodies than did the girls and had more advance arm and hand movements in executing the throwing. As we can see from Table 1, both the practice and control groups made gains in average throwing scores from the initial to the final test. There is, however, a significant difference in the gains of the trained group over those of the control group. The boys improved more in distance-throwing skills than the girls with the same amount of training. Radical changes in style of throwing were sometimes accompanied by power performance. The most marked change in throwing style due to training, however, was found in stance. This is noteworthy for those concerned with guiding children in the development of skills. The importance of good form in the development of simple motor skills is indicated by the results of this study.

There is some evidence, however, that training given at too early an age is largely ineffectual in promoting the development of motor skills. This is shown in a study by Hicks. Children from two and a half to six years of age were given eight weeks of training in throwing a ball at a moving target. Such training produced no greater gains in the skills than were produced in the control group through structural maturation and general practice. There are skills, which should be delayed to permit the child to mature sufficiently to acquire the best methods of performing them. The gains to be derived from deferred practice, however, do not continue indefinitely. For example, training in motor skills needed to perform acrobatic dancing cannot be delayed too long. Such delay may be more detrimental than helpful.

Table 1. Differences Between Beginning and Final Throwing Averages

	Throws in Feet		*Gains*	
Group	*Initial*	*Final*	*Feet*	*Percent*
Trained (Boys)	24.0	30.0	6.0	25
Control (Boys)	23.5	26.5	3.0	12.8
Trained (Girls)	16.3	18.4	2.1	12.7
Control (Girls)	15.7	16.0	.3	2.1

Also, the younger child is at an advantage in learning foreign languages. Penfield and Roberts point out that the child's brain has a specialized capacity for learning language. This neuro-physiological ability diminishes with the years. Also, the child experiences a direct psychological urge, which immensely facilitates foreign language learning. His primary motivation is satisfaction of his curiosity and not mastery of a new language.

Experiences in the schools of Europe and America have shown that, after a certain age—10 or 11—the child approaches a second language by using the already mastered symbols of his own language. He tries to use his own verbal units and thus speaks with an accent. Furthermore, the youth who begins learning a second language during his teens or twenties employs the linguistic units already learned during the period of vocabulary expansion. He therefore *translates* the symbols of the foreign language into his own and then derives meaning. The young child does not do this. He employs the foreign language units directly to get meaning.

Thus, if easy and natural pronunciation together with facility in use is the goal of modern language instruction, such instruction should begin during the early elementary years in classroom situations *where no other language is spoken* for the time being. The impetus then will not be to collect words, nor to acquire language, but to learn about interesting things, to play games and to read pleasant stories. Penfield and Roberts point out that evidence suggests that those who learn more than one language in early childhood find the learning of later additional languages easier.

The neurologists also suggest that speech is not the only new skill, which is more easily and accurately acquired in childhood. Learning the piano and violin and learning to ski also come into this category.

In this connection a comment from Pearson is interesting: Perhaps definite instruction in the specific skills of various games—batting, catching, and pitching in baseball; stance, swing and putt in golf; tennis strokes; techniques of basketball, bowling, boxing, wrestling, swimming, dancing, fishing, hockey, whatever game the individual selected would accomplish more toward the development of coordination and rhythm than the usual physical training of the gymnasium, and it would also enable the child to learn a recreational sport which he would continue in adult life.

One should not oversimplify the factors involved in the acquisition of skills, however. The dynamics of the individual child operate at all stages and in all aspects of his development. One six-year-old child will persist in a skill-developing activity in spite of difficulty and failure while his classmate with equal maturity and opportunity for learning gives up quickly. Materials bearing on the role of emotions and motivation on behaviour and learning will be presented in subsequent chapters.

In general, it may be stated as a fundamental principle that beyond the early years most of the differences in learning complex skills-especially the higher initial scores—are a result of the wide range of experiences and differences in motivation. Where gross motor skills involving the large muscles are concerned, differences in strength at different age levels give a significant advantage to older children. Also, the older individual has greater ability to sustain attention and follow directions in the performance of complex motor skills.

Learning the Task as a Whole. It has been noted earlier that learning is usually more efficient when the learner grasps the major relationships. The whole, when understood, gives meaning to the parts. After one has gotten the general pattern of the plan of a city, such as Washington, D.C., it is easier to learn the location of important buildings and parks in that city. Thus, formal training on specific items of a task may be very helpful in overcoming a specific difficulty.

Although experimental results favor the whole method of learning, they are not sufficiently conclusive to permit a simple and generalized statement of the relative efficiency of the whole and part methods in the learning of skills. Even when applied to specifically perceptual-motor skills, the results vary from person to person. There is some evidence that the more capable students are likely to do better with the whole method. Certainly the size of the unit to be learned should vary with the capacity of the learner. This was noted in a study by Lemke of motor-esthetic learning. His study was concerned with children's improvement in playing the violin through instruction in phrasing. The importance of distinguishing the rhythmical phrases in the interpretation of music is analogous to the value of punctuation and accentuation in written and oral expression.

Two groups of intermediate-grade children were used in Lemke's study. The experimental group was given instruction in phrasing three periods a week for ten weeks, while the control group was given no such instruction. The experimental group was given the task of perceiving and executing this smallest unit, in contrast to a larger measure of unit which beginners are usually taught. The experimental group showed marked improvement over· the control group—improvement which was reflected not only in phrasing but also in tone, time, pitch, and technique. The conclusions drawn from this and other studies bearing on the whole part method of learning may be summarized as follows:

1. No one method is superior for all learners or for all tasks. The length and complexity of the task may make learning by the purely part method superior in some instances to learning by the whole method.
2. In general, students should be oriented to the problem before practicing special details.
3. The size of the learning unit should be influenced by the maturation and capacity of the learner.
4. In complex perceptual-motor tasks or complicated skills, special attention should be given to difficult parts.
5. The learner's attention should be focused upon the task as a whole and the perceptual cues rather than upon special movements to be made.
6. Attention should be given to the total performance of the task, leaving "the rough edges" to be smoothed out later in additional practice.

The Effects of Practice. To be effective, practice must be sufficiently long for the learner to identify cues and make discernible progress on the task. Further, practice must be so arranged that there is a minimum lapse of time between cue and response and between the response and reinforcement. The learner must know when his response is correct.

The importance of adequate spacing of practice is a fundamental principle of learning. This is most important in acquiring skills.

Research findings at the present time do not support a simple definitive decision to mass or to distribute practice solely on the basis of categories of verbal or motor learning. A more workable distinction lies between *serial* (verbatim) and paired-associate types of tasks. A distinction must also be made for idea learning, which is .in a separate category (underlying both serial and paired-associate tasks). Evidence suggests that distributed practice is better in verbatim *learning* than in paired associate learning. Massed practice, on the other hand, produces better *retention* for serial tasks than for paired-associate tasks.

In general practice periods should be short and well spaced at first, but not so short that the learner will be unable to grasp the act as a unit. In the precision stage, practice periods may be longer and more numerous. A study by Fulton attempted to compare the effect of placing emphasis on speed and accuracy in the initial stages of a training period of a ballistic movement. Results obtained from the comparison of two equated groups given fifteen training periods at the rate of two a week revealed no significant differences in speed of strokes at the end of training period. However, the group, which emphasized speed developed greater accuracy than the group which made accuracy the primary aim. This finding is in accord with other studies, which indicate that the correct order of emphasis in teaching skills should be technique first with speed and accuracy being achieved as the result of control.

The importance of practice in the development and fixation of a skill will also depend upon the motivation of the learner. Practice, as mere repetition, may create unfavorable attitudes toward a task and may thus act as a barrier to the development of a high state of efficiency. We can see this with the student who finds practice periods in typewriting unpleasant. He will not reach as high a level of performance as he could were he adequately motivated. This is one of the potential dangers in over-learning. When practice is carried to the point where it is distasteful to the learner, or when it is carried on in a mechanical, repetitive fashion, efficiency in learning will be adversely affected. The value of over-learning is largely dependent upon the motivation of the learner and the optimal distribution of practice time.

Guidance in the Acquisition of a Skill

Skills are learned by practice. It has been noted that at certain maturation levels in human development, there are developmental tasks whose practice gives the child such satisfaction that the mere repetition of the activity seems to be an end in itself until the task-skills have been adequately mastered. This is almost naturally achieved before the child will get the opportunity to practice the next sequence of skills. At the same time there is usually a naturally motivated "teacher" in a parent or family member who constantly motivates and demonstrates by talking to the child, praising, and illustrating. This practicing takes place in natural life situations and is purposeful. The same principles should be observed in the more formal settings where skills such as writing, reading, swimming, skating, and typing are taught.

Of paramount importance is the teacher or instructor. He must not only know the whole constellation of the skills involved with their clusters of sub-skills but he must be able to demonstrate the correct pattern of performance, not only in its entire, smooth performance, but also in its individual and involved parts. Furthermore, he must be able to observe the student's weaknesses and strengths as he practices, and he must be able to capitalize on the student's strengths to aid him in overcoming his weaknesses. The instructor has the responsibility to know the best methods of teaching the skills and how they can be best practiced.

***

4

Psychology of Creative Thinking

The idea, frequently expressed, that creative ability is related to the activities of gifted individuals results perhaps from one's conception of what constitutes creative expression. The notion of what constitutes creative expression may best be understood from an examination of behaviour involving creativeness. A little girl at play was recently observed by one of the writers. She was gathering blocks left over from some recent construction and placing them parallel to each other in two rows about eight inches apart. She later constructed two small make-believe houses near the parallel rows of blocks. Upon questioning the little girl it was learned that she was constructing a railroad, and two railroad stations.

The little girl had relatively recently been on a trip by train to see her aunt. This trip had no doubt made quite an impression on her, and this furnished the dynamics for her activity. There is discernible in the play of this little girl some of the important characteristics of creative expression. These include the following:

1. Prolonged attention related to some absorbing experience.
2. Heightened motivation to discover, test, or interpret for one's self the meaning related to the experience.

3. Expressive behaviour resulting from the heightened motivation.

4. Variations in behaviour as an outgrowth of experimentation to discover ways of expressing one's self.

5. Tension reduction through successful experiences in creating ways of expressing one's self.

Applied to the play life of the typical six-year-old, any activity into which children enter wholeheartedly will probably have some characteristics of creative expression. Creative activity may take place through a great variety of media. The kindergarten child who uses bright blue tempera (a paint) to portray his family, the first-grade child who makes up a silly jingle to sing, and the third-grader who plays cowboy all are demonstrating creative expression. Likewise, the dramatic "skit" of the sixth graders may be the creative product of several pupils. Not all school activity is, or should be, creative, although the various aspects of school life should furnish opportunities for creativeness. As in problem-solving, thinking is also involved in creative behaviour. Through the process of thinking, the learner will grasp new relationships, give a new interpretation to a problem or fact, or improve creatively existing conditions or standards. In this connection it should be pointed out that the learner must discover before he can create.

Children, as they develop, seek to explain the world, particularly aspects of the world they live in. Out of a wide variety of experiences the learner discovers the nature of the physical world and the culture in which he lives. Such a discovery is essential for creativeness.

Factors Influencing Creative Expression

Various factors in the child's physical and social environment affect the extent and nature of his creative expression. The principles of growth and learning applicable to other aspects of the child's growth and learning are also applicable to creative ability. Important differences may be noted in the creative ability of children of the same age level. Also, the same child will vary in his creative expression from one situation to another.

It has already been suggested that the creative expressions of the child will be limited by the extent to which he has discovered the physical and social world he lives in. Creative expression cannot take place without ideas and thoughts, and ideas and thoughts are not nourished in a vacuum. Since creativeness involves a new interpretation and a reorganisation of experiences, the wider the experiences and the greater the wealth of ideas and thoughts, the greater may be the creative activity.

A second factor influencing the creative expression of the child is environment. Environments, which furnish the child an opportunity to express himself and encourage him to do so while supplying media in harmony with his interests and abilities is most important. In the elementary school considerable use is made of paints, crayons, drawing paper, scissors, paste, blocks, and the like.

Closely akin to the second factor, and perhaps part of this factor, is a condition or situation, which stimulates creative expression. An attractive room with good pictures and other materials furnishes a good setting for creative expression. A bird, goldfish, flowers, window curtains, and other materials in the room will likely add to the stimulating effect. The children should be encouraged in their efforts. In some cases a display of their products may be stimulating. However, the best motivation will be a feeling on their part that they are growing, that they are reaching a goal—a feeling of accomplishment.

A fourth factor influencing creativeness is the social climate. Where the child does not feel inhibited, he will be freer to express himself. Criticism from the teacher and others in such a manner as to lead to loss of interest and confidence is extremely harmful. If the child comes to feel that he can't do acceptable work, he will stop trying. There is nothing more harmful to creative expression than the feeling of inadequacy. It is at this point that an understanding teacher is most important.

Self-expression *versus* Imitation. It has already been suggested that many forms of creative expression are observable in the activities of children. On one occasion, a first grade child, when requested to draw a man, drew a house with one window and one door. When the teacher asked where the man was, the child replied, "He was behind the window, but he has gone away." The understanding teacher will take advantage of such a situation to direct the growth of creative ability, rather than to discourage it 'by demanding stylized responses in activities. The beating of the tom-tom by Frank may show all the characteristics of creativeness when he is allowed to beat out the frenzy of an Indian war—dance or the fury of the approaching storm.

Self-expression may be contrasted with imitation. In self-expression, the child's responses are on the level of his own ability and age, motivated by his own feelings and ideas. This does not mean that there is no place for suggestions and guidance from others. It has been observed that considerable help may be given the child in his creative efforts through suggestions from the group-perhaps truer in creative activities than in most other forms of behaviour.

In imitation, the child's responses are patterned. For example, the teacher may have the children draw some picture hanging on the wall or may have them write a short story, furnishing them with all the data and requesting them to put the facts together. In these activities there is little opportunity for self-expression. Lowenfeld has presented the following contrasts of self-expression and imitation:

Self-Expression	*Imitation*
Expression according to child's own level	Expression according to strange level
Independent thinking	Dependent thinking
Emotional outlet	Frustration
Freedom and flexibility	Inhibition and restriction
Early adjustments to new situations	Going along set patterns
Progress, success, happiness	Leaning toward others, dependency, stiffness

Emotional Release through Creative Activities. Many students of child psychology have emphasized the importance of furnishing children with favorable emotional outlets. The inmost self of children, which they often have difficulty expressing in an adult-dominated environment, is often released through creative activities. Such was the case of Louise.

On the playground Louise frequently quarreled and had temper outbursts. She was described by the playground supervisor as "a ball of fire." However, in her art activities (clay modeling and painting) another self appeared. These products depicted a child with considerable originality, and with the orderliness and quality characteristic of the poet.

Aesthetic Appreciation. The development of the ability to accomplish things regarded as worthwhile is accompanied by the building of an appreciation of similar things created by others. Thus, appreciation develops as a result of growth in creative expression, and may be regarded as one of the values to be derived from growth in creative expression. The purpose of appreciation is enjoyment. Many teachers lose sight of this in their teaching and often miss the close relationship to be found between the development of certain skills and the appreciation of the aesthetic elements involved in the products.

There are common as well as specific problems involved in the acquisition of aesthetic appreciation. Studies show that the transfer of appreciation from one area to another is not automatic. If the art instructor wants the pupils to increase their appreciation of the dance or music he must relate the classroom activities in art to the dance or music. There are certain fundamental principles in common, but the pupils need to be guided in seeing and understanding these common fundamental principles.

The traditional grading system presents one of the most frequently observed barriers to training for aesthetic appreciation. This, perhaps, results from the relative difficulty involved in evaluating growth in aesthetic appreciation. It is much easier to measure a pupil's ability to recite a poem or name the principal characters in a play than to measure his aesthetic appreciation of the poem or play.

If we are interested in increasing a pupil's appreciation for fine arts or music we must keep appreciation as an important objective and make use of learning procedures designed to develop appreciation. Aesthetic appreciation involves both emotional and intellectual development. An intellectual understanding of the conditions under which a song was written or a painting produced may be most important in the development of appreciation among more mature pupils. However, this intellectual information alone is insufficient. The development of appreciation for the poem includes increased understanding, a feeling tone, and in many cases a sharpened imagery of the situation. Actual experiences in writing poems, use of visual aids, dramatizations, good oral readings, and group projects in writing are useful in the development of the components making up what is termed *aesthetic appreciation.* The beginning point for teaching the pupil to appreciate things encountered in his physical or social environment is a social climate that does not interfere with creative expression. Also, a teacher who has developed aesthetic appreciations and who is able through sound learning principles to lead others to develop aesthetic appreciation, will significantly affect the learning and development of aesthetic appreciation among her pupils.

Guiding the Child in the Development of Creative Ability

The Motivation of Creative Expression. The fundamental principles of motivation and learning are as applicable to the development of creativeness as they are to other aspects of the child's growth and learning. Creative expression does not appear in a vacuum; neither does it appear without motivation and effort. Students of psychology have emphasized the value of the fine arts in satisfying basic needs. Likewise, the creative expressions of children through drawing or other media have been found useful in studying the personality dynamics of individual children.

There are many opportunities available for creativeness in motor and language skills. The dance, dramatics, and writing as media for creative expression are frequently used in the modern school programme. The language arts offer one of the best mediums of expression for the intelligent school-age child. However, all school-age children should be encouraged and stimulated to express themselves through the language arts as well as through other media. Stimulation may be provided by having children relate certain aspects of their experiences-how they spent the summer, what they would like to do during the Christmas holidays, and the like. The children may be asked to respond to such propositions as:

What I would like to do when I grow up?

What I would do if I had lots of money?

What I would like to do next summer?

Atmosphere for Creativity. We have already pointed out that creative activity does not take place in a vacuum. Neither does it occur in an atmosphere that places too much restriction on behaviour. A suitable atmosphere for creativity will be characterized by certain conditions, some of which are here described.

First, the child must feel that he is accepted. Such a feeling will best develop in an atmosphere where teachers and others in authority recognize and respect the uniqueness of each child's personality. Closely related to this need for acceptance on the part of both teachers and pupils is the feeling of personal worth which grows out of a recognition that what he is doing is a worthwhile contribution.

Second, a child needs to feel secure. Children who are inhibited, who feel insecure, or who are not interested in the activities at hand are not likely to display creative thinking. Gillilies presents a good description of how one teacher by gaining the confidence of a group of underprivileged children, was able to secure their participation in creative dramatics. Preparation for creative dramatics includes such activities as guided reading and listening to other children's stories. It is also dependent upon the proper set or attitude, which can only be secured in an atmosphere where the children feel that they are wanted and are part of the total group. Studies of the dynamics of child behaviour show various causes underlying security; however, there is no substitute for an inner-contentment fostered in an atmosphere where the individual is not inhibited through fear of severe censure or disapproval.

Third, the child does his best creative efforts in an atmosphere of freedom. The child who is told what when, and how to do something will not have the opportunity to exercise his own initiative or give expression to his own feelings and ideas. This does not mean that guidance is necessarily a barrier to self-activity. When guidance is presented in a democratic spirit of helpfulness it becomes a source of encouragement to the child. Parents and teachers have the responsibility for providing opportunities for children to act on their own purposes toward satisfying the need for self-expression. The parent or teacher who sets an example for the child through his own creative activity need not expect the child to be inspired to duplicate this effort or activity. Control and direction, whether they are by example or by teaching, will inhibit self-expression and destroy originality and creativeness.

The Danger of Stereotyped Procedures. Educators are becoming more aware of the deleterious effects of unimaginative or stereotyped school work. Also, there is an increased recognition of the importance of creativeness in the lives of growing boys and girls. Educational psychologists have recognized, since the early teachings of William James and others, that stereotyped procedures in school tend to produce stereotyped products. We can see the results of these stereotyped procedures in the drawings of children who are taught to imitate rather than to express themselves. We also pointed out that stereotyped procedures may evolve as a result of imitation of things observed on television or heard on the radio. The extent to which children will develop stereotyped procedures will depend largely upon how teachers and others who guide them in their educational growth proceed.

Problem-solving

Master teachers have constantly interspersed the learning experiences of their students with problem-solving. However, despite the virtues claimed for the problem-solving approach to teaching and learning, most teachers rely upon memory procedures and recitation because first, most of the studies in problem-solving-conducted in laboratories—have limited application in the classroom. Second, the results of these studies have not been presented to students of education in a form useful for classroom teaching. Two yearbooks of the National Society for the Study of Education have devoted considerable attention to this problem, and have had some worthwhile effects. The student of educational psychology will find the materials of these yearbooks useful. A study of problem-solving behaviour, steps involved in problem-solving, and the problem-solving behaviour of school-age children should give the student of educational psychology better insight into the role of problem-solving in learning at school.

Thinking and Problem-solving. Many early writers assigned to the "mind" the function of thinking. There are many people today who merely assign thinking to the mind without offering any explanation of what they mean by mind or how thinking is carried on by the mind. On the human level, thinking and problem-solving are so closely related that it is well-nigh impossible to conceive of problem-solving behaviour without some consideration of the thought processes. Children as well as adults constantly encounter problems, which demand clear thinking.

Problem-solving behaviour is here regarded as those activities an individual pursues in trying to reach a goal or solution to a problem. The problem situation may vary in complexity from a child's attempts to stack two or three blocks to a scientist's calculations of space and time relationships. Differences in the complexity of problem situations have contributed to different explanations of problem-solving behaviour. At least two processes appear to be common in all these explanations. These involve *(1)* an analysis of the goal, and *(2)* an analysis of the situation.

Analysis of the Goal. The nature of a problem situation features a goal to be attained, but the individual concerned has not figured a way of attaining the goal. Sometimes the learner suggests solutions before he understands what the goal is. This may result from failure to understand the problem or from the development of faulty habits in problem solving. Certainly the development of students as problem-solvers is one of the most important functions of the school. Many learning experiences are so arranged that students are given training in solving problems similar to the kinds of problems they are likely to meet later. The elementary school child who learns to use the dictionary is learning a problem solving technique that will likely be useful on many occasions. The boy who learns to follow directions carefully in the physics laboratory is learning a technique of problem solving that will be most useful in many aspects of life. The first step in any problem is for the pupil to have a goal and to grasp an understanding of the problem. This requires careful thinking.

Analysis of the Situation. The problem-solving process requires the individual to analyze the situation. This may be thought of as the second step, if an analysis of the goal is regarded as the first step. By analyzing the situation the learner determines some of the things he must do to solve the problem. Logical analysis of the problem-solving situation usually involves a series of steps, which we will describe later.

Problem-solving Among School-age Children. Concrete, direct experiences are important to the school-age child's problem-solving activities. However, as he grows older there is a significant increase in his ability to state a problem in words and to verbalize its solution. An important difference between the problem-solving behaviour of younger and older children is that the older children recognize the problem as a problem, whereas the younger children tend to emphasize the objects used in the problem rather than the problem situation. This was apparent in a study reported by Heidbreder in which the problem was to find a small celluloid doll concealed in one of two boxes. The children were to solve the problem by responding to different clues, such as the design at the top of the box. Heidbreder noted that three-year-olds were concerned only with obtaining the doll from the box, that some four-year-olds appeared to react to the problem as such, and that children six to ten years of age definitely responded to the problem as a problem.

Using a problem box built by Parcy Taska, Hensley compared the problem-solving ability of bright and dull children and the methods they used. Criteria for selecting the subjects were: *(1)* chronological age, *(2)* mental age, *(3)* sex, *(4)* level of intelligence, and *(5)* no apparent emotional disturbance. The younger groups (approximately seven years of age) were superior to the older groups (approximately twelve and one-half years of age) of the same mental age in number of problems solved. A comparison of subjects of the same mental age but varying in chronological age revealed a significant difference in the number of solutions with verbal generalizations, indicating that younger subjects are superior to older subjects with similar mental age in verbal generalizations. This is important to teachers of bright and dull children.

Thinking and problem-solving abilities do not develop in a vacuum. Children need guidance in the development of problem-solving ability. There are many opportunities for developing such ability in the classroom. Some conclusions about problem solving among elementary-school children are:

1. Much of the problem-solving activities of pre-school children involves the manipulation of concrete objects in the environment.
2. The use of trial-and-error in children's problem-solving activities varies with the nature of the

problem and the intellectual development of the child.

3. Increased language development is an aid to problem-solving. There is a positive relation between language development and growth in abstract problem-solving ability.

4. There is some evidence that children often solve subordinate parts of problems before integrating them into the total problem.

5. Children are often impetuous in their problem-solving, jumping from an awareness of the problem to a solution without careful testing of the information and data available.

6. With age, there is an increase in problem-solving ability, both in accuracy and speed.

Barriers to Problem-solving. A study reported by Kersh was designed to test the idea that learning by independent discovery is superior to learning with direction, because it is more meaningful. Based on retest data and reports from the subjects Kersh concluded... the superiority of the discovery procedure of learning over procedures of learning with external direction is not adequately explained in terms of "meaningful learnings." The results of this experiment suggest that when the learner is forced to rely on his own cognitive capacities, it is more likely that he will become motivated to continue practicing the task after the learning period. Consequently, the learning becomes more permanent and is more effectively transferred than when the learner is not so motivated.

An important barrier to the development of problem-solving ability and to the solution of a problem is lack of motivation. Because of lack of motivation, both attention and practice are likely to be limited.

Students frequently acquire attitudes, which are barriers to critical thinking. The following incident in an education class illustrates how prejudice limits clear thinking. The instructor was discussing problems and methods involved in teaching respect for rules and, particularly, the law. In the midst of the discussion a student raised his hand and said, "But don't you think that each state should have the right to run its own schools?" This was the first mention of states rights or the public schools, but the student's attitudes were so strong that they colored his thinking on related areas and interfered with his concentration upon the problem being discussed. A second barrier to critical thinking, closely related to the first, is the complete dependence upon authority. Students accustomed to the autocratically managed classroom are likely to be more dependent upon their textbook, the teacher, or some other source of authority than students trained in a freer classroom atmosphere. Students should be guided in evaluating materials being studied in light of their experiences, previously learned materials, and other available evidences. They should be taught that people frequently differ in their interpretations of what they observe and of what they read. Thus, different interpretations sometimes occur in textbooks. They should be taught, however, that scholars are "truth-seekers," and that they should be continuously interested in trying to learn the truth from all available sources. If the teacher is going to be effective in training students to be "truth-seekers," he must first of all be one himself. Teachers tend to pass on to their students their prejudices and ineffective methods of solving problems.

A third barrier to good problem-solving is a lack of a relatively systematic method of attacking the problem. Poor geometry students—relying almost completely upon trial and error—frequently start trying to work out a solution to the problem before they have carefully analyzed it. Some science students begin a laboratory experiment before they have secured a good understanding of the problem and procedures to follow in the experiment. It is here that teaching as guidance can be very effective.

A fourth handicap to problem-solving is rigidity in thinking. This rigidity may be a result of previous experiences in which pupils are taught to perform a problem in specific ways. This may result in negative transfer when the subject attempts to apply the same method to a different problem. This was noted in an experiment reported by Birch and Rabinowitz. The problem consisted of Maier's cord experiment, described earlier. Twenty-five students were divided into three groups, a control group and two experimental groups. The results showed that specific prior experience limited the perception of object properties and made the experienced materials less available as aids to solving problems.

A fifth barrier to problem solving is the learner's lack of confidence. A person who has continuously failed in solving science or mathematics problems will not likely approach a new problem with a feeling that he will be able to solve it. Teachers need to guide students not only in problem-solving techniques but also in the successful solution of problems. This procedure would take advantage of success as a motivating force and of reinforcement as a means of aiding the learning process.

Guiding the Learner in the Problem Solving Process

The question may be asked, what schoolroom procedures will teach pupils how to solve problems most effectively? The answer will be found in the application of the principles that have been presented in this chapter and in previous chapters to problem-solving in the classroom. The preceding chapters have emphasized that learning is a product of behaviour. What is learned depends upon what is done. Therefore, school procedures must consist in guiding the child in the correct methods of mastering what we teach as well as in content. If we want him to be able to solve problems after he gets out of school, he must be given the experience of solving problems while he is in school. More attention in education should be given to the *problem-solving method.* The schools must be concerned with *how to do* as well as with *what others have done.* It is important for the junior-high-school pupil to learn how his ancestors built their houses and earned a living more than a century ago; but it is equally important for him to learn how he is going to solve the problems of the future.

The Problem-solving Process. A number of investigations have been concerned specifically with how people go about solving problems. Experimental studies dealing with the nature of problem-solving by humans suggest that people use a variety of methods which can be roughly grouped into three categories: *(1)* trial-and-error behaviour; *(2)* insightful behaviour; and *(3)* analytical behaviour. These three methods are not qualitatively different, but may be arranged on a continuum; subjects shift from one method to another quite readily during the problem-solving process. The individual attempting to solve Maier's two-cord problem may first resort to trial-and-error behaviour. Insight may be noted when the individual observes the pair of pliers, not as a tool to hold objects, but as an object to be made into a pendulum bob. The learner will likely analyze the problem at different times during the problem-solving process. This tends to furnish him with ideas or hypotheses that become the bases for new or revised ways of attempting to solve the problem.

The results of studies suggest two kinds of learning that may be useful in problem-solving. The first of these involves the acquisition of certain broad, non-specific notions about the object, situation, or method experienced. We see this with the child who gains experiences in mounting insects. A second type of learning is one in which the pupils take general ideas and convert them into more limited functional characteristics. The pupil who spends much time and effort-mounting butterflies illustrates this. The learning involved in the mounting of butterflies may be of such rigid pattern that it interferes with other activities in nature study or science involving different kinds of insect life. If pupils are to become efficient problem-solvers they must be taught to vary their methods of dealing with problems in harmony with the nature of each problem encountered.

The results of studies reported by Luchins suggest that repetition may exert harmful influences on the individual's ability to solve problems, especially problems requiring originality. Luchins experiments showed that even young children can learn several methods of solving problems within their grasp. He concludes: "This suggests that a means of combining the possible blinding effects of repetition is to teach more than one thing in a given lesson and to allow practice in more than one response in a given practice period." Such experiences would give the pupils the feeling of being creative, the satisfaction of understanding something of the formulation of problems, and better understandings of different methods useful in solving problems.

Essentials in the Problem-solving Process. Considerable psychological research has been concerned with how students solve problems. Dewey's analysis of the stages of the problem-solving process has had an important influence on the thinking of many educators. Other investigations have also dealt with how people solve problems. The result of these investigations indicate that the problem-solving process involves four essential functions: *(1)* an orientation function—understanding of the nature of the problem; *(2)* an information gathering function; *(3)* an hypothesis-formation functions; and *(4)* an hypothesis-testing function. Although these processes are identifiable in most problem-solving situations, they do not necessarily appear in this sequential order. For the teacher to demand that the learner always follow this sequential order would not contribute to creative thinking, important in difficult problem situations.

Educational psychologists are concerned with the problem's influence on the problem-solving process and the influence of the characteristics or the problem-solver on the problem-solving process. In the solution of simple problems, the child depends upon obvious cues present in the immediate environment; in the solution of more difficult problems hypotheses are likely to be set forth and tested. Investigations show that the more complex the problem the more apparent the differences appear in the problem-solving process.

One of the differences to be noted between intelligent and unintelligent problem-solving behaviour is the degree of accuracy each kind of behaviour attains in evaluating possible solutions. The intelligent subject is more likely to "think a possible solution through" and to foresee whether it will work. This does not mean, however, that intelligence is synonymous with good problem-solving ability. The ability to imagine a possible solution to a problem grows out of training and experience, and not simply out of superior intelligence. Basically it is clear thinking that involves reasoning. The effectiveness of reasoning will depend upon innate mental ability, the amount of information at hand, and the extent to which good habits of thinking are applied to the problem at hand.

Creating the Problem. The first essential in guiding the child in the development of problem-solving ability is to guide him in the recognition of problems. This can be done by raising one or more thought questions of interest and concern to the pupils. Such a question should not be one that can be answered by repeating something that may be read from some assigned source, although this is highly important for certain types of problem-solving. The problem should call for clear thinking and insight, the outgrowth of knowledge and understanding. The problem may be to determine an effective Christmas program, to invite parents to the school program, or to decorate the schoolroom for Halloween.

Whatever the nature of the problem, it must be adapted to the experience and maturational level of the pupils. Also, while the teacher may suggest the problem, it is not a real problem for the pupils until they accept it and are motivated to find a solution to it. The teacher's question should be designed to set off a chain of suggestions from the pupils. Unless these questions appeal to the interests and curiosity of the children so that they have a felt desire to solve the problem, they are ineffective. Thus, it takes the teacher's skill, initiative, and originality to provide thought-provoking questions that will challenge the interests and abilities of the pupils.

Understanding the Problem. Once the problem is stated, the next step in its solution is for the pupils to understand it. Sometimes, when pupils fail to make headway with a problem, teachers frequently admonish them with the words, "you aren't thinking." Actually, the pupils may be thinking intensely, but perhaps, not on the problem, nor in the way the teacher wants. A problem not clearly understood, or one vaguely defined leads to mental fumbling. Thus, it is very important from the beginning that pupils have a clear idea of what the problem is. To assure this, pupils may be asked to repeat the problem. The teacher may also feel the need to point out some significant aspects of the problem that they are overlooking. Sometimes a well directed question to the pupils will help them to clarify the problem.

There are times when children and adolescents must be urged to "stick" to the problem or to "keep on the subject." Without such guidance irrelevant materials are likely to be introduced, and may lead to a discussion far a field from the problem under consideration. Clear thinking about a problem depends ultimately upon seeing the relationship between the relevant facts leading to a solution of the problem.

Gathering Information about the Problem. On problems where the relations between the different elements are not clear, the child resorts to trial-and-error behaviour. Children ordinarily need more trials and make more errors than adults in solving problems, although their thinking and reasoning processes are generally similar to those of adults. While reliance upon trial and error is justified, the solution to the problem will not be found through "blind" trial-and-error behaviour. Problem-solving is a goal-seeking process in which the individual knows what he is looking for and is aware of the solution when he finds it. If the problem falls within a field where the pupils have much information, they can arrive at a solution by recalling relevant information about the problem. When the problem situation contains aspects of problems with which the children are familiar, relations are more apparent and insight appears.

In many cases the pupils will need additional information before attempting to solve the problem. They should be encouraged to use their past experiences in seeking additional information about the problem. The teacher should guide the pupils in becoming acquainted with sources of information and in how to use such sources. He may suggest that they contact certain people, visit certain places, write to authorities, or make a trip to the police station, court—house, hospital, or factory to get the information they need. He may suggest library source material and the librarian's help may be enlisted. The development of problem-solving ability will not take place automatically.

Seeking and Evaluating Suggestions for the Solution of Problems. Language and symbols provide the means for solving most of the problems students encounter at school, although actual experiences are often essential. The good teacher will not give the student answers, but will guide him in seeking possible solutions. Pupils should be encouraged to do their own thinking. It is out of such thinking, fumbling, and reconstructing that insight usually appears. The teacher can best guide the pupils by directing their attention to important elements in the problem that have been overlooked.

Sometimes the pupil will get off on the wrong path or lead. At this point he should be encouraged to re-examine the problem to see if that approach will lead to solution. He should be encouraged to vary his attack on the problem. Because pupils sometimes give up very quickly, they should be urged to try different approaches once or twice more. If they are very discouraged, they should be permitted to drop the problem and return to it later. After a period of rest, they may be able to return to the problem with new zeal and perhaps with new ideas.

An evaluation of the solution of a problem requires that the learner—have the problem clearly in mind. Failure to understand the goal one is striving for may lead to an inadequate or incorrect evaluation. Guessing does not, in itself, solve problems. Neither do "blind" trial and error attempts. An evaluation of the solution requires a critical and open-minded attitude, which grows through maturation, experiences, and careful guidance in suspending judgement and maintaining an open-minded attitude.

Group Dynamics in Problem-solving. Studies indicate that group situations have an important bearing on learning and problem-solving. Group solutions to problems tend to be superior to individual solutions. A friendly group situation seems to contribute to the solution of problems, particularly those requiring originality. Heise and Miller noted that the success of group activity in problem-solving was dependent upon the channels of communication in the group, the nature of the problem, and the stress or tension of the total situation. It was further noted that problem-solving was most efficient where communication was unrestricted, and least efficient where there was one-way communication among all pairs.

A study reported by Hudgins was designed to test the hypothesis that problem-solving experiences in a group improve individual ability more than does individual experience. The subjects of the study were 128 fifth-grade pupils. In the first phase of the study the pupils worked on arithmetic problems in subgroups of four students; in the second phase the pupils solved the problems individually. The results of the study did not substantiate the hypothesis that group problem-solving behaviour was superior to the individual behaviour. It appears that any problem-solving superiority present in small groups will depend upon the efforts of the most able member of the group to communicate his knowledge and understanding to others of the group.

The question of the superiority of group versus individual problem-solving behaviour must be considered in terms of the needs of pupils and the nature of the problems involved. Too much emphasis on group methods may be wasteful in terms of developing competent individual problem-solvers. Furthermore, much "group work" in school is actually work by one individual, usually the one considered most able m the area, since the students problem is to secure a passing mark. Some characteristics of a classroom that promotes problem-solving behaviour are:

1. Teacher-pupil planning
2. Thought questions and effective discussion procedures
3. Good techniques for presenting data, such as blackboards, bulletin boards and reports
4. Cooperative effort in projects involving group-problem solving
5. Discussion, debate, criticisms, and suggestions
6. An emotional climate of friendliness, cooperation, and the sharing of ideas

Experiences Basic to Successful Problem-solving. It has been already pointed out that concepts grow as a result of experiences. For instance, the child evolves a set of concepts related to fairness, to family life, or to safety. These groups of concepts guide his thoughts and constitute a useful frame of reference; they are also essential for solving problems. Unless the child has had some experience or experiences that furnish meaning, he will be confused and unable to find solutions to problems. His inability to understand terms and his failure in reasoning often stem from his lack of experiences. In these circumstances, exhortations by the teacher to "think" will be quite futile. Home and school should therefore strive to furnish him with a variety of experiences using pictures, radio, television, stories, pets, toys, books, excursions, opportunities to explore, answers to questions, and contacts with persons from different backgrounds.

As long as life moves along familiar channels where no new demands are made on the individual, habit is sufficient. However, when the individual is faced with a goal he cannot reach without special help or consideration, habit is insufficient and he is faced with a problem. Thinking seems to occur when the individual, confronted by a problem, endeavors to find a solution based upon relevant past experiences. In this connection language is very important. Even the pre-school child tends to verbalize while attempting to solve a relatively complex problem. This verbalization increases with age.

5

Intelligence Tests

The modern psychologist has been taking more interest in measuring the intelligence than defining it. The processes of measurement and their result have helped us a lot in discovering the nature of intelligence.

Binet defines intelligence as "judgement or common sense, initiative, the ability to adapt oneself, to judge well, understand well, reason well." He stresses that "intelligence is a capacity to enable the individual to take and maintain a definite direction, to make adaptations for attaining a desired goal and to be able to criticise oneself and others."

Freeman defines intelligence as a capacity of successful adjustment in all sorts of situations. Intelligence tests lead us to this definition. But it is too general. Intelligence is more than the ability of adjustment.

According to Terman intelligence is an ability to think in terms of abstract idea.

This definition has also been criticised very much. No doubt 'to think in terms of abstract ideas' is a significant aspect of intelligence but this is not at all. All intelligent persons can deal with abstract ideas quite successfully but they can handle objects and concrete jobs also with the same success. Moreover, even insane persons think and talk in terms of abstract ideas but they are devoid of intelligence, because their ideas are not directed to some useful goal.

Tharndike is content to define intelligence as the power of "more association or connection forming ability." But this explanation is quite incomplete. Even feeble-minded powers have enough connection forming ability. They too can associate ideas to some extent.

After analysing these definitions it may broadly be said that intelligence consists of the following mental traits:

(i) Ability to do the maximum in the minimum period of time.

(ii) Ability to solve problems independently.

(iii) Ability to think in abstract terms.

(iv) Ability to take benefit from personal and experience of other.

(v) A proper sense of discrimination and relationship between objects and persons.

What is Intelligence. This is perhaps the most difficult question over posed to psychologists. This question has not been so far satisfactorily answered inspite of various seminars and conferences. No body knows what is intelligence. The nature of intelligence is compared with the electricity. Everybody knows about the utility of electricity, but nobody knows about its nature. In the same way people know about the importance of intelligence, but they are unknown to its real meaning. Different psychologists have given different definitions to clarify the concept of intelligence. We can divide these definitions in three groups:

(1) Ability to Adjust. It means that intelligence is not to adjust but it is ability or capacity to adjust. This definition has been given recognition by following psychologists:

According to View of **Burt**, "It is the capacity of flexible adjustment."

According to **Stern**, "Intelligence is the ability to adjust oneself into a new situation."

According to **Ross**, "Conscious adaptation to new situation is Intelligence."

According to **Woodworth**, "Intelligence is an acquiring ability, it is capacity to acquire capacity."

(2) Ability to Learn. It means that intelligence is not to learn but capacity or ability to learn. In this regard views of various supporters of this definition are as follows:

According to **Woodro's**, "Intelligence is an acquiring capacity."

According to **Buckingham's**, "Intelligence is ability to learn."

According to **Dearborn's**, "It is the capacity to learn or profit by experiences."

According to **Thorndike's**, "Intelligence is the ability to make profitable use of past experiences."

(3) Ability to Carry on Abstract Thinking. It means intelligence is the capacity to carry on abstract thinking. This definition has been recognized by the following psychologists.

According to **Spearman's**, "Intelligence is rational thinking."

According to **Terman's**, "Intelligence is the ability to think in terms of abstract ideas."

According to **Binet's**, "Intelligence is the capacity to think well, to judge well and to be self-critical."

It is very difficult to separate all these definitions into three separate categories. Wechsler's definition seems to combine and extend the above these groups of definitions.

He says, "Intelligence is aggregate or global capacity of individual to act purposefully, to think rationally and to deal effectively with the environment."

Vernon classified all these definitions into three different approaches, namely:

Biological Approach. Man is an organism and his survival depends upon adaptation to the environment. This category of definition lays stress on adaptive nature of human beings. If psychology can be interpreted as a biological science, intelligence can be interpreted as an adaptation to the environment. This approach emphasizes that intelligence is the ability of an individual to adapt to new situation of life. From practical point of view, the biological concept is not useful in the study of individuals within a culture.

Operational Approach. Operational approach is important to understand the concept of intelligence in clear and definite terms. Scientific terms are not defined in terms of isolation but by stating the observable conditions under which the statement is true or false. Instead of defining the word itself it should be defined under conditions in which it occurs.

Psychological Approach. This approach emphasizes the role of both heredity and environment in the development of intelligence. It is very difficult to isolate the relative effect of heredity and environment in the development of intelligence.

A close look at all the above definitions suggest that intelligence is the ability to do a thing. Intelligence is the capacity to acquire knowledge, but it is not knowledge. Intelligence is not thought but the capacity to think. Intelligence is not a skill but is a capacity to acquire skill. Thus the nature of intelligence may help us to desire a workable definition of intelligence in the following form—'Intelligence is the mental ability of an individual which helps him to cope with the new life situations effectively and efficiently.'

Types of Intelligence

Thorndike has classified intelligence into 3 categories namely:

1. **Abstract Intelligence.** It is the ability to understand words, numbers and letters and to use them effectively. Abstract intelligence is required in ordinary academic subjects in schools such as reading, writing an solving academic problems. The highest level of abstract intelligence is manifested in the thoughts of poets, philosophers and writers.

2. **Social Intelligence.** It is the ability of an individual to deal effectively and efficiently with his social and cultural environment. Social intelligence is revealed when a person is able to establish and develop desirable social relations in confirmity with his social and cultural norms.

3. **Concrete Intelligence.** It is the ability to understand and deal with things as in skilled trades or scientific appliances. This is also known as mechanical or motor intelligence. In education concrete intelligence is required in learning dances and participating in games and sports.

Characteristics of Intelligence

1. It is an endowment to the individual child, which has been given to him by nature.

2. It helps the child in the learning process and to achieve the goal of maximum learning in the minimum period of time.

3. Intelligence gives an insight to the child to evaluate the future and act according to the requirements of the situation.

4. It enables the child to proceed from concrete to abstract. It is in abstract terms that ideas remain in our mental make up.
5. It helps the child to acquire the capacity to profit from his previous experiences and the experiences of others.
6. Though the development of intelligence is fixed by heredity, yet it is also determined by the environment as well. In a healthy environment the child is able to develop his intelligence better in comparison to a hostile one.
7. The child is able to face the future with success and solve the difficult problems of life.
8. It enables him to distinguish between the right and wrong, truth and falsehood, social and anti-social activities.
9. There are very minor differences in the development of intelligence between boys and girls.
10. The development of intelligence proceeds from birth till the end of the period of adolescence.

THEORIES OF INTELLIGENCE

There are three theories of intelligence which explain the nature of intelligence:

1. Spearman's Two-Factor Theory. The English Charles Spearman (1904), who was the inventor and first user of factor analytic methods developed a two-factor theory of intelligence from his own experimental work.

The theory was expounded in his book *"The Abilities of Man."* This book was published in 1927.

The essence of his theory in his own words was, "That all branches of intellectual activity have in common on fundamental function (or group of functions), whereas remaining or specific elements of the activity seem in every case to be wholly different from that in all the others." We can say that on the basis of this intelligence is composed of two factors—one 'g' factor and the other 's' factor. This 'g' factor is involved in all walks of life and 's' is a special factor which is exclusive and is shared by none. The Examples of 's' factor are: Artistic ability, 'Musical ability'. These 'special abilities' are independent of 'g' factor. There are 9 's' factors.

Spearman wisely refused to identify 'g' with intelligence or any other quality whose definition was controversial, he suggested that it depends upon the general mental energy with which each individual is endowed. The 's' factors he compared to a large number of mechanisms or Engines which could be activated by this energy. 'S' are largely affected by education and training whereas 'g' is innate as well as ineducable.

The chief criticism that can be raised against Spearman's work is that he failed to allow sufficiently for types of abilities, which while less general that 'g', are certainly not specific. The reason was that he was unable to get at 'group factors' and his samples were small. Towards the end of his life, Spearman had begun to realize the existence of 'group factors' but could not formulate his views.

2. Thorndike's Multi-Factor Theory. E.L. Thorndike's multi-factor theory stands in sharp contradiction of Spearman's two-factor theory. According to this, intelligence is a name conveniently given to infinite number of specific abilities combined together. It can be stated that intelligence is the sum total of all the specific capacities with regard to every separate act. It also means that E.L. Thorndike denies the existence of a general factor. Intelligence is a host of highly independent factors. This theory was given to us in the beginning of the present century.

Types/Kinds of Intelligence. Thorndike concluded that there were three types of Intelligence:

(i) Social Intelligence of ability to understand and deal with persons.

(ii) Concrete Intelligence referring to dealing with things, as in skilled trades and specific appliances.

(iii) Abstract Intelligence or ability to understand and deal with verbal and mathematical symbols.

Abstract intelligence is the one that receives the greatest weight.

3. Thurstone's Group-Factor Theory. Intermediate between the theories of Spearman and Thorndike is the Group-Factor Theory or the P.M.A. (Primary Mental Abilities). Theory given to us by Thurstone.

It was in the year 1938, that Thurstone gave us this theory after giving 56 types of tests to students of Chicago University. All these results were subject to factor analysis. He concluded that in all these tests, seven types of factors were working. *i.e.,* Intelligence is composed of those seven primary mental abilities which are working in all tests. Thurstone does not believe in 'G' and 'S' theories. Thurstone concludes that certain mental operations have a common primary factor that gives them psychological and functional unity and also differentiates them from other mental operations. These mental operations constitute a group. A second group of mental operations has its own unifying primary factor, and so on. In all , there are seven such groups which cover the entire range of mental abilities. Each of these primary factors, is independent of others.

(1) V—Verbal (2) N—Number (3) S—Spatial (4) W—Word F—frequency (5) R—Reasoning (6) M—Memory (7) P—Perceptual.

Educational Significance of the SI Model

This is the most comprehensive model taking into consideration all possible aspects of intellectual activity. This is the only theory which considers creativity (Divergent Production or thinking) along with intelligence. Convergent production or thinking in the same model. At least there are two very significant educational implications of it.

1. In the present world, the body of knowledge is expanding very fast, forcing specialization even at the earlier stages of the educative process. We know already that special aspect of intellectual activity are involved in the different specialization processes, both academic and professional. We therefore need an *a priori* knowledge about the specific ability of each student to place himin the right line of specialization. SI Model and analysis of the individual under its guidance can just pinpoint the individual's abilities and provide us a secure base on which his future learning is to be based. This sounds like the theory of 'Perfect Niche' in educational and vocational guidance where square pegs are placed in square holes and round pegs in round holes. Probably the fundamental human creativity and freedom will elude it, but surely this is so far the most scientific step as compared to previous attempts. We are aware that the theory of 'human multipotentiality is also there where an individual may capable of a group of jobs or activities, rather than a 'unilinear occupation', but in that cease his attainment on the various tests constructed on SI model should show corresponding results. After all the day psychology ceases to attempt to predict human behaviour, it will cease to be a science. Of course there are no such studies which can establish the empirical predictive validity of SI

model. This can be carried out by testing young students on SI Model Tests. Predicting their future success on certain abilities, putting them on those trainings or educational streams and finally evaluating whether they come up to the expectations as held out by the test battery.

2. When some students with adequate intelligence fail to learn, corrective teaching (also known as congnitive therapy) in that case first requires an accurate measure of his abilities, and some concrete steps for utilizing his strengths and developing him where he is weak. Merely a knowledge of IQ here is of little use. Only assessment made by SI Model tests can provide here an academically acceptable method of dealing with the problem. This can be a great diagnosis use of this theory.

MEASUREMENT OF INTELLIGENCE

Many attempts have been made to measure intelligence by various methods. The measurement movement has passed through various stages.

(i) Phrenological. Gall discovere phrenological approach to measure intelligence. Gall held that intelligence is directly proportional to the size of the head *i.e.,* the larger the head the greater is the intelligence of the individual.

(ii) Stage of Physiognomy. Physiognomy is the science of shape of features of the face. Features of face were taken to be an index of intelligence. According to this view it was held that an individual having sharp and bright facial features is an intelligent individual. But it was found that many students having bright faces did not fare well in the school. So this view was also rejected.

(iii) Brass Instrumental Stage. Psychologists tried of find out certain instruments to find intelligence known as aesthiesometer. With this instrument psychologists calculated

Aesthiesometric Index of the skin. They held that the lower the Aesthiesometric Index, greater will be the inelligence. This view was also rejected because skin index (resistence) differs from individual to individual.

Modern Intelligence Tests

Psychologists have been interested in knowing the specific mental abilities of the individuals right from the beginning. Intellgience tests provide useful information about these mental abilities such as in academic, vocational, personal and counselling situations and in many diverse areas.

Inelligence tests have been divided into two parts:

- Classification on the basis of Administration.
- Classification on the basis of form.

On the the basis of Administration, these tests can be divided into two groups.

Individual Tests. The tests which are used to test only one individual at a time are known as individual tests. These tests are Binet Simon Test of intelligence and Terman Test of intelligence. In these tests examiners can pay more attention to the examince, he can observe and encourage him more closely during the test. They are preferred by psychologists in clinics and hospitals. These tests are time consuming and require trained examiner.

Group Tests. Tests or intelligence which can be administered to a large number of individuals (groups) at a time are called group tests. They can be verbal or non-verbal performance tests. These tests are preferred because they save time and do not require trained examiners. Army Alpha Test, Army Beta Test and Raven's Progressive Matrices are the examples of group tests.

Classification on the Basis of Form

Verbal Tests. The tests in which language is used to give response to the question is called verbal tests, *e.g.*, A bird does not always have:

(1) Wings (2) Feet (3) Bill (4) Nest.

Non-Verbal Tests. In these type of tests the language is used only in giving necessary instructions to the subjects. These tests involve such activities in which the use of language is not necessary. These tests include itmes on picture completion, picture arrangement, block design, object assembly and digit symbols.

Individual intelligence tests are further divided into two parts:

Individual Verbal Tests. Individual verbal tests are those tests which are administered to one individual at a time. Binet scale is the example of this test. Individuals are required to use language as well as paper and pencil for giving the responses. The test content is loaded with verbal material. Some of the verbal individual intelligence tests are as under :

Benet-Simon Tests. French psychologists Binet and Simon have done a pioneer work in the field of intelligence testing. In 1905, they published a scale of intelligence tests, known as Binet-Simon scale. In this scale some 30 tasks, from the simplest to the most complex, were prescribed in a serial order. The scale was prepared to test feeble-minded children. The scale contained tests for the age group of 3 to 15 years. There were 6 items in the test meant for each age. This scale was being extensively used in almost all the European countries—America, Canada, Australia, New Zealand, South Africa, China, Japan and Russia. Some of the items which were included in Binet's scale are as under :

At An Age - 3

(i) Points to nose, eyes and mouth.

(ii) Repeats two digits.

(iii) Enumerates objects in a picture.

(iv) Gives family name.

(v) Repeats a sentence of syllables.

At An Age - 4

(i) Gives own sex.

(ii) Names key, knife penny.

(iii) Repeats three digits.

(iv) Compares two lines.

At An Age - 8

(i) Counts from 20 to 0.

(ii) Notes omissions from pictures.

(iii) Gives day and date.

(iv) Repeats five digits.

At An Age - 12

(i) Composes one sentence containing three given words.

(ii) Names 60 words in three minutes.

(iii) Defines certain abstract words.

(iv) Discovers the sense of a disarranged sentence.

At An Age - 15

(i) Repeats seven digits.

(ii) Repeats a sentence of 20 syllables.

(iii) Interprets pictures.

(iv) Interprets given facts.

In 1916, Terman of Stanford University had given a revision. Terman made some modifications by avoiding certain draw-backs in Binet's test. He placed six tests in each age group from 3 to 10, eight tests at the age of 12, six tests at the age of 14, six at 16 and six at 18. In 1937, Terman revised the Stanford Binet Tests with the help of Merril and published the Revised Stanford Test. It became useful for the age range of 2 to 18 years. In Stanford-Binet scale 1960, language was used to the highest degree. In it certain items were deleted which were criticised to be out of date.

Individual Non-verbal Tests/Performance Tests. Individual non-verbal tests are mostly performance tests. In performance tests, the content is in the form of material objects and the individual's response depends upon what he does or perform. Generally, following activities are used in performance tests.

(a) ***To Fit Block in the Holes.*** The material consists of a board having holes and numerous blocks. The subject has to fit the blocks in the holes.

(b) ***Picture Completion or Picture Arrangement.*** In picture completion tests, the subject completes the picture with the help of given pieces cut out of each picture whereas in picture arrangement, the pictures are to be arranged in series from the given picture *i.e.*, Hally Pictorial Completion Test.

(c) ***Block Building.*** In these types of tests, the subject is asked to make a structure or design by means of blocks.

Bhatia Battery Test. The battery has been standardised by Dr. Bhatia to be used under Indian conditions with the purpose of providing differences and comparisons of illeterates and school going children, and for providing useful information for school going children as a supplement to verbal tests. The battery includes 5 tests each with its own sub-tests and time limit.

Minnesota Pre-School Scale. This scale is used to test the intelligence of the children in the age group of 18 months to 5 years.

Group Verbal Intelligence Test. The tests which necessitate the use of language and are applied to a group of individuals at a time come under this category. It includes the following tests:

Therman Group Test. It was prepared in 1920. It includes 10 sub-tests.

Army Alpha Test. This test was applied to the new recruits in the American Army in the First World War. It includes 8 sub-tests.

Army General Classification Test. This test was developed during Second World War to serve the same purpose as the Army Alpha. It contains nine (9) number of vocabulary, arithmetic reasoning and block counting items.

In India, many attempts have been made to construct group verbal intelligence tests. A complete list of standardized tests in Indian conditions is available with NCERT, New Delhi. Some of the popular intelligence tests are :

- The Group Test of General Mental Ability (Samuhik Mansik Yogyta Pariksha) by Dr. S. Jalota.
- General Mental Ability Test by P.S. Hundal (Punjabi)
- Group Intelligence Test by Prayag Mehta
- Group Test of Intelligence prepared by Bureau of Psychology, Allahabad (Hindi).

Group Non-Verbal Intelligence Test

Terman Mcnemar Test of Mental Ability. It was prepared in 1941. It includes 5 sub-tests.

Army Beta Test. It was developed in World War I in U.S.A. The Army Beta includes tasks such as cube analysis digit symbols, geometrical construction, mazes and picture competition. This test was primarily prepared for use in military selection, however, it subsequently proved useful for civilian workers.

Cattle's Culture Free Test. It is available for three levels—4 to 8 years, 8 to 12 years and high school to adult. Each series consists of 4 sub-tests which are series, classification, matrices and conditions.

Raven's Progressive Matrices. The progressive matrices was developed in U.K. to measure Spearman's general factor of intelligence. The original test consists of series of sixty matrices involving abstract figures and designs. Each matrix contains a blank section and the subject (student) is directed to select the missing piece from eight choices.

Chicago Non-Verbal Tests. This test has been proved most useful for the young children of age 12 and 13 years. C.I.E. non-verbal group intelligence test (adopted in Hindi medium schools). It was originally prepared by J.W. Jenkins.

Intelligence is only an idea, and an abstraction. It is not a thing. Therefore it cannot be measured in the same way as we measure a piece of cloth, wood or temperature of our body. The measurement of intelligence is not as simple, valid, reliable and definite task as the measurement of a piece of a cloth or temperature of a body. In case of a piece of cloth and temperature of the body it is convenient to use the measuring instrument when ever we like, but is difficult to use intelligence test with the similar convenience. The administration and interpretation of intelligence tests require sufficient skill, labour and competency on the part of the examiner.

Uses/Advantage of Intelligence Test. Intelligence tests are widely used in schools and colleges due to following reasons :

(a) ***To Identify Individual Differences.*** On the basis of intelligence scores we can identify the individual differences among students and provide them individual guidance *i.e.,* we can advise students to select subjects keeping into consideration their intellectual abilities.

(b) ***Selection.*** Intelligence tests can serve a useful purpose for selecting students for different purposes *i.e.*:

- For admission to school.
- For awarding scholarship.
- For selection in jobs.

(c) ***Predictions.*** On the basis of intelligence test results, it is possible to predict the future academic achievement of a child because I.Q. remains constant. If the child is dull, his academic achievement is bond to be low and for this, planning can be done in advance, and the child can be advised to opt vocational courses.

Classification of Pupils. Children can be classified into various categories on the basis of inelligence tests. We have children who are of superior intelligence, average intelligence, dull and feeble minded. Children having the same I.Q. may be grouped together and constitute a class. This will endure the uniform progress and avoid educational wastage.

Detection of Various Types of Pupils. Various types of pupils *i.e.,* gifted and feeble-minded etc. can be detected with the help of intelligence tests. Moreover causes of backwardness, delinquency and problematic behaviour can be found.

Award of Scholarships. Scholarships may be given to suitable and appropriate students on the basis of intelligence tests. The Government of India selects some students for the award of scholarship or studying in public schools on the basis of intelligence and achievement tests.

Promotion of Pupils. Intelligence tests can be used to promote pupils.

Use in Clinics. Intelligence tests are used in clinics and mental hospitals in order to find out how far the disease has impaired intelligence.

Use in Research. Intelligence tests are used to a very large extent in educational and psychological research. For example, to find out the causes of delinquency, slow learning and maladjustment among children, intelligence tests are used to see the effect of mental abilities in these abnormalities. Intelligence tests specially individual tests are used for research with young children, emotionally disturbed cases and cases with special educational disabilities.

Use in Educational and Vocational Guidance. Every vocational and educational course pre-supposes certain levels of intelligence. On the basis of intelligence testing, we can guide the students, whether they should go for studies or adopt some vocational course.

Understanding Personality. Intellectual ability is one of the most important aspect of personality. Intelligence tests help us to understand the personality disorders among students. These are used to understand delinquent and problem children.

Use in the Study of National and Racial Differences. With the help of intelligence tests we can know the intelligence level of various races and nationalities. Intelligence tests scores show that I.Q., scores of Germans, Japanese and Americans are more than those of Africans and Maxicans.

Use in Industry. Intelligence tests are very useful in industry *i.e.,* in selection of the employees in industries, in locating workers who require training and to study working conditions which lead to efficiency.

Use in Army and Civil Services. Since the First World War intelligence tests are extensively used in the Army. Army Alpha and Army Beta tests have been used on lacs of persons. Army General classification tests have been used on millions. In India, intelligence tests are used in the selection of army officers. Moreover, they are being used in various competitive examinations.

Helpful in Assessment of Teacher's Work. Teacher's work can be assessed with the help of intelligence tests. When the achievement of the pupils in a subject does not correspond to the scores of intelligence tests, it indicates that the subject has not been properly taught by the teacher.

Evaluation of Methods and Material of Instruction. Intelligence tests are useful in evaluating the results of the experiments conducted by a school in the relative importance of different text-books or with a certain text-book with extensive reading material.

QUALITIES OF A GOOD PSYCHOLOGICAL TESTS?

Following are the qualities of a good psychological tests:

1. **It is Reliable.** A test is reliable only when the results remain constant whatever the environment or on different occasions. It also means consistency of the scores of the subject when tested again and again. If the results change, the test is inconsistent and unreliable. How to make a test reliable? There are three important methods :

    (a) Tes/Retest Method.

    (b) Split-half Method.

    (c) Parallel Forms.

2. **It is Objective.** Objectivity means freedom from personal opinion or bias of the examiner. A good test is free from the linkages and personal whims of the scorer. Essay type examinations are not objective—personal opinion counts.

3. **There is Ease of Administring and Scoring.** Readymade keys are available for calculating result. Administration can be easily done. Directions are clear.

4. **It is Valid.** An index of validity shows the degree to which a test measures, what it purports to measure when compared with accepted criteria. The first esesential quality of a valid test is that it is highly reliable. If the reliability of a test is zero, it will not correlate with anything. A test that yields inconsistant results (low reliability) cannot correlate with a measure of another variable.

5. **Norms.** Class/age/percentile norms are available. This helps in quick comparison of results.

6. **A Standardized Test in Less Time Counselling.** We have the example of 3 hours essay type examination with us. It is just miserable to stand guard duty for three hours.

Some More Facts About Intelligence Tests

1. The correlation of intelligence tests scores with school marks is substantial (0.5 to 0.6 is average).

2. Intelligence tests and achievement combined in a battery give still better prediction about future achievement.

3. Intelligence tests correlate higher with standardized measures of achievement than with school marks.

4. Previous school achievement gives correlation with later school achievement to be equal or higher than the correlation between intelligence and later school achievement.

5. The degree to which intelligence tests are related to academic success depends upon the subject matter.

All the individuals differ in mental traits as much as they do in physical features. Whatever the conception of intelligence, all the psychologists and educators and even common people have been believing since ancient times that there are various levels of intelligence. Some individuals are more intelligent than the others. We come across some men who are giant intellects and at the same time there are some unfortunate people who are devoid of intelligence and cannot count up to ten even after full maturity. Between the genius and the idiot there lie all grades of intelligence both above average and below average.

With the advent of the 20th century there appeared a ray of hope in this connection. The educational authorities of Paris were very much disgusted with the leakage of students in Primary Schools due to their backwardness in studies. They wanted to know the basic causes of the backwardness. The problem was entrusted to Alfred Binet, renowned medical practitioner interested in psychology. Alfred Binet worked on this hypothesis that children fail in studies due to poor intelligence. Now he wished to ascertain if the intelligence of such children who had left school was really very low and that of those students who were doing well in schools was quite up to the mark. There was no objective instrument of measurement of intelligence so far. There arose the need of some reliable objective tests.

Both the psychologists prepared the first objective test of Intelligence in 1911. After laborious experiments and thorough research, Binet reached the conclusion that no single performance could measure this faculty adequatly. Therefore, he included many small problems concerning various situations in his test. He soon discovered that intelligence develops gradually with age. Therefore, many tests suitable for many grades of children according to their age were constructed. They were tried on large samples and were standardized for various age levels.

Mental Age. Binet and Simon discovered that all children could not attempt the test standardized for their particular age level although a large number out of the same could do the same. For example, a nine-year old should be able to do the test standardized for his age group. But sometimes a child could not do well in it. He was then offered the test for lower age groups. Suppose he succeeded in a doing well in the test prescribed for the seven year age group. Then his mental age was declared to be seven years although his chronological age was nine years (chronological age is the actual age of the individual counted in days, months and years from the day of his birth). Similarly, a child of nine years could have mental age of nine, ten, eleven or more years.

All such individuals whose chronological age corresponded with their mental age were thought, to be normal or average in intelligence. All the individuals whose mental age was more than their chronological age were declared to be of supperior intelligence while individuals with less mental age were believed to be below normal in intelligence.

Intelligence Quotient. Terman gave a new concept of Intelligence Quotient to the world. Binet gave the mental age along with the chronological age of the individual. One could know the intelligence level of child by comparsion of both the ages. Terman went a step further. He multiplied the mental age with one hundred and divided the result by she chronological age. It gave intelligence Quotient (I.Q.). The formula is given below:

$$\frac{M.A. \times 100}{C.A.} = I.Q.$$

Suppose the C.A. of a child is 10 years while his M.A. is 12 years; then his:

$$I.Q. = \frac{12 \times 100}{10} = 120$$

Why Individuals Differ in Intelligence? Individuals differ as much in mental features as they do in physical aspects. In fact, no two individuals are alike physically or mentally in the world. This difference is due to heredity as well as environmental influences.

Influence of Heredity. Let us take heredity first of all. As individuals differ in intelligence, therefore, their offsprings are not expectd to be similar. If both the parents are very superior in intelligence, their children are expected to be intelligent and similarly mentally weak parents beget dull children. If one of the parents is superior in intelligence and the other one is dull, the young ones will be mixed generation, some of them intelligent, others dull, still others in between and most of them having reverse influences in themselves in latent forms apt to influence the coming generations only. Due to this fact we come across some intelligent children whose parents both mother and father are dull. The heredity influence may be coming down from distant forefathers either from father's side or mother's. Ordinarily we do not find dull children with parents who are both superior in intelligence, or a genius born in the house of dullards.

Influence of Environment. Environment, too, affects intelligence tests although to a very limited extent. Injury to brain, constant bad health, long and continued emotional disturbances either impair intelligence or make it ineffective in life.

MEASUREMENT OF INDIVIDUAL DIFFERENCES

Individuals differ in intelligence. No two children can be quite similar in intelligence or in any other mental trait just as no two individuals can be quite the same is any physical feature. However, individuals, can be graded in large groups of intelligence level with small differences.

There are standardized tests for every age level. Every standardized tsts has many items to be attempted. The child to be assessed is given the test of his age level to do. It is then evaluated. Every standardized test has its own norms. There is no need of finding out the Mental Age first and then calculating the I.Q. From the marks secured by the child in that particular test his I.Q. can be found out directly with the help of its norms. Suppose a child of 10 years attempts a test standardized for the group of 10 years chronological age. He secures 70 marks in it. The norms will show what his I.Q. is in that case.

We can divide the tests in the following way:

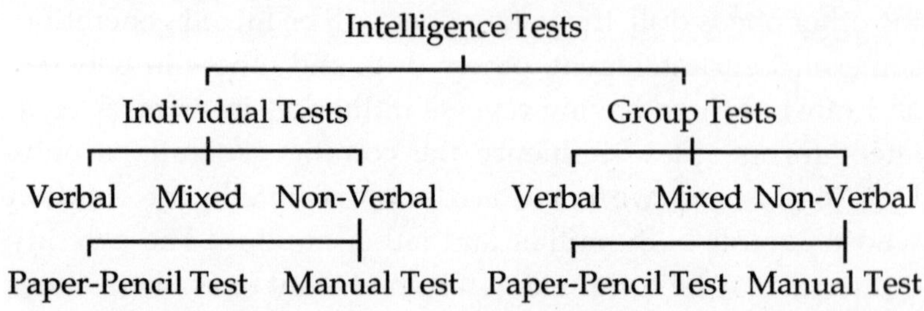

1. Individual Tests. These tests are administered to one individual at a time. These cover age group from 2 years to 18 years. These are : *(a)* The Binet-Simon Tests, *(b)* Revised Tests by Terman, and *(c)* Mental and Scholastic Tests of Burt.

2. Group Tests. Group tests are administered to a group of people. Group tests had their birth in America—when the intelligence of the recruits who joined the army in the first World War was to be calculated. These are : *(a)* The Army

Alpha and Beta Test, *(b)* Terman's Group Tests, and *(c)* Otis Self-administrative Tests.

3. Performance Tests. These tests are administered to the illitrate persons. These tests generally involve the construction of certain patterns or solving problems in terms of concrete material. Some of the famous tests are : *(a)* Koh's Block Design Test, *(b)* The Cube Construction Tests, and *(c)* The Pass Along Tests.

TERMAN'S CLASSIFICATION

On the basis of I.Q. Terman gives the following classification on American tests:

Near genius or genius	above–140
Very superior intelligence	120–140
Superior intelligence	110–120
Normal or average intelligence	90–110
Dullness	80–90
Borderline cases	70–80
Definite feeble-mindedness which has been further classified as under:	below 70
Morons	50–70
Imbeciles	25–50
Idiots	below 25

The Bombay-Karnataka Revision Tests. Dr. V.V. Kamat revised Binet's scale to suit Indian conditions and administered intelligence tests to 1,074 children and adolescents of all ages from 2 to 20 of both sexes. The locality selected for the experiment was the town of Dharwar in the Bombay Presidency. The children selected were fairly representative of the general population of Indian children. Dr. V.V. Kamat classfies Indian children as under:

Class	Range of I.Q.s
Near genius or genius	140 and above
Extraordinary	130–139.9
Very superior	120–129.9
Superior	110–119.9
Average or normal	99–109.9
Backward	80–98.9
Very backward	70–79.9
Borderline	60–69.9
Morons	40–59.9

Role of Home and School to Build the Personality. Psychologists now will agree that social factors are the most important in shaping our personality traits. The members of the family, playmates, school and class-fellows, society at large all these in a way determine and influence his personality.

(a) Home Atmosphere. Fundamental patterns of personality are formed during childhood. A congenial home atmosphere, with good relations between the parents and the child, is essential for a well-adjusted personality to develop. If parents provide a stimulating environment and a great degree of freedom, children will grow into strong, independent and self-reliant individuals. If, on the other hand, they are domineering and strict, children will be timid, lacking initiative and self-confidence. Over affectionate parents make children too dependent and overstrict ones make the too timid or too rebellious. Similarly disrupted homes often produce unstable, badly-adjusted personalities. The child has close emotional tie to each parent. Hence their quarrels cause serious conflict in his personality.

The position of the child in the family has much to do with the pattern of his personality. The only child, the youngest child, the adopted child, the favourite child, the only son in a family of daughters or the only daughter in the family of sons-grows differently and develops emotional attitudes which makes a difference to his or her personality. For example, the only child is likely to be pampered or over-protected. The parents give him extra protection and love and unknowlingly teach him to expect more from the social environment. The child grows self-centred, obstinate and less cooperative.

(b) School Atmosphere. The share and responsibility of the school in forming the personality of the child is equally important. The school makes the man in more than one way. It gives him more knowledge, more opportunities to think and reason and a broader outlook on life. It helps the emotional development, cultivates tastes and attitudes and offers material for building up ideals and aims in life. The schools of today have realised that mere instruction is not enough. They are providing opportunities for social competitive and cooperative work and experience. N.C.C., A.C.C., scouting games, social service leagues, co-operative stores, school banks, art clubs, hobbies, trips and the like give opportunities to the growing young people to dominate over some and yield to others, to play the role of leaders and followers as the occasion demands.

6

Psychology of Growth and Development

Narrowly conceived, growth is sheer increase in size, height, degree, power, etc. For example, growth from conception onwards is a natural thing. It is in this sense used for physical change. As such we speak of muscle growth, brain growth, bone growth and the growth of body in general. The changes produced by growth processes accumulate and are measured directly.

Development is the direction in which growth takes place as a result of factors outside the maturing individual. In this some while growth is a natural process; development is a result of the environmental factors that affect the organism as he grows. So far as his body organs are concerned, the organism grows; but simultaneously there is a change in the expression of his emotion's fear, anger, sympathy, love, apathy, etc. As the individual grows in size or in weight, there is a change in the way he carries his social behaviour. There is a growth in emotional, mental, social aspects, but it cannot be directly measured as we measure growth in physical aspects. The growth in these areas is qualitative in nature and hence we term it differently as development.

In educational and psychological literature growth includes development as it includes maturation and learning. Growth and development are related because both occur together. Hence, there is a tendency on the part of educationists and psychologists to use both interchangingly. Both concepts appear to be synonymous and often are confused. When we speak of physical growth and physical development we are quite clear as regards the difference in the two terms—physical growth is structural and is physiological change that takes place within the individual during the process of maturation. When physical growth takes a certain direction and is facilitated or checked by the environmental factors, which stimulate the growing individual, it becomes physical development. The two terms growth and development are used one after the other in psychological literature; for example, we speak of reading readiness as a stage of growth and development at which reading instruction will probably be effective and before which instruction is relatively fruitless. We speak of readiness as a stage of growth and development not only because there is a change which can be directly measured as in mental age and sensory perception needed for reading but also there is a change in emotional control, in desire to read, and in experience which cannot be measured.

The task of applied educational psychology is to point out ways in which growth is facilitated, or the ways in which development takes place. The task of the educator is to provide conditions that are favourable to growth: for education is a growth process. The task of the educational psychologist is to discover and create those conditions, which tend to facilitate growth of the individual child. The duty of the teacher is to work in accordance with growth principles rather than against them.

Principles of Growth and Development

The teacher should clearly understand the nature of growth and its principles before he launches upon the task of educating children. These principles are:

(1) Growth and development result from an interaction of Heredity and Environment.

(2) Growth is continuous and gradual.

(3) Growth proceeds more rapidly in earlier years.

(4) Growth is a regular step-by-step process.

(5) Growth moves from Generalisation to Differentiation and Integration.

(6) Each child and adolescent has his own rate of growth.

(7) Traits are correlated as a general rule.

(8) Maturation influences the results of training.

These principles will be discussed in detail below because they have a far-reaching impact upon principles and practices of education.

1. Growth as a Functions of Heredity and Environment. The development of an organism is a product of two interdependent factors 'what he is' and 'what he has.' 'What an organism is' is determined by his hereditary potential and 'what he has' is fixed by his environment. Both interact on the individual and growth takes place.

2. Growth is a Regular Step-by-step Process. Growth is never haphazard. There is order and sequence. For example, the baby creeps before the crawls, and he crawls before he walks, and the child walks before he runs and he runs before he dances. What is true of physical growth is true of every mental process. For example, the child babbles before he utters words; he utters single words before he speaks in sentences; he speaks before he writes; he writes simple: stories before he creates a work of art.

3. Growth is Rapid in Earlier Years. In early childhood any structures and functions grow at a much faster rate and as the child grows, the rate of growth slows down. The rate of growth is then negatively accelerated as shown by general forms of growth curves for size, weight, intellect, etc. (see Fig.)

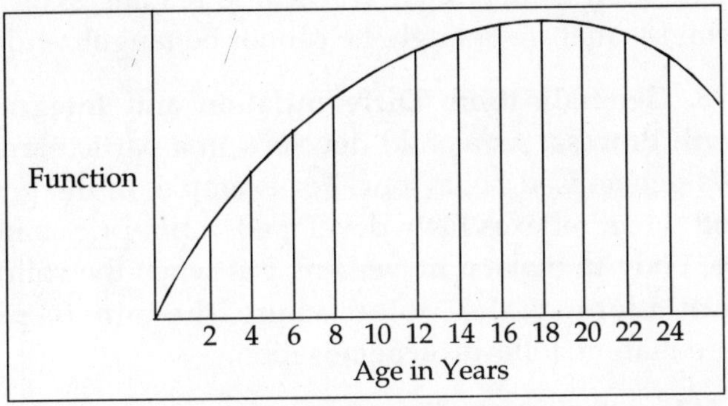

4. Growth is Continuous and Gradual. Growth or development does not occur in spurts. We may talk of stages of development or of growth as infancy, childhood, adolescence but it does not mean that when one stage stops and the other starts. There are no breaks in the process of development.

5. Traits are Correlated. As growth and development, of traits takes place, they grow in a correlated manner. For example a gifted child grows physically, socially, emotionally at the same; rate as he grows mentally.

6. Each Child has his Unique Rate of Growth. Some children grow rapidly. Some are slow. Some travel by an ox cart, some by a car and some by a jet plane. Some become prominent when they are still children, some, when they are adolescents and, some never. The rate of growth is not only unique for an individual child for a particular trait, but the rates of growth for all different traits of the child are unique. One child may grow rapidly in one trait in early years, and then may seem to have reached a plateau. The other child may show a regular and gradual pattern of growth. The third child may experience a slow rate of growth in early years and then show a spurt, which carries him beyond what is regarded as an average for all.

7. Maturation Influences Results of Training. The role of maturation is illustrated in teaching reading skills. Unless the child is mature enough, he cannot be taught reading.

8. Generalisation, Differentiation and Integration in Growth Process. As a child develops in a particular trait, he shows generalised behaviour. For example, in the post-natal period when reflexes have developed, a pin-prick causes the whole body to make a movement, but when the child grows he can identify the point where the pin is pricked. Differentiation follows generalisation.

When the baby is shown an attractive toy it tries to catch it with gross muscles, but when he grows older he is able to pick up the object with his thumb and forefinger. There is differentiation. Integration means that all parts are work in harmoniously towards the goal and it takes place concurrently with differentiation.

Growth as a Functions of Heredity and Environment

Growth and development depend upon the hereditary and environmental factors so much that the growing individual is regarded as a product of both. The growing child's behaviour is influenced by his genetic structure, physical body build his rate of maturation. It is also affected by his cultural mileau-the values, ideals, goals and the specific situations, the typical or general environment of home, school and society.

Most educational psychologists now believe in the interactive process of heredity and environment. Heredity provides the potential and environment acts upon this potential and produces what the child is. For example, intellectual growth and development are the results of the interaction of the two. No psychologist now believes that I.Q. remains constant; that is, the rate of mental development for a given person can change under certain conditions. For a group of persons it is believed that rate of mental development possibly cannot he extensively changed by providing a stimulating environment. But, however, beneficial and stimulating an environment may be, the change in the rate of mental development is limited by hereditary potential. The less stimulating environment causes a child with high hereditary potential to develop to such an extent as a more stimulating environment can do to the same child. That is why identical twins reared apart show a difference in I.Q. When two children with different hereditary potentials are given equally stimulating environment, they do not develop equally, meaning thereby that even the most stimulating environment cannot affect growth beyond the hereditary potential.

Educational Implications of Heredity-Environment

The teacher has to start with the student where he is. The student has come to school with some hereditary potential and it is the teacher who is to be charged with the responsibility of realisation of his potential to the maximum.

Each child has differential amount of hereditary potential; hence the teacher will have to first assess that potential. For this he may use what are known as intelligence tests, achievement test batteries, interest inventories, readiness scales. If he can wisely use the data obtained from such tests about each child he may start well and well begun is half done. How disappointing it is to note that in spite of the importance of such tests, teachers in our schools do not know anything about them. If some Psychological Bureaus have tried to break the ice, and have taken tests, the data obtained are simply filed way.

As growth is the result of interaction of the organism with the environment, it means that the teacher should help each child to achieve the greatest possible realisation of his potential. His help may be in the form of encouragement, praise and direction. Every child should be encouraged to do more and to read more, to write more, and to perform more intricate tasks and solve more difficult problems. Each child should be praised for good work and given proper guidance. The more stimulating the environment, the greater will be the realisation of hereditary potential. For example, if the child meets better birth conditions, gets more immediate and intimate mothering, faces little emotional stress in the home, gets better schools, and is taught by more appropriate teaching techniques, he will not only get rapid and vastly increasing knowledge, but will develop emotionally, socially and morally in more desirable directions.

Child's work even when it is below average should not be deprecated. He should be given an experience of success in what he does. The teacher's duty is to direct him to areas where he can get more success. In short, the teacher has to adapt learning experiences to the needs of individual pupil so that he may realise his hereditary potential to the maximum.

The relative influence of heredity and environment on the all round development of the child has been a disputed concern of biologists, educationists and psychologists. But can heredity be sharply differentiated from environment? Are they not influencing the child co-operatively and concurrently? Can the single cell, which is at first the fertilised ovum and later the entire organism, grow without being influenced by both its pre-natal and post-natal environment?

The course of development is influenced by what the organism is (his inherited potential) and by what he has (his environment). Heredity and environment are welded together as interdependent influences by the way one reacts to what he is and has. His reaction to them determines the aspect of development.

Four things are clear now:

(1) The organism gets some hereditary potential. (What he is.)

(2) It interacts with environment. (What he has.)

(3) The environment interacts with hereditary potential.

(4) As a result the organism increases, expands and grows.

Educational Significance of Early Rapid Growth

The pre-school period is characterised by rapid growth. The infant, from 2 to 5 years of age, shows tremendous improvement in coordination, perception, differentiation of behaviour and acquisition of skills. The growth in this period is so rapid that you can tell a difference between a 2-year old and 3-year old baby, but it will be difficult to perceive a year when the child grows into adolescence. There is faster rate of language development; there is greater speed of getting along with his brothers, sisters and adults; there is quicker crystallisation of fundamental personality traits. All these developments occur within a short span of four years.

The fact that growth takes place more rapidly during the early years does no mean that it stops after a certain age. The child is continually growing. Even when broad features of personality traits become nearly established during early years, they are subject to modifications later. The idea that in pre-school period broad fundamental patterns of behaviour are determined once for all and no modification needs be done is erroneous. The primary school teacher who is entrusted with educating the child should not feel that his efforts will bring no fruit for much has taken place in the child's life before he enters the classroom at 6+. He should recognise his responsibility to mare the first school experiences as happy as he can.

It is not enough to teach the child reading, writing and arithmetic skills. Acquisition of academic skills such as these, is useful and desirable but more fruitful are the emotional adjustment and social development. The child, who does not meet his social and emotional needs in the primary school, cannot learn academic subjects efficiently. An adequately trained teacher feels the need of making the first few years of school life happy and enjoyable and practises what be feels.

There is rapid growth in the primary school life though not so rapid as in pre-school life. This does not mean that schooling should begin at an earlier age or social experiences should be given in greater amount at the age of 4 or 5. An immature child should not be fitted into a school system. Individual differences must be realised. It means that even if a child is 6+, he should not be forced to enter the classroom if he is not mature enough.

During the early school years there is rapid growth. Though the child is quite active yet he gets fatigued soon either because his body tissues have not become so mature or because rapid growth requires more expenditure of energy. Fatigue causes loss of appetite, restlessness, and inattentiveness. The child of class I, becomes restless or inattentive earlier than that of class VI. The primary school teacher should shorten the length of periods. A child, who is growing at a much faster rate and spending much energy, suffers from fatigue so much that he does not learn as well as the one who is not growing so fast. The result is that he becomes backward and a slow learner. Primary school teachers should recognise this phenomenon and therefore provide a balanced programme of rest and activity in the school.

Individual Growth Rates and Teaching Practice

The principle that each individual has his own rate of growth asserts that some children grow rapidly and others grow slowly. Growth rates for mental, physical, emotional and social traits are different for different children. For example, the rate of mental maturity (Mental Age) is different for different children. What is true for mental age is true for other ages. Besides, particular child has many ages: mental age, social age, emotional age, organismic age and so on. Individual growth rates, however, remain constant. A child, who is above average in intelligence when he is 6+, will remain so when he is 15+. A child who is tall for his age at 3 will remain so when he is an adult.

The phenomenon that each individual child has his unique rate of growth so far as a particular trait is concerned implies that teachers should deal with the problem of individual differences effectively. Each child should be provided with the type of training and education best suited to him as an individual and to his expected needs as an adult. An effective teacher realises the nature and extent of individual differences. He recognises the fact that there are individual differences in learning ability, in temparaments, in needs, in interests, in background experiences, in home conditions, in ideas and in attitudes. He adjusts his instruction to these differences.

A good teacher provides a variety of activities to his class. He groups pupils of similar interests and mental development. He schedules his classes of varied difficulty. He teaches out materials fit for different levels of reading readiness.

A bad teacher is contented with giving the same dose to all and sundry. Hence there are failures, dropouts, frustrations and poor results.

Physical Development of the Learner

Physical development is studied horizontally and longitudinally. Horizontal studies gives us data regarding growth patterns of children at specific stages of development. Such studies do not give us information about individual growth patterns. Longitudinal studies are progressive studies of an individual and can be used to compare him with himself at various stages.

Different stages that a child passes through from birth to 16 years of age are the infancy (on the average, from birth to 5 or 6 years of age, during which the sensory channels begin to function and the child learns to creep, to walk and speak), the childhood (on the average from 5 to 12 years during which permanent teeth appear, and the child learns to read, write and care for himself), the adolescence on the average from 12 years to 18 (in some cases to 20 or 25 during which the development of sex organs bring about the appearance of physical sex characteristics'.

The specific growth changes from birth to adolescence occur with regard to height and weight, body proportions and growth or internal organs.

During infancy a normal child tends to follow certain definite patterns of growth. Height and weight increase tremendously. The infant boy grows on the average 7 "by the age of 9 months and the infant girl grows to 6 3/4" by that age in heignt. Weight is doubled during the first 6 months. During childhood and adolescence the height goes on increasing. Hereditary background and environmental factors combined determine height-weight ratio for a particular child. For example, children of short and stoct parents are generally short and stocky those of the tall and slender are tall and slender.

Different component parts of the skeleton do not grow at a regular rate. When the child is born, the size of bones of arms and legs is smaller than that of the skull. As he grows, the head and torso become proportionally shorter than before and arms and legs become longer. At birth there are no teeth. But as the child grows he gets baby teeth and then a second set of teeth which serve him all his life.

From birth to adolescence all the body systems have different rates of growth. At time of birth the nervous system is developed sufficiently well. The circulatory system has a balanced functioning too. But with growing years, the heart grows in size and volume. The lymphatic system becomes active at birth and increases rapidly after 12 years of age. The genital system develops slowly during the childhood but grows rapidly from 11 or 12 years of age onwards.

Environment plays a significant role in physical growth and development. Favourable environmental conditions, planned recreation and rest, proper diet, well-ventilated living quarters, freedom from care and anxiety are beneficial for proper physical growth. Better nutrition, better shelter, more adequate life necessities are conducive to better health. Behaviour problems in our children spring up because of malnutrition, unhealthy home environment, lack of rest and recreation anxiety and trouble at home.

The individual is first and foremost a physical being. Therefore, any programme of his education revolves round his physical growth and development. The primary aim of education would then be the development of excellent body, good health, active neuimuscular system.

The knowledge of characteristics of physical growth and development is very essential to the teacher. He should not only be conversant with subject he teaches but he should also study the growth characteristics. The learning equipment, the curriculum, the techniques of teaching have to be geared to the proper growth of the child. He has to be careful to the normal physical growth of the child as he has to be careful of his normal intellectual growth. The child who seems to be growing beyond his years as well as the child who seems to be growing shorty, need his special attention. Even a slight physical abnormality during the childhood creates trouble to the individual. Attitudes, interests and emotional behaviour grow out of physical status. Above normal height or weight or uneven physical growth rate, produce emotional strain and stress in the child. The teacher has to help such a child in solving emotional difficulties and problems.

Many children come from poor homes. Their parents are illiterate and do not know how to take care of them. Children are either normal or undernourished. They lack of adequate shelter. Living conditions are far from satisfactory in villages and in some urban areas too. Proper attention has to he given to the nutrition of the average school child. A mid-day meal or some other programme with state or public aid may be launched and the problem of maturation can be solved.

Every school has a responsibility for preparing able-bodied youths to serve the nation. Sanitary conditions of school premises, a provision of well-ventilated school rooms, sufficient and well-planned program of sports and games, periodical medical examination and dental care, are a must for a good school.

SOCIAL DEVELOPMENT

Social development is the development of social behaviour. It may be defined as the progressive improvement of the individual in the understanding of social heritage and the formation of flexible conduct patterns of reasonable conformity with this heritage. The social heritage is made up of social institutions and mores and customs of the groups. It stimulates the child. It changes conduct in one way or the other. This change is known as social development.

Social development cannot be studied apart from intellectual, physical or emotional aspects of development. The social behaviour of the person at any stage of development affects and is affected by his physical, mental or emotional development.

Social Development in Infancy

The infant's first social responses are with the adults and are self-centred in nature. At first he is mainly concerned with fulfilment of his basic needs. Soon he acquires the skill of attracting adults and making them fulfil his needs. At the age of six months he begins to take note of others but he gives more attention to his surroundings and play materials than to other children. At the age of 15 months there is a change. Now more attention is given to other children rather than to play things and his surroundings.

The play activities of young children show a change from individualisation to socialisation. For example, upto two years age the child works upon the principle of what is mine is mine and what is yours is yours. At the age of 3 years he begins to know what is yours also. During the pre-school years a child gradually assumes behaviour characteristics which show a slow growth of social consciousness. His social behaviour with others is affected by interest in self rather than by interest in others. He lives in his own world. He develops such social response patterns as may check desirable modifications during later life.

Social Development in Childhood

Cooperation or competition is developed according to the home and community influences. If the home gives more importance to competition, the child develops rivalry which influences his youthful behaviour. If the home gives more stress to cooperation, the child becomes uncompetitive. The other agency which affects his social behaviour is the nursery school. The child begins to take interest in self in association with others when he is exposed to an enlarged environment. When he begins to attend nursery or kindergarten school he begins to feel presence of other youngsters, gets social diet from them, imitates directly their behaviour patterns, and experiences tensions in their mere presence. The teacher in the nursery or kindergarten school takes the position of parents. If the teacher gives a sense of security and affection to the child, the child develops better social attitudes.

In the stage of elementary school the child is interested in satisfying his own needs but he tries to satisfy them more according to social customs of his group. He develops a strong desire for belongingness to the family, the neighbourhood and the school. He appreciates the concept of right and wrong but follows the adult model. Like the adult he learns that ethical values of right and wrong are advantageous only so far as they serve one's purpose.

Social Development during the Later Childhood. During this stage of development, the child is confronted with a new environment, many new children, and a teacher substitute for his father. The social world expands. At 6 when he enters this world he gets confused. By twelve when he leaves the primary school he becomes quite adjusted to his ever-expanding social world.

When the child is in the first or second class of the primary school he forms a peer group of 5 or 6 youngsters. He fights for the group in and out of the classroom. When he grows further, the size of the peer group increases. Boys and girls are now separated by social taboos or by difference in social interests of the two sexes. Boys join boys group, girls join girls group. Boys begin to take interest in sports, adventures and out of-the-home activities; girls take interest in domestic activities. From the age of 12 to 14 the peer group becomes a gang or club.

Social Development in Pre-Adolescence

The age from 12 to 14 is the age pre-adolescence. The gang or club plays a very important role in the process of social development now. This pre-adolescent social group has secret passwords, badges, rules and special places for meeting.

The child feels freedom when he is in the group but he works according to the instructions of the leader. Interest in forming a gang is evidenced by the interest shown later in forming associations, societies, political or social organisations. The child achieves certain social values through such group relationships. The gang is not always a socially undesirable group. Many gang activities are highly desirable: Some gangs have active sports, hobbies, etc. Some gangs are notorious for actual defiance of law and order, gambling, petty thieving, fighting, smoking and various types of vandalism.

Role of School in Socialisation of the Child

Educators all the world over are stressing the need of proper social development from infancy onwards. In fact the whole civilization rests on the understanding and adjustment of an individual with anothor. What we call character is constant social behaviour. It is the socially adaptable being who can adjust in any kind of life situation and lead a happy life. It is the socially developed person who abides by rules that govern social conduct, who appreciates the rights of others and who realises his own responsibilities as a member of the social group. It is the socially developed individual who appreciates the value of good government, the importance of the home relationship and the value of cooperative living.

The school has to assume a wide responsibility in developing in its pupils social consciousness. It is the only institution, second to family, which is charged with the responsibility of socialising the child and the youth. The teacher who has to responsibility of becoming parent substitute as soon as the child enters the school.

A sympathetic and skilled teacher encourages the development of socially desirable behaviour. He who gives him a sense of self-esteem and feeling of security. He who provides opportunities to children for organised group living.

He who leads the retiring child to assert himself and the aggressive child to learn the art of submission.

In a well-organised high school social activities and projects are undertaken. Student self-government under able guidance, community projects, a well-planned house system are some of the features of good school for socialising the pre-adolescent and the adolescent pupils. Every student is given a chance to take an active part in co-curricular activities. Radio programmes, T.V. lessons, the press, and current magazines are provided to develop social attitudes and ideas among young boys and girls. Summer camps, scouting and girls guiding, outings and excursions, autumn break tours are organised to train children and youths in personal responsibility, leadership and group living.

Emotional Development of the Learner

Emotion may be defined as a state of being stirred-up or aroused in one way or the other. Such a stirred-up slate involves mental, physical, physiological, situational and habitual factors. An emotion has strong and mild, pleasant and unpleasant states. On the one hand, emotion means an upset condition of hate or fear in which physiological functioning prepares for fight or flight; on the other, it may mean the condition of love or sympathy in which physiological functioning leads to a feeling of well-being for self and others. It may mean a mild feeling such as friendliness towards one's own chum; it may mean a strong feeling such as paralysing fear during a flood or an air-crash. It may mean a happy laughter or an unpleasant chronic anxiety at the threat of losing one's job.

Aspects of Emotional Experience

The total emotional experience has three aspects :

(i) overt behaviour (bulge of the eyes, the flow of the tears, the flush of the face).

(ii) visceral behaviour (a decrease in the flow of saliva, flow of blood).

(iii) emotional experience (feeling of joy or sadness).

When one is in the stirred state, one shows some behaviour which is openly displayed. Then there is an extensive visceral disturbance in the interior organs. At the same time there is feeling of a varying degree of emotional experience.

Emotion is, therefore, an affective experience that accompanies generalised inner adjustments and mental and physiological stirred-up states of the individual, and that shows itself in his overt behaviour. Emotion is a feeling state accompanying an upset condition of the organism. It is a stirred-up state of mental and physical aspects of the individual.

Arousal of Emotion. An emotion is aroused at the perception of a stimulus which has a potential for arousing it. For example, we hate our enemy. The very sight of the enemy is a stimulus to arouse the emotion of hate. An object that arouses one emotion cannot arouse another emotion at the same time. The presence or absence of emotion-arousing stimulus determines the presence or elimination of emotion. Present the stimulus; emotion is aroused. Remove it: the emotion is reduced.

The stimulus that arouses emotion produces visceral changes. Adrenin or adrenalin is released into the blood stream. This causes an increased rate in heartheat, raises blood pressure, causes more rapid respiration, and constriction of the blood vessels on the surface of the body. The flow of digestive juices is inhibited. These are the physiological responses to the stimulus (enemy); and their function is to prepare the organism to fight or flight. These physiological changes inside the body do not cause emotion but they are simply a part of it. The emotion is caused by the stimulus situation only. Mere injection of adrenin in the blood stream causes some to feel a variety of emotions, some to feel none, and some to feel that they are about to have one.

The visceral changes affect the skeletal muscles, and the organism who is face to face with an enemy shows skeletal behaviour (or overt behaviour) as the bulge of the eyes or the flush of the face or an attack on the stimulus. The emotions experienced are conveyed to others by the overt behaviour. Thus we have in an emotion overt behaviour, visceral changes, and an emotional experience.

Below are given three important facts about the physiological aspects of emotions, the cumulative effect of the stimuli that arise them and the suggestion to deal with them.

1. Every Emotion has Physiological Aspects. W.B. Cannon (1929) propounded a theory that emotions have philological changes which prepare the individual to meet an emergency. For example, when the child is faced with an anger producing situation, there is an increased rate of heartheat, and an increase in blood pressure to cope with the emergency prepares to fight or take flight. When he cannot burn up the extra energy made available to him because of present day customs not permitting him to get rid of such an emotion through violent conflict, a kind of poison is created in his system. Similarly, when a teacher is reprimanded by the Principal for no fault of his, he prepares to avoid the situation and does not give vent to his feelings through violence. Such a repression of emotional reactions becomes hazardous for mental and physical health.

Educational Significance of Cannon-Bard Theory. The Cannon-Bard theory has educational implications for improving learning efficiency and for better emotional development of the child. Fear and anger are not only bad for effective learning, but they are evils for his mental health also. Fear of examinations or punishment should be replaced by more positive means of motivation. Anxiety about status caused by failure may be avoided for it causes mental ill health. Every teacher should seek to understand the extent and nature of imotions that arc generated in the school through improper handling of children. Each member of staff should seek to find out what emotions the children are bringing from outside (home or external society) to school. If a child is worried about family problems, his emotional state would inhibit learning. He will show mental inertness or mental ill health: both the conditions may force him not to achieve what he is capable of. A conference with the parents may be organised to explain to them the evil effects of emotional tension. A greater tolerance may be cultivated to meet the disagreeable circumstances in the home (or in the society). Personal Guidance can be offered. Emotional needs of pupils, who have minor personally disturbances may be satisfied. Then the amount of reading gain will be proportional to the gain achieved in emotional adjustment.

2. Arousal of Disruptive Emotions is Facilitated by Physical Conditions. A teacher should realise that disruptive emotions are caused by certain stimuli and become intense as the stimuli pile up. He should not only try to find out those stimuli and avoid their piling up, but he should try also to find out and appreciate the effect of physical conditions, home circumstances and school environment upon the emotional development of his pupils.

3. Emotion Arousing Stimuli have a Cumulative-Effect. The longer the emotion arousing stimuli persist the greater is the intensity of the emotional reaction. A teacher may insist on pupils to work hard in English or Mathematics at times, but as the insistence increases, the resentment and hostility mount up. The autocratic Principal may demand from his pupils strict discipline in the assembly or in the school, but as the demand increases persistently, there is a greater and greater hostility expressed. Minor irritations in the classroom cause greater emotional stress after-wards. Similarly, we have accumulation of positive emotional experiences. The wise mathematics teacher creates and sustains enduring interest in the subject by giving daily a sense of satisfaction to his children from what they accomplish, however small it may be. The success of programmed learning, in which the pupil gets reward for correct answers on brief bits of material, may be ascribed to this piling up of positive emotional experiences.

Some children are ill-fed or inadequately fed at home. Others are suffering from defective vision which has either not been detected or corrected if detected. Still others may be tired, ill or hungry when they come to school. These physical conditions and many others may cause irritation, worry or emotional disturbance.

Pupils may also be irritable because they might have troubles at home. An unwise father or mother might have blocked their desires. A strict autocratic guardian might have placed his difficult demands at home. Or, the school may be causing emotional stress and strain on the child by imposing an autocratic discipline or by offering curriculum that does not meet the needs and interests or by threatening failure at the examination.

A good teacher has an awareness of all these factors. He remains calm when his pupils display temper tantrums. He does not answer back when they become hostile. He does all that he can to help them control the disruptive emotion. He creates in the school and helps the parent to create in the home an environment conductive to the development of constructive emotions, such as affection, love, sympathy, friendliness, humour and respect for individuality. He advises parents to make the child's daily life enjoyable at home by giving him adequate nourishment, proper amount of sleep, a balance between work and rest, and correction of sensory difficulties. He tries to give small daily satisfactions and creats an enduring love for learning at school. He helps the child in building happy relations among peers.

CONTROL OF EMOTIONS

Emotions are either constructive or disruptive, pleasant or unpleasant, positive or negative. For example, love is a positive emotion and hate is a negative one. Humour is pleasant but anxiety is unpleasant. An emotion may be constructive or disruptive or both. For example, excessive anxiety about examinations is disruptive but slight anxiety may cause pupils to apply themselves more assiduously to hard work. Some of the disruptive emotions are: fear, anxiety, hate, prejudice, aggression, anger.

Fear. Fear may be defined as a tendency to take flight from certain objective situations. In such situations the element of insecurity is important. The natural overt behaviour from a fear arousing situation is that of flight. Children under seven years of age display fear response to noises, falling or danger of falling, pain or persons and things associated with painful experiences, strange objects, persons and situations. An infant does not fear the dark, the fire or the snake unless it is conditioned. Fear is thus learnt through conditioning. There is a carry-over of fear response from one situation to another. Once a child has responded to situation by fear, he is likely to repeat that response in similar situation later.

Fear is aroused by a certain situation. But there are various factors that contribute to its development. We fear to approach a too busy street with heavy traffic because it is associated with accidents. We fear the dark not because of the darkness itself but because of insecurity in darkness. Children fear a policeman or a teacher mainly because some parents deliberately teach their children to fear these persons. Children fear to speak before an audience because they have learnt that anyone who addresses a group is almost certain to be criticised by some of the listeners.

The emotion of fear is very intense and sometimes has a very damaging effect on the child. Though some fears are irrational, yet can't be explained away. The teacher should become alert when he finds fear response in a child for his classmates, or for the examinations or for the teacher himself. He should not ridicule a pupil for being afraid nor should he force him into a fear producing situation. To reduce or eliminate this emotion the teacher should encourage confidence in the child, develop skills, enhance feelings of worth. He should make an attempt to find the cause of feared situation, set a good example in the presence of a feared situation, provide some enjoyable accompaniments parallel to the fear-inducing situation, praise the willingness to try and practise skills to cope with fear. For example, when the child fears to speak before an audience, he should support the chiid, produce confidence in him, develop the skill of speaking, set an example of how-to-speak, and reward the child for his performance however small.

Anxiety. Mild anxiety is a light concern for a thing. There is an earnest desire for a thing when we are anxious about it. But there are also uneasiness and trouble attached to an anxious state. And the negative handicapping emotion that is most often present in the classroom is extreme anxiety. The mildly anxious individual is alerted and sensitive to stimulations. The mildly anxious child applies himself very assiduously to the learning tasks for he is desirous of getting success in it. But intensely anxious child gets low scores because it handicaps achievement.

When anxiety becomes extreme, it takes the shape of fear and like extreme fear it inhibits action, narrows the perceptual field and impairs constructive responses. (O. H. Mowrer, 1960) Like fear anxiety is a response to danger. In fear the danger is objective. In anxiety the danger is subjective. Anxiety is a response fearful in nature, but is out of proportion to reality.

The arousal of anxiety among children has been explained in a number of ways. Freudian psychologists believe that separation of parents or non-gratification of instincts causes anxiety in children. The child depends on parents for care and protection. When separation takes place through quarrel or tight or divorce so that care and protection is withdrawn from the child and he becomes anxious and worried. Similarly, when cultural demands do not permit him to gratify his instinctive tendencies and needs, he becomes uneasy and troubled. Sullivan (1948) also regards parents responsible for arousing anxiety in their children. Anxious and self-rejecting parents make their children anxious and self-rejecting. They have low opinions of themselves and doubt their ability to succeed in any situation and the same happens to their children. Sometimes they try to make up their own shortcomings or inadequacies by insisting on greater accomplishment than can be expected of them. They set so much higher a goal before their children that they are unable to reach and anxiety is generated. A third explanation of anxiety among children is given by Horney (1945). Chronic anxiety in school children (as in other individuals) is caused by an inconsistent, unjust or harsh environment. The organism in such an environment does either of the three things :

(i) moves with people by being meek or self-efficacing.

(ii) moves against people by being aggressive or competitive.

(iii) moves away from people by being aloof or withdrawn.

Educational Implications. Anxiety generally stems from sources beyond the school. The child who is coming to school may be troubled by the threatened or actual separation of parents. He may be anxious because he is not getting the love and affection of the father or of the mother or both. He may be anxiety-ridden because his instincts are not being satisfied. The anxiety in the child may be due to the inconsistent and unjust demands made on him by the school or the home or the society. Anxiety may be caused by the teacher or the parent who is pessimistic, self-rejecting and neurotic.

But what should a teacher do? Should he eliminate anxiety in the child or tolerate it? Anxiety is an inevitable thing. A balance has to be struck. Mild anxieties have to be tolerated, extreme and chronic anxieties have to be eliminated. Mild anxieties facilitate and enhance learning, whereas severe and very low anxieties retard learning. (Reed, 1960) Chronic anxieties can be reduced by counselling and personal guidance. Anxieties about examinations can be reduced by giving frequent tests and assigning them a proper place in the total evaluation scheme so that no one examination becomes a main thing. Teachers are generally found ridiculing, ignoring or shaming children Such practices should be avoided because they unnecessarily generate anxiety and are bad for mental health also.

Aggression. Aggression is an emotional response to a frustrating situation. A situation is said to be frustrating when it more or less, blocks or thwarts the activity of the organism toward a goal. When aggression occurs, the organism either attacks people or things about him or retreats, withdraws and ceases to struggle. For example, when people become aggressive they attacks the person who frustrates the satisfaction of their needs. They also express their hostility by destroying things or property or persons other than those-who cause blocking or thwarting. Pupils destroy school property, break furniture or remove fixtures from the school building. This is displaced aggression.

Aggression is aroused by the person who causes frustration but it is also aroused by home or school conditions. Parental behaviour and home backgrounds are a source of aggression. When school's social demands conflict with what they have learnt at home, there is aggression. A child whose parents allow him to wear gaudy dresses every day, finds a conflict in the school which turns him out for not wearing school uniform. The child, therefore, becomes aggressive toward the teacher who turns him out of the school and sends him home. The child also brings with him the parents' pattern of behaviour into the school. The common response to a permissive parents' attitude toward the child, is the child's delinquent, aggressive behaviour. School conditions are also a source of aggression in the child. If a mentally less-than-average child is required to achieve a certain standard which he possibly cannot attain, he shall become aggressive.

Controlling Aggression. Aggression may be reduced or eliminated by removing the cause or source of aggression. Aggression may be expressed in a constructive way also. Play therapy has been used for reducing aggressiveness of seriously disturbed children. Substitutes of play therapy have been employed. By asking children to write stories of violence and thus express their hostility, aggression becomes reduced. By letting an aggressive child talk out his difficulties, he will be given a chance to express his feelings and reduce aggression. The teacher or the Principal to whom the child is sent should listen to what he says and understand his viewpoint. The aggressive child will throw off much of aggression if he comes to know that there is some one who wants to listen to him, who cares for him and understand him.

Anger. It is a state when an organism displays his hot displeasure towards another. In its milder from anger is simple resentment; in its intense form it is rage. The anger-arousing stimuli are varied. When the small infant is not allowed to suck his or her mother's breast, it displays resentment. When he grows up into childhood and his interests are denied he shows his anger in screaming, kicking, stamping, crying. When he is an adult the expression of anger takes the shape of attack, criticism, violation, insolence.

Temper tantrum, however, is displayed by an individual of any age. The main objective behind the emotional expression of anger is to get what one wants. In childhood temper tantrum takes the shape of striking, tearing, kicking, crying. In adolescence or adulthood we have the expression of temper tantrum in protruding lips as a sign of displeasure, in using sarcastic and biting language, and in withdrawing oneself with dignity from the group. The child, who is angry, shows his anger physically by disobeying and resisting or by expressing his resentment in words. The adolescent or adult uses taunts, ridicules, sarcasms. Truancy, rebellion, delinquency are various forms of expressing anger in school children and boys.

Anger like aggression can be reduced or eliminated when the source of anger is removed. Divert the attention of the angry person from the anger-arousing, situation to something else. A pleasant remark sometimes diverts the individual away from the state of rage and resentment. Never try to argue or reason with an angry person. Let the storm pass. Then you can succeed in giving him suggestions, or ideas. But we never act according to the above precept. When enraged we turn the child out of the class, send him to the principal's office, and punish him at once. We ourselves do not let the storm pass.

Anger is sometimes a useful emotion. When the child is not doing what he is capable of or when he is faced with injustice or unfairness, anger should be aroused. Anger with oneself increases learning efficiency. Anger with the unjust gives him moral strength.

7

Psychology of Achievement Tests

Every class-room teacher wants to find out the progress made by his pupils in the subject he teaches; for example, in Arithmetic, History, Georaphy, Hindi, English, Science, etc. Achievement in a subject measures the status of the pupil in that subject. An achievement test measures the learning objectives in a subject-matter field. The following are the purposes of achievement testing:

(1) **The Subject-Matter Achievement Tests are Single Subject Tests.** *They give the picture of a student's status in a specific subject*—his performance level in that subject only. They give a more detailed pictured a student's knowledge of concepts, facts, principles generalisations. They can be devised to help the teacher make a preliminary diagnosis of areas of weakness in a particular subject-matter field.

(2) **A Subject-Matter Test is Usually Given at the End of a Particular Course.** But it may be also given as a pre-test. It is also given as a diagnostic tool to students whose performance does not match their ability Sometimes various parts of a content-area are tested in different parts of a subject-matter test. The sub-scores on these tests are used to *give us a more clear picture of the student's achievement.*

(3) The main purpose of achievement testing is to *find out the progress that a given pupil has made as an instructional outcome.* If an achievement test is given when the child begins a course at the beginning of a term and another equivalent achievement test is given at the end of the term and if a child is below average in both tests, there is no cause of concern to the teacher because it is not the fault of the teacher's teaching. The fault lies somewhere else. With the scores obtained in an achievement test both the superior and the slow learner can see objective evidence of their growth.

(4) **Scholastic Achievement Tests are, Therefore, Needed to Find a Student's Standing in One or More Subjects.** They are required to find pupils' strengths and weaknes and to diagnose why these weaknesses exist. *They are used as diagnostic tests.*

(5) General achievement test batteries are also prepared to measure a student's standing in a number of subjects at a given grade level. An achievement test battery is divided in to parts that yield separate scores in such subjects as languages, arithmetic, science, social studies.' The purpose of an achievement test battery is manifold, It *surveys the whole field of achievement at a particular level.* It is comprehensive test, so it presents a general picture of the student's performance. The information gained from an achievement test battery is useful also in diagnosing specific difficulties of a pupil. A poor work in one subject field, *i.e.*, arithmetic may be a reflection of the fact that the child has a difficulty in understanding the language of the question in arithmetic; hence, it indicates his weakness in reading.

The superior pupil will feel probably encouraged if he keeps the relative position (the position as he had at the beginning of the term and the position he has at the end). The slow learner will see that he is growing even though slowly by comparing his status at the beginning with the status at the end of the term.

Uses of Achievement Testing

Achievement testing, is useful to the teacher and the student in a number of ways. An achievement test measures the *status* of the pupil as explained above in a subject-matter field: an achievement test battery measures the level of performance in different areas.

(1) Instructional Aid. An achievement test is used as an *instructional tool* in day-to-day teaching to facilitate learning. It is, therefore, closely related to learning activity. The simplest example of such an instructional tool is the set of examples given at the end of the chapter of a book. The problems and exercises given at the end of a chapter or a topic test what the learner has learnt. Many work books have such an instructional value. An instructional test may be taken under the supervision of a teacher's guidance or it may be taken at home or it may be done in the library. Practice exercises are also instructional tools.

A very interesting use of achievement testing as an instructional aid is made in teaching machines. A teaching machine is a mechanical device developed to tell the student whether a particular answer is correct or incorrect. When the student starts the machine without the teacher's assistance, reviews material, tests himself at the end of the instructional unit, we call the process machine teaching. In a language laboratory, when the student plays a tape recording of a foreign language and tries to learn the vocabulary, speech structure, and the accent, there is machine teaching.

A teaching machine is a very simple device. A number of questions in a sequence are fed into the machine. These questions are set on a carefully selected subject-matter. The programme begins with something familiar and easy and proceeds to increasingly difficult and less well-known material.

(2) Prognostic Use of Achievement Testing. Prognosis means foretelling, prediction, forecast. The test scores gained through achievement testing indicate not only pupil's present level of achievement, but they also tell us something about the future. They tell the teacher as to what extent his pupils can get advantage of further learning experiences. Suppose, for example, a student wants to take up a course in Higher Algebra. If he has mastered the fundamentals of elementary algebra, he can be expected to succeed in taking that course. An achievement test in fundamentals of elementary algebra can be given to him to predict his future success in the advanced course. An achievement test, therefore, can be used for prognostic purposes. For curricular many guidance prognostic tests have been developed.

(3) Measuring Aptitude through Achievement Testing. An aptitude is a capacity, plus a probability that a student will develop an ability in a specific field. Aptitude therefore refers to a rather narrow field of behaviour; for example, to musical ability or to mechanical ability. An aptitude test is designed to measure the probable future performance. Any test that, can estimate the probable future performance may be designated as an aptitude test. An intelligence test may be used as an aptitude test and in fact there are many intelligence tests called Differential Aptitude Tests, Factored Aptitude Tests, General Aptitude Test Batteries.

An achievement test can also be used as an aptitude test. The distinction between achievement and aptitude is not very strictly absolute. The only difference lies in their uses. When an achievement test in Physics is used to find out the present status of the student (the present performance in the subject), we call it simply an achievement test. But when it is used to predict the future performance of the student in some profession, it is caused an aptitude test. Such aptitude tests are given to pupils seeking admission to medical colleges.

The tests which are used to measure the results of training are known is achievement tests. But the tests which are used to measure a person's ability before he has been given a chance for special training are known as aptitude tests. The achievement testing looks to the present and the past, the aptitude testing looks to the future.

The testing practices of secondary school teachers do not aim at either prognosis or at prediction of probable future success. The practical uses which the school teacher makes of achievement testing have little to do with such purposes.

Practical Uses of Achievement Testing. There are generally two uses for which a school teacher prepares and administers an achievement test: *(i)* to help him in determining the pupil's marks in a subject; and *(ii)* to find out what parts of a topic need to be retaught.

But achievement test scores may also be used *as a guide* to find out the approximate quality of' work each pupil should have done or should do and to discover what units or topics should be taught again or revised. Achievement testing should help the teacher to make value judgments about his teaching effectiveness. It should indicate the strengths and weaknesses of teaching techniques and teaching methods. It should help the teacher to classify his pupils into superior or slow learners so that he may be able to deal with the two distinctly different classes of pupils adequately.

A very practical use which the teacher can make of achievement testing is '*diagnosis*.' For example, if a teacher of mathematics finds that his whole class has missed how to solve simultaneous equations by substitution method, learning the solution of simultaneous equations has been incomplete. Perhaps the students did not recognise that certain questions cannot be solved if one does not use this method or perhaps they did not study the method seriously at all. Reteaching becomes in such case very necessary.

Achievement test scores also *help the student in knowing his present status* in a particular subject field. An achievement test, where it is objective and fair, stimulates students to do better work. Performance on an examination always stimulates the interested child toward further accomplishment. It tells him where he has succeeded and where he has failed. He tries to relearn what he failed to learn when he took previous test. Progress in subject-matter achievement is the final goal of all schooling.

Objective Test Items

The essay-type items are usually indefinite in meaning. They vary in scope. Their scoring is characteristically subjective. In order to compensate these weaknesses, simple, easily and quickly answerable forms of short questions are set in scoring the answers of which the subjective element of the scorer 'is eliminated or reduced to a minimum. The essay-type question is generally long and the items so formed to offset the, weaknesses inherent in the essay-type questions are generally short. The various forms of short answer type questions are True and False (Yes and No), Modified True and False, Multiple choice, Matching-type, Simple recall, Completion tests and their other modifications.

To illustrate these types a few examples are given below. A teacher will have to acquire skill in preparing these short answer type questions:

(A) True-False Items. A true-false type question involves a statement. The statement may be true or false. The student is required to indicate whether it is true or not by writing T if true and F, if false. The symbols T, F, Yes or No, + or 0 are placed in front of or in the end of the statement as shown below:

Direction. Place a sign plus (+) in front of each statement that is true; otherwise place a zero (0).

1. Growth is a function of interaction of the organism and environment.
2. If you want transfer, teach for transfer.
3. Goals should be attainable and pupils should feel that they are able to attain them.
4. The field theories of learning take a molecular view.
5. Affection is a destructive emotion.

When the symbol T (True) or F (False) occurs in front of the statements, the pupil has to encircle T if the statement is true and F, if it is false.

The above statements are so clear and definite that there can be no debate over them. There is also no rhythm in the answers as there is rhythm in + - + - + or + + - - +. In constructing such an item the teacher should avoid statements which are neither true nor false, or which are indeterminate or which contain words or expressions giving a hint for correct response or which have too many negatives. He should avoid stating personal opinions and meaningless generalisations. The true and false items should be balanced.

The greatest drawback of such items is that the pupil guesses and even when he does not possess a knowledge of subject-field being tested, some of his answers are sure to be correct. The chances are 50:50 for an answer given on guessing to be correct. Hence some test builders apply the following correction formula:

Score = Number right minus number wrong.

But what about a student who knows the subject-matter correctly? He will be penalised unnecessarily and the one who is guessing will be rewarded. Hence, some test makers ask the student to indicate why he thinks a statement incorrect or false. This type of test item is known as Modified True-False item. As example follows:

Direction. Encircle T if the statement is true and F if it is false. In the latter case give your reasons why the statement is false.

1. A test that is administered to several subjects is a group test. T.F.

   Reason for falsehood:

2. Adrenin is a hormone secreted by thyroid gland. T. F.

   Reason if false:

Another modification in True-False item is to increase the number of alternatives: True/False/Do not know.

Direction. Tick True if the statement be true, False if false and Do not know if 'it is not known to you. But do not guess.

1. It is unlikely that learning will be effective without knowledge of results. True/False/Do not know.
2. Dalton plan was originated in the city of Dalton. True/False/Do not know.

(B) Multiple Choice Items. A multiple-choice item is designed to offset the weaknesses of the alternate choice True-False item. Instead of two choices, the student is offered 4 (or 5) choices and he has to select the best answer. The choice has to be indicated by crossing out, underlining or ticking or entering the letter or number of the choice made on a line to the right or left of the statement.

Direction. Place in the margin the letter of the word or phrase that indicates the correct answer.

1. When I am thinking about the accident T saw Yesterday I am:

   (a) Reasoning.

   (b) Imagining.

   (c) Thinking.

   (d) Reading.

2. Teaching is most effective when the teacher bases his teaching upon:

   (a) Reinforcement theory.

   (b) Learning by insight.

   (c) Conditioning.

   (d) All theories of learning.

The test builder who prepares multiple choice items should take care that no answer should be far-fetched or patently wrong. There should be a gradation in the correctness or suitability of answers and the student should be challenged to find the best answer. Only one answer should be the best. The statement should not be either ambiguous or liable to educe difference of opinion as regard the correct answer as in the following statement:

The Psychological factor, Machine teaching or programmed learning lays the greatest emphasis upon, is :

(a) Learning is an individual process.

(b) Learning is an active process.

(c) Knowledge of results facilitates learning.

(d) Law of effect.

(C) The Completion Test Item. A test item (question), which requires the student to fill-in the blank, is called a completion test item. He has to supply the word or phrase omitted. Either a word or two are omitted in a sentence or many words are omitted in a phrase and the student has to supply the commissions so that the meaning of the sentence or the paragraph becomes clear.

Direction. Fill-in the blanks.

1. The mental process in which the mind wanders freely is ....
2. The word .... means shape or form or configuration. Configuration, in part, depends upon the figure-ground relationship. Typically, what is clearly outlined is .... and what, is vague is .... Thus, in a landscape painting the barn though small is .... while the sky, the field in front, the forest in the back are ....

In scoring such a test the more important factor tested being the logical reasoning there may be a difference of answers. Hence, credit will have to be given to answers that are most logical and correct.

(D) Matching Tye Tests. In a matching test the student has to associate a word or phrase given in one column to a word or phrase given in another column.

Direction. In column A you are given the names of some psychologists and in column B you are given certain psychological facts or principles or phenomena associated with them. Associate the true place number of the psychologist in the margin of column B most nearly associated with the phenomenon.

	Column A	Column B	
1.	E. R. Gutbric	Transfer of Learning	( )
2.	E. L. Thorndike	Programmed Learning	( )
3.	Koheler	Genetic Studies of Genius	( )
4.	Alfred Binet	Emergency Theory of Emotion	( )
5.	Charles Judd	Law of Readiness	( )
6.	W. B. Cannon	Learning by Insight	( )
7.	Terman	Intelligence Testing	( )
8.	B. F. Skinner	Law of Contiguity	( )

(E) Modified Essay Type Questions. In order to make the response of an essay-type question. The examiner sometimes tries to reduce the subjectivity by requiring the answer in a short sentence. He scores the answer according to its adequacy of thought and content.

1. The aims of education in the modern democratic set-up of the country are:

   (a)

   (b)

   (c)

   (d)

   (e)

2. The five recommendations made by the Education Commission, (1964–66) are given as under:

   (a)

   (b)

   (c)

(d)

(e)

3. The forms of short answer type tests are:

(a)

(b)

(c)

(d)

Merits of Objectives

The short answer type questions have been found to be a psychologically sound technique of evaluating pupil achievement. A number of uses have been claimed for short answer type questions.

(1) Easily Scorable. One of the great merits of short answer type questions is that they can be easily and quickly scored. The correct answer to every objective-test item is found out and a key is prepared for the entire test. The answers which agree with the marking key are scored as correct: those that do not agree are scored as incorrect.

In scoring an objective test the problem of reader reliability does not arise. The person-to-person correlation of evaluating answer scripts is + 1′00 (plus one point 0, 0), because anyone who scores the answer scripts arrives at the same score an any other person does because both have to follow the same scoring key.

(2) Subjective Element Reduced to the Minimum. The subjective element of the examiner is either eliminated altogether or reduced to the minimum. The examiner has no chance to apply his personal idiosyncrasy or individual point of view because an objective test item (true-false, matching, multiple choice or any other form) is definite in wording and not so variable in scope as the essay-type questions are.

The only subjectivity that can enter is involved in selecting the form of the items to be included in the test or in making the key. In modified True-False test items where the student has to enter his reason why an item is False, subjective element enters from the side of the examinee who has to offer his own opinion. In constructing multiple choice items greatest care is taken to word the items in such a way that there is perfect definiteness and no ambiguity. Care is also taken to see that no two answers are considered to be appropriate and wherever there is difference of opinion as regards the best answer such a question is removed from the test.

(3) **A Very Good Tool for Testing Factual Material.** An objective test is a very good technique of measuring factual material. A large amount of study material can be tested in a very short period of time. Knowledge exists and functions on four levels—recognition, recall, interpretation and appreciation. The first level—recognition—is best tested by multiple choice and matching type questions.. The last three levels are best tested by recall type questions. Recognition tests, if they are constructed carefully can also measure understanding, evaluation, application and other aspects of thinking. Poorly made tests simply measure memory.

LIMITATIONS OF SHORT ANSWER TYPE QUESTIONS

The critics of short answer type questions and the adherents of essay-type testing have pointed out certain limitations of the objective test items.

The short answer type questions were devised to offset the limitations of essay-type questions. Though short answer type questions are in the form of being easily and quickly answered, though subjective clement of the essay-type questions is eliminated or reduced to the minimum, yet their use and construction has certain limitations.

1. Too much emphasis is placed on petty details and broad concepts are excluded. Relatively unimportant learning material is stressed. This criticism becomes more valid when the test constructor pays little heed to the worthwhile learning outcomes and more heed to the form of questions. Where the learning objectives are stressed and pupils have to give thought to answers, the above criticism does not hold good.

2. Correct answers to short answer type questions can be guessed easily. It is quite true in the form of True-False items. No guessing can be checked. The only alternative that remains is the use of modified true and false items.

   In the other forms also the student proceeds by eliminating wrong and apparently wrong answers which is not a desirable learning outcome. Anyone who does not know a correct answer to a multiple choice or matching type question may so proceed and by a process of elimination may arrive at a correct answer. In order that a student may not use a process of elimination more items are placed in one column of the matching-type question and care is taken not to offer cues through the wording of items. In the multiple-choice questions care has to be taken so that no answer seems too far-fetched or patently wrong because in that case it would be most liable to being eliminated by the student. Again, one may use the correction formula:

$$\text{Score} = R - \frac{W}{n-1}$$

The application of this correction formula again is subject to criticism because the pupil whose response represents knowledge rather than guessing will be unnecessarily penalised.

3. The short answer type questions are easy to score but difficult to construct. The error is moved from the scoring process to the constructing process.
4. In America even, where the test writing became an industry on a large-scale there were many poor tests with questions of alarming triviality. There is no use asking a worthless question only because it can be marked objectively. Even in such countries where objective tests became very popular, there are teachers and administrators who favour essay-type questions because of their greater advantage. The essay questions require from the pupils a greater mental effort. Taking a short answer test is simply pointing or ticking the correct answer. It calls for the least effort of the mind above that of keeping awake.

Limitation of Essay-type Tests

Essay-type Test Item Defined. An essay-type test item is a free response test item. The student is free to give the answer of a question as he likes. Stalnarker defines an essay question as a "test item which requires composition by the examinee usually in the form of one or more sentences, of a nature that no single response or pattern of response can be judged subjectively only by one skilled or informed in the subject." An essay question, which requires a student to think, to organise and to apply his knowledge, can be defended on the ground that it serves educational purpose, but an essay question which is so general that the student is unable to answer it satisfactorily or the teacher finds it difficult to score it with confidence is not a good tool of measurement.

It is the form of the essay question that creates difficulty to the student as well as to the teacher. Consider, for example, the following question:

"Describe the causes of Indian Mutiny of 1857."

The student here is expected to describe all the causes that led to the political upheaval in 1857, in India, but the problem before him is what causes he should name and what amount of answer he is to give. To describe all the causes is as impossible as it is ridiculous. The most informed student of the High School in history writes all that he remembers and the teacher grades the answer as he likes. There is no criterion either before the student or before the teacher. Such an essay-type question does not serve any useful educational purpose.

A more useful essay-type question may take any one of the forms suggested below but the main idea behind setting an essay question should be to require from the student some thinking and mental exertion and not rote memory. A mere recollection of information from the text-book is generally called for and all essay-type questions suffer from this handicap. They are neither thought provoking nor challenging. If the teacher had placed the above question in the form given below, some mental effort would have been required of the student and he would have been led to think, organise and apply his knowledge of Indian history—In what ways was Indian Mutiny (1857), different from the Quit India Movement (1942)?

A Suggestive List of Good Essay-type Question. The following is the list of forms of questions which may be used to encourage thinking, organisation and application of information gained in a subject field:

1. Explain and interpret a process.
2. Apply principles and rules.
3. Criticism and evaluate.
4. Make comparisons and define relationships.
5. State and define reasons and purposes.
6. Illustrate by examples.
7. Draw conclusions.
8. Cite causes and results.
9. Generalise and discuss.

The defects of general essay-type questions have caused a great concern to the examiners, teachers, and administrators all the world over and a great revolution has occurred in the field of educational measurement in the first two decades of the present century. The limitations of essay questions that we have been highlighted are as follows:

1. **Difficulty in Scoring.** The major difficulty in using an eassy question lies not in constructing it but in scoring the answer scripts of the examinees. The problem of scoring answer sheets is really a formidable one. Extraneous and undesirable factors tend to enter scoring of an essay-type question; for example, the quality of hand-writing and ability in composition of the answer influence the teacher's evaluation of the answer script. When such factors are not allowed to operate, answers may vary a great deal in scope and in that case it becomes difficult for the teacher to decide as to which answer is satisfactory to a question.
2. **Subjectivity in Scoring.** The subjective opinion or personal bias of the examiner enters the scoring to

such an extent that there is always a person-to-person variation of making an answer. The teacher's liking of students and grades given to them are found to be positively correlated. It means that the students whom the teacher likes most get higher scores than their measured proficiency warrants and the students who are liked least by the teacher get lower score than their measured proficiency warrants.

3. **Unreliability of the Essay-test.** Besides the readers' unreliability the essay-tests have an inherent unreliability also. When a second administration of the same test takes place or when an equivalent form (equivalent in terms of length, difficulty, subject-matter area, and type of questions) is administered to the same group of pupils, the two sets of scores so obtained do not correlate highly.

4. **Unreliability of Scoring.** The subjectivity of scoring leads to unreliability of scoring. When a teacher reads an answer script at different intervals, the scores given to the same script vary a great deal. There is thus a time-to-time variation in scoring a single paper. This is known as reader's unreliability. By unreliability of scoring we mean inconsistency. A number of researches indicate the presence of this phenomenon. Even when the examiner is given enough guidance to score in several practice-sessions, a single essay-type answer has been given grades varying from one to eight by one examiner when he was asked to rate the same paper at different times.

5. **Essay Tests not Comprehensive.** The content coverage of every essay test is low. In a limited time of 3 hours' duration only a limited number of essay questions can be answered. The results is that the

whole question paper covers a small area. The number of questions in an essay-type question paper cannot be kept more than 5 or 6 because it becomes difficult for the teacher to mark all the answer scripts in the time given to him for marking.

6. **Unimportant and Undesirable Factors Entering the Scoring.** A number of strange factors begin to operate while scoring a test paper in which essay questions have been answered. Clear legible hand-writing has a greater advantage over a handwriting which tries the teacher's patience. The student who knows little but who gives a systematic answer gets more credit than the one who knows more but whose answer is not so arranged.

7. **Encouragement of Cramming.** The limited content coverage of the essay-type question papers leads to another evil practice of cramming or of question spotting (consequently of cheap notes). In almost all public examinations this evil recurs. Teachers also single out those areas of the syllabi which they consider most likely to be asked in a particular year and then they concentrate intensely on those areas only.

8. **Essay-type Paper Unfair to the Students.** When the paper cannot be expected to cover the entire field, the student has to be judged by a small sample of questions which is not always representative. The test then becomes unfair for the student who knows all the subject-malter except the one that he is required to answer. Those who can guess better and whose guessing comes out to be correct happen to score high.

Suggestions to Improve Essay-type Testing. The weaknesses of the essay-type examinations have been too much laboured upon. Still they have survived the attacks. It seems therefore that there is something good in them which we are not able to capitalise upon. Many teachers and administrators still favour essay examinations. They claim that a pupil is given greater opportunities in essay questions to organise his material and to present his point of view. He is more able to express his ideas in written form and essay-type examinations serve more useful educational purposes.

There is therefore a greater tendency to reform essay examinations than to discard their use altogether. It is now believed that if essay-type questions are constructed more carefully, and are scored move objectively and are prepared in such a manner that they cover more content area, they can be more useful than the short answer type questions.

Suggestions to Improve Essay-type Test Scoring

The teacher has to decide very carefully what grade he would give to a particular answer. A model answer to each question should be written by the teacher first, and it should be divided into sub-parts, and definite numbers of points should be given to each sub-part depending upon its relative importance. The answer to a question given by a student should then be read keeping in mind the numerical scores for each sub-part, and each sub-part should be marked.

Another method of reading the essay examination papers has been suggested by Ruch. He says that all the essay examination papers should be read first, and each question should be graded separately. It has been said above that personal bias enters scoring by the teacher. If, however, he grades the paper, question by question, the liking or disliking of students cannot influence his scoring. It means that the teacher should read and grade question number one in all the papers, then the second, and then the third, and so on.

Public examination boards try to solve the problem of unreliability in scoring. A closely coordinated team of examiners under a chief examiner is appointed. Examples of answer made are considered and the team decides on a common standard of marking. The marking of the answer-book by the team goes on with continuous checking of examiner's standard of marking by the chief examiner. Such a co-ordination may be helpful in achieving consistency.

The last but not the least criticism of essay-type questions is that they favour verbal fluency. If language is an obstruction the question intended to discover how much the student knows about the given subject will not be a fair condition. Language is only an instrument of expression. In some examinations language difficulty puts barrier between what the student knows and how he conveys his knowledge to the examiner. If ability in the use of language is taken to be a part of examination the language barrier may not be regarded as a cause of anxiety. But if the essay-type examination is intended to test the candidate's knowledge only then this examination difficulty would not permit the examiner to discover the true amount of candidate's knowledge.

STANDARDISED ACHIEVEMENT TESTS

A Standardised Test Defined. A standardised test is one for which norms have been established. It means that the test has been given to a large number of students and scores have been given definite expectancy values or norms for given groups of pupils. A norm is an average or topical score which measures achievement (any trait or behaviour such as intelligence). So every standardised test has norms. It is prepared by a test specialist according to certain definite rules or standards of construction. It is intended for general use and covers a wider scope of material than is covered in an ordinary teacher-made test which is needed only to evalute the achievement of students of a class.

The forms of questions in a standardised test are generally short-answer type or object test items. A particular standardised test serves a particular populous. It has to undergo a number of processes. The preliminary form of the test contains more items than are to be included in the final test. The specialised test constructor consults school people, school administrators, administers, the tests once, twice and sometimes thrice also. These administrations are called first, second and third try-outs. A try-out is done in order to find the reliability, validity of the tests, its usability and scorability.

A statistical treatment is applied to the data. The preliminary test is revised in the light of investigations and the final form is published for use by school people.

Difference of Teacher-made Tests and Standardised Test. A teacher-made test is intended to measure the outcomes of learning which a teacher in particular has in mind. The standardised test intends to measure the educational outcomes aimed at generally by a number of schools.

A teacher-made test is not a published test as it is to be used by a teacher for his own school to measure the attainment of objectives which he himself has laid down for class-room teaching. A published standardised test is prepared to measure the objectives of teaching a subject by a number of schools. So all school people are consulted and therefore it is more comprehensive.

The standardised tests are more accurate than all the teacher-made tests put together because in their construction much expert thought has been employed. The teacher-made tests are not so carefully prepared. The items of teacher-made tests are seldom edited. The types of behavioural changes covered are limited in scope.

The standardised tests can be used by headmasters to compare the achievement of their pupils with that of the pupils of other school. But a teacher-made test cannot be so used.

The chief characteristics of standardised tests that differentiate them from teacher-made tests are:

Objectivity. All standardised tests make use of objective test items which are definite in wording, limited in scope as regards response, simple in construction, easy and least subjective in scoring. These items are true-false, modified true-false, matching, completion, recognition, identification and multiple choice. Maximum objectivity is attained through strict use of scoring key after it has been prepared with due consideration and thought.

Reliability. A test is said to be reliable when it gives consistent results on the second administration of the test itself (or of an equivalent form) on the same pupils or group of pupils. A test is said to be reliable if a group of students take the test second time and obtain approximately the same scores again. The only condition is that no learning should interpolate between the two administrations of the same test to the same group.

Several statistical methods have been suggested to measure the consistency of an achievement test. A consideration of these methods required a pertinent knowledge of statistics. If the rank order of scores obtained by a group of students on the second administration changes materially from the one achieved on the previous testing, the test would be designated as an unreliable test. The extent to which the two ranking have greater agreement is measured by finding out the correlation coefficient between two sets of scores got on two different administrations.

The greater the coefficient of correlation, the greater the reliability of the test. Since there is always a chance of interpolated learning in between the two administrations of the same test at two different intervals of time, another method of finding out the reliability of a test has been suggested. This reliability is known as internal consistency. The test is administered only once to a group of children. The odd and even numbered items are scored differently. Two scores for the same student are arrived at-one for the odd-numbered items and the other for the even, numbered ones. The correlation coefficient between the odd and even-num-bered scores gives the extent of reliability of the test.

Still another method has been, employed to find out the reliability of a test. After constructing a particular achievement test, another equivalent test is also prepared. By an equivalent test we mean a test which contains items of equal difficulty level, the same subject-matter area, the same type of questions, and the same length of the test also. These two tests are administered one after the other and the correlation co-efficient between the two test scores gives the reliability co-efficient of the test.

Validity of a Test. An achievement test is said to be valid when it measures what it purports to measure. It means that in order that a test may be valid it should be constructed with specific objectives being kept in view. A test of application, for example, will be valid only when it measures the ability of students to apply facts and principles to problem situations. Conversely, a test which measures the know ledge of concepts, facts, and principles would not be a valid measure of applicational ability. A test of history is a valid test of history if it measures knowledge of historical facts. But if, however, it measures student's ability to read rapidly or if it lays special emphasis upon verbal intelligence, it would not be called a valid test of historical facts. So an achievement test is valid only as far as it measures achievement and is constructed with specific objectives.

The validity of a test is measured by the extent to which it agrees with the criterion measures. The application test of literature should agree with the number and quality of good books of literature one has read in spare time. The criterion of achievement in a subject may be the teacher's opinion regarding a class because through daily contact with the individual members of the class the teacher gains knowledge about the status of performance of its individual members.

The validity coefficient of an achievement is computed by finding out correlation coefficient between:

(a) Either the criterion measure and the scores obtained on the test.

(b) Or between the two test scores obtained by administering the proposed achievement test and the standardised achievement test already existing in the field.

Scorability. A standardised test has to be scored by machine so that the test results may be given at once. A test which takes too much time of the tester becomes useless when it is needed for wide use. Essay-type tests waste much time and consume needless energy of the examiners; hence they are not usable.

Objectivity. When a standardised test is developed, the exact and correct answer to each item is designated and a key is prepared for the entire test. The test papers then can be scored objectively, simply by marking those answers as correct which agree with the key and those answers as incorrect which do not agree with it. Hence, when a standardised test is given to a group of children one arrives at the same total score for each child as any other examiner does. Thus, person-to-person (*i.e.*, examiner to examiner) correlation for a set of items is +1.0. If the same examiner happens to score the test papers he will arrive at approximately the same scores. The standardised test, therefore, is completely foolproof.

There may be subjectivity in a standardised test, but as far as scoring of the answer scripts is concerned, there is perfect objectivity. If there is any subjectivity involved in a standardised test it is in-volved in selecting the items for inclusion and in making the key but not in scoring.

Norms. Every standardised test contains norms—age norms, grade norms, geographical norms, etc. Norms present the to-be-expected performance of average student on a specific age or grade or region.

Administrability. A test is said to be administrable when it can be given accurately and easily. If the directions to solve the test items are simple, the test can be taken easily. If the directions are complicated and difficult to understand, the test becomes difficult to administer. A test, which is not administerable, becomes unreliable because of the incorrect grasp of the instructions or because of the misunderstandings that arise while the test is being given.

***

8

Personality

There are three phases or aspects of personality, which account for much of the apparent disagreement among psychologists and educators. These are really different points of view of the same thing. 'What is true of one aspect (viewed in isolation) may or may not be true of another aspect.

First, there is the action aspect of personality concerned with how a person acts. Using this aspect as a guide, some personalities are called emotional while others are considered calm, intellectual, and so on. Thus, personality is sometimes defined as the sum total of a person's action patterns. Using this definition, a person who acts in a wide range of situations with jovial and felicitous behaviour is said to have a happy and jovial personality. Any personality may be described from the standpoint of the action or behavioural aspect.

Second, there is the social aspect, or the stimulus effect a person has on other people. "John has a good personality" in every day speech means that John has a favorable effect on one or more people. This aspect is the sum total of all those things about a person that affect other people. The social aspect of personality, then, simply describes the characteristic effect a person has on others.

A third aspect of personality is the cause or why aspect. This is the aspect of personality, which makes a person act in social or unsocial ways and makes people react accordingly.

People like a person (the social aspect) because his actions are interpreted as friendly (the response aspect) which, in turn, is the result of his positive attitudes (the cause aspect). All three aspects are important. None of them alone nor even all of them together describe the whole of personality. No aspect definition, no aspect measurement will give more than a partial understanding of personality. Our effect on others, the effect on us of things and events in life, our deepest thoughts, feelings, and attitudes are all interesting and important aspects of our personalities. But, personality cannot be identified with anyone of these aspects. It is all of these and more.

Meaning of Personality

Personality is the whole of man: his inherited aptitudes and capacities; all his past learnings; the integration and synthesis of these factors into characteristic behaviour patterns; and his ideas, values, and expectations. Since personality is a generic term involving intelligence, emotion, motivation, learning, memory, thinking, perceiving, and other factors, some psychologists believe it would be better to drop the word personality entirely. These psychologists assert that explanations of these components leave nothing further to be said.

In the organic world, however, the whole is more than the sum of its parts. A synthesis of dynamic parts produces something unique. There are so many cross-relationships involved in an organic combination of living, interacting parts that very small differences can produce very great effects. Therefore, a synthesis of psychological factors into a personality, living and dynamic as it is, is not a mere assemblage of components. The whole personality becomes something quite different from the psychological factors composing it.

The Self-concept. From the emergence of the notion of self or individuality, indicated by the suggestibility of the last stage of infancy to the awareness of his own identity in late childhood, the child gradually develops the power to enter into the reality of his environment. Progressively, he gains understanding of the process through practice in a number of roles (pupil, group member, team leader, member of a family, etc.) until he becomes less disturbed by changing moods. A person's self, as defined previously, is an objective reality. His ideas of himself or his understanding of himself, with all his strengths and weaknesses, however, is a learned product which is always subjective. This learned concept of self may be realistically and precisely correct, or grossly erroneous. As in the development of all concepts, knowledge gained through the cognitive activities of his life's experiences, colored deeply by his complex, individually developed emotionality, conditioned by his constitutional equipment, and determined by his personal choices relate and interrelate in the evolution of the self-concept. Combs and Snygg describe the self-concept as the way a person perceives or knows himself, especially concerning the fundamental aspects that are very important and central to himself and which are involved in a great deal of his behaviour. It is the very essential me whose loss is regarded as personal destruction and whose disorganization is vigorously resisted. These writers apply the term phenomenal self to the person's awareness of what he is at the precise moment of action. To an "outsider" who can never know a person as completely and intimately as he knows himself, the phenomenal self is an inference from the individual's behaviour. It is a useful concept in assessing personality and predicting probable behaviour.

An important aspect of the self, then, is that it represents the way in which the individual sees himself. Usually the individual's behaviour, including his thoughts, feelings, motives, and values, tends to be consistent with this self-concept or the way he sees himself. Lecky has suggested that a basic need of an organism is the need for self-consistency. In other words, the individual's behaviour will tend to be consistent with his self-concept. A simple case may illustrate this point.

Tom, a six-year-old first grader, hostilely refuses help from his teacher in putting on his rubbers when preparing to go home after school. Tom's teacher was motivated by kindness and a sincere desire to help the boy after watching his unsuccessful struggles. Tom, however, saw her efforts to help as a threat to his self-concept as a "big boy" who was able to dress himself and care for his dressing needs. On the other hand, Sally, a classmate, sees in the teacher's helping hand a gesture or sign of affection and welcomes such assistance.

Growth in Concept of Self. It has been pointed out that the child's concept of self is influenced by a great many factors: his parents' social status and class membership; their attitudes, values, standards of behaviour, and moral and ethical beliefs; the practices under which he is reared; cultural patterns which ascribe the various roles he is expected to play; personal qualities such as body size, weight, strength, agility, physical assets and defects; his sex, race, religion, and mental ability. Naturally all these factors are not developed at anyone time, but result from the varied experiences he encounters throughout life. It must be emphasized that the child's self-concept, to a large extent, is the result of the reactions of others to him. In the case of Tom, for instance, perception that the other children welcomed the teacher's aid in preparing to go home could change Tom's reactions. Tom would redefine his self-concept to include help from others as part of being a "big boy." If actions of others suggest that a child is stupid, inept, insincere, etc., then it becomes difficult for the child to hold on to a self-concept of adequacy.

The developmental nature of the child's self-concept has been revealed by a number of investigators: Generally the child's experiences at home, in school, and in the community lead to fairly accurate insights concerning his abilities and achievement. Brandt had a group of sixth graders and a group of eleventh graders estimate how well they expected to do in certain academic and physical tests in comparison to the group as a whole and in comparison to each classmate. He concluded from his study that self-rating accuracy may be developed and that it tends to increase with age and grade in school. Students with self-concepts of inadequacy (not good students, not good in school, etc.), which have been built up through experiences with parents, classmates, teachers, etc., often perform less well than they potentially could. They also manifest lower aspirational levels relative to tasks at school. In a study by Bledsoe and Garrison fourth and sixth-grade girls were found to have significantly higher self-concept ratings (by themselves) than fourth- and sixth-grade boys. It was also noted that self-concepts of elementary-school pupils were related to cultural forces in their backgrounds.

In an investigation of the self-concepts of potentially delinquent and potentially non-delinquent boys from similar physical environments, Reckless, Dinitz, and Kay found significant differences. Boys who were deemed non-delinquent saw themselves as obedient. They liked school, rarely played "hookey," felt that their families were as good as most families, and believed their parents to be neither overly strict nor too permissive. In most cases, their families were striving to achieve the "middle class" norms of behaviour. Therefore, these boys found their actions confirmed by teachers-persons in authority-and peers whom they considered important. Such confirmations (responses of approval) strengthened their self-concepts, which supported non-delinquent behaviour.

Boys who were delinquent, however, saw society as set against them. Many came from broken homes; most came from homes in which parental behaviour was inconsistent. Expectations transmitted by the parents led the boys to expect inconsistent, unfair treatment from persons in authority. The self-concept of the delinquent was one of revolt against established authority (because it was unfair and did not allow him to meet his needs).

The child is born into a particular general culture as well as subcultures. His personality is both enlarged and restricted by these cultures. These subcultures overlap the general culture and thus restrict or enlarge the child's world. The family, religious group, social group, and neighbourhood make for a diversity of culture and contribute to personality differences.

The Ideal-self. Some investigators have resorted to the use of the concept ideal-self as a means of determining the self-aspirations of children. The ideal-self is usually thought of as an expression of the type of person a child would like to be or resemble. The term ideal-self has been shown to be valuable in determining the relationship between how the child sees himself and what he thinks he should be like. Havighurst, Robinson, and Dorr have hypothesized that the ideal-self may be developmental in nature. They suggest that the ideal-self begins when the child identifies with a parental figure. During middle childhood and early adolescence it moves through a stage of romanticism and glamor, and culminates in late adolescence as a composite of desirable characteristics which may be symbolized by an attractive, real, and visible young adult or perhaps even an imaginary person.

Elements of Personality

There are several factors that contribute to our personality. These factors have received greater or less importance at the hands of different psychologists. Here we shall discuss some of the important elements. These elements generally stated are :

1. Personal Appearance. The size and shape of a person influences his personality. If a man is tall, of good physical proportions, and well-muscled, his personality is likely to be affected favourably. He is likely to be respected by his fellows and popular with them. A physical "deviate" on the other hand, has his own personality problems. By a 'deviate' we mean some one who varies or deviates considerably from the average. A person who is very small, very tall, too fat or too thin is a deviate. Being a deviate lessens the feeling of confidence and personal worth.

It is true that there can be a relationship between physical development and certain personal attitudes, especially in the case of deviates. But the fact is that no one can judge personal and intellectual qualities by physical appearance.

2. Emotional Life. The core of an emotional experience is feeling. When feelings violent and the composure of our mind is disturbed we have no longer feelings but emotions. An emotion is thus noting but an intense and violent feeling. Emotions play a very important part in the individual and social life of man. They determine to a very great extent his physical and mental health. They also determine whether a person will be liked in the society or will be treated as a nuisance. Emotions are to be sublimated. They should not be repressed.

3. Intelligence. Intelligence is an inborn capacity to perceive the right thing, at the right place, at the right moment. It is the general mental adaptability to new problems and conditions of life. Intelligence is certainly an asset. It enables easy adjustment even under difficult circumstances and thus helps in building up personality. Intelligent people are able to adjust themselves to changing environments with great ease, efficiency and speed and hence they are said to have good personality.

4. Temperament. Man may be rational animal, but at times he is extremely emotional also. Intense and violent feeling is emotional long drawn out emotion is a mood. Mood when it becomes permanent influences our temperament. Temperament is partly physical and partly mental. Diet and climate also effect our temperament and temperament affects personality. Differed types of temperament have resulted in different types of personalities:

> ***Choleric Type.*** He is also known as the violent type. He is energeting, full of ambition and courage but easily excitable to anger.
>
> ***Melancholic Type.*** He is humble, sad, depressed and pessimistic.
>
> ***Sanguine Type.*** He is active, cheerful and optimistic in his pursuits.
>
> ***Phlegmatic Type.*** He is slow, dull and unemotional. He is also known as 'apathetic' or 'indifferent type.'

Cyril Burt holds that majority of the cases belong to the mixed-type. Thus, there is a considerable overlapping of these temperament.

5. Character and Moral Traits. Character is the sum of all those tendencies, which the individual posesses. It is the organisation of instincts and habits under the sentiment of self-regard. If this organisation is strong, character is strong. It it is weak, the character is weak. Character includes our sentiments and habits in the widest sense of the term. It is the product of the interaction of instinctive dispositions with the physical and social environment under the guidance of intelligence. Character and the personality of the individual are very closely related.

ASSESSMENT OF PERSONALITY

The following methods and devices are used to measure personality and its various traits :

(1) Observation Method. The experimenter has simply to observe the behaviour of the individual. If he finds that good traits are present in his behaviour, he tries to know to what degree they are present in him. Thorndike's studies are famous in this line. To get one index of leadership, for example, we could merely count the number of elective positions which a student has held.

This device needs much time and is liable to error.

(2) Interview Method. For information which cannot be obtained through observation, investigators make great use of the interview. In such an interview, of course, the experimenter may use many supplementary devices. Used by trained and judicious, inquirer it can bring to light information which could be obtained in no other way. He may rely largely on rather simple discussion, basing his estimate on the answers to his questions and on the information volunteered by the person being interviewed.

The informal interview, of course, is no device for the untrained inquirer. He may miss much that is significant and may mis-interpret a good deal of what he observes. Secondly, the informal interview does not yield a quantitative score.

(3) Personality Questionnaire of Inventory. Personality, frequently is measured by questionnaries. Woodworth devised a "personal date sheet" in 1918, to determine emotional instability among soldiers. It had 116 questions, each to be answered by 'yes' or 'no.' Woodworth choose items relating to various physical symptoms, fears, worries, feelings and attitudes known to indicate mental or nervous disorders.

Some of the questions are—Do you usually feel well and strong? Does liquor makes you quarrelsome? Are you troubled with the idea that people are watching you on the street? Did you ever have a nervous breakdown?

A variation of the personality questionnaire is Sidney Pressey's Crossout test" to measure emotionality. On a long list of words the subject is asked to cross out those unpleasant to him; on another list those he considers wrong or unethical; on another items about which he worries. This test is generally used to get information about a person's emotions.

There are, of course, many objections to the questionnaires. The person taking the test may see through the questions and check the answer which he thinks will give him a good score rather than the answer which be regards as true.

(4) Performance Tests. Obviously persons may answer questionnaires wrongly or dishonestly and there lies a serious weakness of this kind of test. To avoid such errors, performance and behaviour tests are often used. It is possible to put a student in a test situation and to see how he actually performs. It is possible, for instance, to give him a test in which he has an opportunity to cheat and to determine whether or not he overcomes the temptation. He could copy from a neighbour's paper, change answers when scorring their own tests, 'peep' in a blind-fold game.

(5) Projective Techniques. Most of the measuring devices discussed so far are designed to cast light not on the integrated personality but on various isolated traits of personality. Now we will discuss those tests which reveal an integrated pattern of personality. Prominent among these are the so-called projective techniques.

Allport and Vernon show that handwriting and other expressive behaviour like walking and reading, speed or ability to estimate areas and distances, show rather consistent personality patterns. Yet there is no evidence that anyone expressive movement, or in fact all of them together, relate very closely to personality traits.

Meaning of Projective Techniques

This title is derived from projection, meaning reflection of one's own inner-self upon the external objects. Freud first used this word. According to him perception of the outer world is determined largely by the feelings, desires, fears, thoughts and ideas of the inner world which is unknown. This is based on depth psychology or the psychology of the unconscious. According to it the quality of personality is much affected by the unconscious motives and emotions. To test the whole personality we must have technique to measure this unconscious. Projective technique makes this possible. Through this technique is let out the hidden quality of the personality. This tells us as to what lise at the back of our conscious behaviour. When a person tells what a cloud looks like to him, or gives him his own interpretation of a picture containing people, he 'projects' into it something of his own personality. If he interprets several items in the same general way, this may reveal important trends of his thinking, attitude, interest and emotion.

Following are the devices used in projective technique:

(1) Dream Analysis. Dreams, according to Freud, are wishful-filling. The reperssed wishes of the individual come in a disguised form in dreams. Thus the analysis of the dreams of the individual reveal the type he is.

(2) Story Telling. The individual is asked to narrate stories which have been of special interest to him. This device is used to elicit the hidden and unconscious whishes, ambitions, fears, judge-ments, etc.

(3) Free Association. You give a casual word to the individual and ask him to give out all those words which come to his mind. A study of this chain of words will help us to assess his personality.

(4) Story Completion. An incomplete story is given to the individual and he is asked to complete the story in any manner he deems fit.

(5) Expressive Movement Tests. This is a technique to judge personality through :

(a) the handwriting of the individual,

(b) painting,

(c) picture completion test.

(6) Visual Tests. Out of the projective techniques the best known is the "ink blot test". The 'ink-blot test' was prepared by a Swiss Psychiatrist Herman Rorschach. It consists of ten cards, each containing a rater elaborate ink-blot. Five blots are in colour, five in grey and black. Those ink-blots are made by dropping some ink in the fold of a paper and squeezing the paper together. These blots suggest various pictures to different people, and since one is free to see almost anything in them, the reaction is supposed to indicate tendencies in the person. Subjects study one blot at a time and tell what each resembles. They can think as long as they like over each card. The examiner records their responses, then shows the card a second time asking the subjects to elaborate ambiguous interpretations and explain which parts of the ink-blots led to their responses.

Results are scored by three main criteria:

(a) Do subjects react to the whole blot, to a part or to a small detail?

(b) Do subjects see human or animal figures or chiefly inanimate objects?

(c) Do their responses involve movement, from colour or the three combined and is the form clear or blurred?

The complete scoring is quite complex, involving many factors beyond mere counting of responses. Seeing whole figures indicates high intelligence and ability to synthesize. A predominance of forms in motion, especially of human forms signifies vivid imagination. Great response to colour means impulsiveness, if not emotional instability. Setting mostly animals, and giving unoriginal responses in general, suggest lower intelligence. On the other hand, noting small unusual details indicates introversion and possible emotional conflicts.

A method somewhat similar to the 'ink-blot test' is the "Thematic Appreciation Technique". In this method, the subject is shown a picture, for instance, of an older man taking hold of the arm of a startled woman. The subject is told that this is a test of the fertility of his imagination. He is asked to give a story into which the picture would fit. The resulting story is supposed to give some insight into the hopes, fears and needs of the subjects.

Limitations of the Projective Technique

1. There is a great dearth of standardised test.
2. They are more subjective. Scoring is difficult and exacting and interpretation is exceedingly complex.
3. There is no proof of their validity. Henry A. Murray of Harvard, himself the creator of several new projective methods, says that their validity is demonstrated with children but some doubts remain about adults. There are many other psychologists who say that these tests lack objectivity and their interpretation is without experimental verification. They feel that the validity of these tests is not yet established for normal persons.
4. These tests are to be administered with great care and that also by an expert. Everybody cannot use them.

FACTORS WITH AFFECT PERSONALITY

The important factors in which the origin of personality lies are:

(I) Heredity. It provides the child with certain endowments to start with. Hereditary factors may be summed as constitutional, biological and physiological factors:

1. ***Constitutional Factors.*** The constitution of an individual is an effective factor in determining the type of his personality. There can be 3 bodily types of personality—*(1)* short and stout, *(2)* tall and thin, *(3)* muscular and well proportioned. We are always impressed by an individual who has a muscular and a well proportioned body. Height, weight, physical defects, health and strength affect personality.

2. ***Biological Factors.*** The working of the nervous system, glands and blood chemistry determines our characteristics and habitual modes of behaviour. These factors form the biological basis of our personality. Adrenal gland, thyriod gland, pituitary gland and endocrine gland affect personality. Adler points out that personality defects lead to the development of inferiority complex and the mental mechanism of compensation. This aspect also includes the mental ability of the child. It is this ability which enables him to mould the social environment according to his requirements.

3. ***Nervous System.*** Development of personality is influenced by the nature of nervous system.

4. ***Intelligence.*** Intelligence is mainly hereditary. Persons who are very intelligent can make better adjustment in home, school and society than those who are less intelligent.

5. ***Sex Differences.*** Sex differences play a vital role in the development of personality of individual. Boys are generally more assertive and vigorous. They prefer adventures. Girls are quieter and more injured by personal, emotional and social problems.

(II) Environment. The sociologists emphasise that the personality of the individual develops in a social environment. It is in the social environment, that he comes to have moral ideas, social attitudes and interests. This enables him to develop a social 'self' which is another term for personality.

The important aspects of the environment are as follows:

(1) ***Physical Environment.*** It includes the influence of climatic conditions of a particular area or country on man and his living.

(2) ***Family Environment.*** Family is the cradle of all social virtues. The first environment, the child moves in, is his home. Here the child comes in contact with his parents and other family members. His likes, dislikes, stereotypes about people, expectancies of security and emotional responses all are shaped in early childhood. The type of training and early childhood experiences received from the family play an important role in the development of personality.

Besides this, economic factors *i.e.*, economic condition of the family and the type of relations between the parents also influence the personality of the child.

(3) ***Cultural Environment.*** The cultural environment refers to certain cultural traditions, ideals, values etc., which are accepted in a particular society. All these factors leave a permanent impression on the child's personality.

(4) ***Social Environment.*** The child has his birth in the society. He learns and lives there. Hence, the social environment has an important say in the personality development of the child.

In addition to the above there are many other social factors which influence the development of personality of a child which are as follows:

(a) ***Language.*** Human beings have a distinctive characteristic of communication through language. Language is an important vehicle by which the society is structured and culture of the race transmitted from generation to generation. The child's personality is shaped by the process of interaction through language with other members of his environment.

(b) ***Social Role.*** The child has to play several roles like son, brother, student, officer, husband, father, etc. throughout his life at different stages of his development. Social roles may be described as the process by which the cooperative behaviour and communications among the society members are facilitated.

(c) ***Identification.*** Identification is an important mechanism by which we try to imitate the physical, social and mental characteristics of our model. It is a very important relationship with others.

(d) ***Self Concept.*** Self concept influences our personality development in two ways—*(1)* If other people hold high positive attitude towards us, this enhances our self and *(2)* If others hold negative attitude towards us, it creates feelings of worthlessness and may lead to self-defence or withdrawal from social situation.

(e) ***Inter-personal Relations.*** Inter-personal relations among the members of a society are important means which help in the development of certain social personality characteristics like attraction towards others, concept of friendship, love, sympathy, hostility and also isolation which is a negative orientation.

(III) Psychological Factors. These include our motives, acquired interests, our attitudes, our will and character, our intellectual capacities such as intelligence *i.e.*, the abilities to perceive, to observe, to imagine, to think and to reason, These factors determine our reactions in various situations and thus affect our personality, growth and direction. An individual with a considerable amount of will power will be able to make decisions more quickly than others.

Thus, we see that hereditary, environmental and psychological factors contribute towards the development of personality.

SOCIAL DETERMINANTS OF PERSONALITY

The environments of different individuals are very much different from one another and so also their effects, but the influence of environment on personality can roughly be divided into that of home; school and society. All these three play an important part in the development of personality.

1. Influence on Home of Personality. The environment of the home has a wide influence on the development of personality. This influence, as a general rule, is according to the patterns found in a particular culture. In the family the relation of child with the parents is the most intimate. The cultural development of the child is very much influenced by the behaviour of the parents *e.g.*, a child brought up in Indian family will be very much different in his behaviour than another brought up in western culture. But even in the same culture much difference can be observed in the parent-child relationship in different families *e.g.*, generally the child has a respectable place in Indian family, but all Indian parents do not sufficienlty love and sympathies with the child. In such circumstances much repression is observed in child's behaviour. He becomes an introvert and often enjoys in his dreams, day-dreams and imaginations things which are denied to him by his parents. The influence of the presence of the parental love is again not the same in the face of all children. A child may become aggressive while another may become submissive in the same circumstances. On the other hand, if the parents show excessive suffocation towards her child, the child may became an extremist and excessively dependent upon the parents. A child excessively ignored shows different types of conflicts in his personality. Children brought in the psychological clinics for the curse of defects of personality showed that an important cause of their defects was the behaviour of their parents towards them. According to segment. Fraud, the tendency to depend upon the parents in the childhood is manifested in the tendęncy to depend upon the leader in the adult age. If the child is allowed freedom in the matters concerning his belongings, food, clothes, books, *etc.*, he will develop a habit of free will, if all these are decided by his parents he will not get any opportunity to utilize his judgment and so become over dependent or submissive.

Parents are more powerful and efficient than the child. Hence, they are the ideals before him. The child wants to become like his parents. Thus, he establishes his identification with either of the parent and tries to follow his manners, ways and behaviour. The child also fulfils his frustrated desires through this identification. It has been observed that the little boy wears the big shirt of the father and walks proudly like him with a stick in his hand. This identification with the parents in the childhood is later on converted into the identification of the individual with the leader.

In the absence of affection and sympathy, the child often turns criminal. While discussing the causes of criminal tendencies. Heavy and Bronner had emphasized three factors: the effort to get rid of the painful circumstances, the tendency to revenge for the misbehaviour of the father, the efforts to satisfy the frustrating desires. Often the child has the curiosity as to from where the younger brother or sister has come. The answer to this question by the parents has an important effect on his personality. The child has a natural curiosity towards the sex tendency. Often the parents try to suppress his curiosity towards sex or they just rebuke when he asks such question. But the child in not silenced by this. He tries to enquire from the servants or friends in the house. But this leads to guilty conscience. The reaction in the parents about the every day matters in the family also effect the personality of the child.

It has been observed that the behaviour of the eldest and the youngest, the elder or the younger is not the same in the family. Similarly, it has been found that the parent's behaviour towards them is not also the same. This has led the psychologist Alfred Adler, to emphasize the importance of birth other in the deevlopment of personality. The birth order of the child fixes the status in the family which decides his roles which affect his personality. The younger child is treated with affection by everyone, hence he becomes over dependent. The eldest child becomes self-sufficient and tyrant, because being the only child for sometime he dose not share his rights and things with others. The birth of another child in the family has an important influence on the child, since it takes away his monopoly in affection and sometimes he is neglected altogether. The above description of the child's problem based upon the conception of birth order has not been conclusively proved. The researchers have found similar conflicts in different birth orders.

2. Influence of School on Personality. School also has an important influence on the personality of the child. In school both the teachers and class fellows mould his personality, just as in the family the parents are ideals before the child so are teachers in the school. The child hates the cruel and strict teacher. On the other hand, he respects good and sympathetic teachers. The personality of the teacher and his behaviour towards the child both exercise important influence on child's personality. The child tends to identify himself with the teacher and tries to imitate his ways, manners and personality traits.

Besides the teacher the classmates and playmates exercise important influence on the personality of the child. These constitute a group in which every child has his own particular status and roles corresponding to it. One can see the leader, the dare devil and the scapegoal child in the group. The leader is the mind of the group. He plans adventures and games. The dare devil executes them while the scapegoat is left to receive the blame and consequent punishment. In different types of groups of children, different traits of leadership are required according to the purpose. Thus, sometimes the intelligent child leads while at other times the leader is theater devil. This particular role in the group determines the future role of the individual in a society. This, however, is not without exceptions.

3. Influence of Society on Personality. Society is a web of social relationship. These social relationships connect men and women with one another. These interpersonal relations influence and mould the personality of the individual. In the society each individual has some peculiar status and roles corresponding to them. For example, in Hindu community, members of different castes have different social status in society. The roles and function of an individual are determined by his status. This mechanism controls the behaviour of the individuals. Social control is further exercised by more, traditions, myths, legends, customs, etc. These determine the style of life of the individual. The individual cannot behave in the society as he likes. Society punishes the individual who breaks its norms. The fear of society is often more powerful than even the fear of heaven and hell or punishment by the state. Therefore, social norms influence been the ways and attitudes of the individuals. This ultimately influence his personality. The individual adopts the prevalent patterns of social behaviour. That is why one notices so much difference in the behaviour and personality of members of different societies. This however, does not mean that there are no individual differences in the same society. In fact, in every society one can find men and women who scarcely care for the social norms.

One's material success is often thought to provide an index of personality. Consequently, having a good personality, in the opinion of many, is the same thing as being well-dressed and wealthy. In spite of the proverb, "The apparel of successful proclaims the man", dress is really of negligible importance, it does not constitute personality. Education, though valuable, is not strictly necessary. Some even hold that goodness is not essential, for they argue, while many great personalities have been saints, a large number have been great sinners; Beauty is an important factor, but by itself it is negligible. Personality is not the same thing as high birth.

There are certain basic qualities to be found in all men who rise above their fellows. Vitality or energy, which radiates outwards, impressing others with a sense power and dominance is one of these qualities. Good physical health is another. Intelligence is another *prerequisite*; other important qualities are courage, sincerity, diligence, tact, enthusiasm originality, enterprise and good judgement. A sense of humour is also a valuable asset, provided its possessor does not become cynical or does not treat life as a huge joke. Self-complacency, unobtrusiveness, quite self-assurance, modesty kindness and character are some additional traits of personality. Sociability, above all, is the most shining trait. The sixth sense called "the social sense" is the most important quality of all. The social sense is the ability to feel at home in any social situation is never overawed by people; he knows how to deal with his fellow beings, for he is acquainted with his foibles and weaknesses. A person possessing this trait may achieve promotion over his more talented workers, because he can handle men and situations better. Tactfulness, and social sense are not learnt from books, but from social interaction, from rubbing shoulders freely with fellow-companions.

Lack of vitality, indifferent health, dullness of wit, timidity, tactfulness, sluggishness, poor judgement, ostentation, selfishness, arrogance, self-disgust, ignorance, indiscipline, lack of originality and lack of enterprise and unsociability are grave defects and they unmake personality.

According to **Woodworth**, a personality trait is some particular quality of behaviour such as cheerfulness or self-reliance which characterises the individual. Personality is the product of these different traits, rather than a mere sum of separate qualities. It has some unity. For example a certain person is not merely cheerful and self-reliant; he is cheerfully self-reliant. Each individual has his own style or quality which is only roughly characterized by naming his traits. Judgment of personality will be better, if the judge observes the most revealing aspects of the individual, and if he has thorough experience in interpreting those aspects.

Personality Profile

The pairs of extremely contradictory qualities are called the "dimensions of personality." For example, honesty and dull-wittedness, persistence and waywardness, sociability and egotism ascendance and sub-missiveness, etc. A diagram can best indicate the personality profile of a person whose various traits of personality have been measured; it conveys an impression of the individual's high or low striding in general and of the evenness or unevenness of his personality.

Sociability is a tendency to behave sociably, to seek company and to participate eagerly in group activities. Ascendancy is to be masterful in any situation. A person, strong in both these traits, would naturally be a good leader. The individual's several traits conceived as tendencies or forces, interact and are combined in his behaviour. These measurements of personality are designed to locate individuals accurately in comparison with other individuals in various dimensions of personality. An integrated personality is one in which the several traits, interests, and desires are combined in an effective harmonious unity. This unity is more characteristics of mature adults than of children. Lack of integration of personality is clearly seen in certain mental disorders, and in extreme cases of double personality, multiple personality and "split personality." Measurement of personality is designed to locate an individual accurately in comparison with other individuals in various dimensions of personality. Rating scales provide a method for indicating intermediate degrees of a trait and permit averaging the judgements of two or more raters. Questionnaries are used to secure measures of traits such as trouble-finding ascendancy sociability, extroversion-introversion, and of interests and attitudes. If questionnaries are carefully constituted, they will be quite adequate, but their validity must be determined for each particular purpose. Situation tests are sample life situations in which certain traits can be observed best by any other test. Projective tests evoke imaginative responses which can be scored to reveal basic personality traits and patterns.

PSYCHOLOGY OF THE UNCONSCIOUS

The psychology of the unconscious was brought into prominence some thirty five years ago by the work of Freud and others working with him, especially Jung and Adler, who afterwards broke from Freud and followed independent lines. Freud's doctrine of the unconscious had both fanatical supporters and violent opponents.

One main idea in Freud's psychology is that unconscious processes have a far greater influence on our conscious life than has been thought of. As a matter of fact, psychologists long ago recognised the influence of the unconscious, especially in regard to dispositions and habits, but Freud went much further. First of all he referred to unconscious processes which never rise to consciousness unless dragged up by a process of psycho-analysis. Secondly, he held that unconscious desires and impulses constantly lead to irrational conduct without our being aware of it. Functioning of the unconscious is more evident when it overpowers our unconscious behaviour as in slips of pen and tongue, phobias, wandering mania, stammering, moralism, habitual lies, habitual thefts, morbid forgetfulness, day dreams, hooliganism, unnecessary fears, feeling compulsion to do or not to do an action, neurosis, etc. Emphasizing importance of the unconscious, he compared mind with an iceberg, only one-eighth part of which is visible, the rest of it being below the surface of water.

The concept of the unconscious is one of the attempts to explain mental diseases or the abnormal behaviour. Abnormal behaviour is the result of a conflict between the conscious and the unconscious functions, or in other words between the 'ego' on the one hand and 'super' ego' and 'id' on the other. The unconscious is the best known concept in the Freudian theory. It is the largest part of mind. It is a huge reservoir which contains all our primitive impulses and strings. It is that part of the mind which is normally inaccessible to consciousness. It is the lumber room of our repressed wishes, tabooed impulses and forgotten memories which are suppossed to have been lost.

Id, Ego and Super Ego

The'Id' is the entirely unconscious striving aspect of personality. It is illogical and inmoral and may be considered as roughly equivalent to the primitive and animal nature of man.

The 'Ego' is partly conscious and partly unconscious. It is the repression of urges that are pushed back into the 'Id' and in general seeks to control the primitive instincts of the latter.

The 'Super ego' consists partly of inherited moralities and taboos and partly of the moral notions acquired by the child from his parents. The principal function of 'Super ego' is criticism. It tries to compel the 'Ego' to repress the tendencies of 'Id' the 'Ego' being the battleground. The 'Super ego' corresponds to the notion of "Consciences".

Conflict, Repression and Complex

Psychoanalysts used the term 'conflict' to describe those struggles between the individual's, interest which result in the repression of many desires, fears and the like into the unconscious. Conflicts are the rule rather than the exception and life is full of contradictions and conflicts. In conflict there is a crossfire of feelings and desires within the individual. We can not both drink in a public house arid maintain our self-respect. Self-assertion tells us to throw away our job when we receive a rebuff but-self-preservation warns us against a hasty step. Conflict of motives is uncomfortable distressing state of mind. The only satisfactory resolution of a conflict is for the person to become aware of it, to face up to it resolutely and to unify the warring motives within his main self.

But a satisfactory resolution of conflict, however, is not always achieved. When the conflict is not resolved, it leads to Repression. The denial of direct expression of a motive is called the repression of that motive. A motive which is repressed is often called a "Complex". Repression is a process of storing up trouble for the future, for it is impossible to bottle up one's complexes without their causing unhappy emotions and undesirable behaviour. The irrational forms of behaviour, which the person himself does not understand, are a manifestation of repressed motives which are thereby finding an out, let.

What is unpleasant, obnoxious, embarrassing or offensive is banished from consciousness. It is said to be repressed and enters into the unconscious. It is not destroyed bit eliminated. These unpleasant experiences are of three kinds:

(a) Unfulfilled desires

(b) Inferiority feeling and

(c) Guilt feeling.

Those, experiences being unpleasant are repressed. Repression is unconscious forgetting of an unpleasant experience. Repressed experience forms a complex. What do these complexes do? They are dynamic and very active. They play, they make fun of us, but we do not know then how do we know the existence of complexes? Through their effects on normal life. One person is abnormally afraid of darkness, lonely places and heights. Another shuns the society of women, forgets engagements, thinks that the whole world is against him or loves to advertise his troubles. They admit that their behaviour is irrational and yet they are unable to explain why they do so.

Psycho-analysis and Education

The reception accorded to the psycho-analytic theories has varied from extremes of uncritical acceptance, to equal extremes of emotionally motivated rejection. Some persons have regarded Freud's theories as divine revelations, others see them as a hideous sexual perversion. All competent and informed persons, however, acknowledge psychology's historical debt to psycho-analysis for some of its problems and concepts.

Obviously with all the elaborate methods of the psycho-analyst the teacher has nothing to do. Not only do they depend a technical training that no practising teacher can hope to attain, but they involve an expenditure of time in their application that puts them forever beyond the reach of ordinary professional teachers. But certain incidental application of psycho-analysis may be made by all teachers. What, then, is to be the teacher's attitude towards the psychology of the unconscious.

1. To begin with he ought to know it. He ought to be aware of what has been done in the way of developing the new doctrine of the unconscious. It is his business to know his pupils as thoroughly as possible and he cannot afford to neglect a whole reservoir of the pupil's experience. The content of the unconscious is an essential part of the pupil's nature and must be known in a general way if the pupil is to be intelligently handled. Even without applying any of the technical methods such as free or the directed association or time reaction, the modern teacher who is acquainted with this subject is in a favourable position to study his pupils with advantage. He knows what sort of things to look for. He knows that the pupil may with perfect honesty give a wrong reason for an action.

2. Teachers do extremely well if they can apply their knowledge of the Psychology of the unconscious to their work in such a way as to avoid the formation of complexes. So far from resolving complexes already formed, the ordinary teacher is very apt to form fresh complexes during the pupil's school course. The unnecessary restraint of school life, the anxieties resulting from overstimulated emulation, the strain of examinations, the humiliations that accompany the teachers thoughtless sarcasms—all these have a tendency to produce unwholesome repressions with consequent complex formation. In the poorer areas, children in elementary schools have often additional sources of danger form their bad home conditions. It is obviously great to the interest of the pupils that the teachers should have clear idea of the possibilities of the

harm that may be done by sheer ignorance and misinterpretation. On the other hand, the teachers must be forever on their guard against reading too much into ordinary reactions of his pupils.

3. Complexes develop from wrong doing and unhappy experiences. One can save oneself from some of these by clean living and—being a good citizen. However, there are circumstances in life—unavoidable failure in school work etc. that will almost inescapably cause complexes. In dealing with complexes produced by unhappy circumstances in the school room it should be remembered that a teacher who gains the confidence and goodwill of his pupils will be talked with by them. His pupils may unburden themselves and rid themselves of their repressed complexes. In talking about a pupil's problems, the pupil is encouraged to bring his complexes out in the open, analyse them and dispose them of. A teacher in order to be effective must be liked by his pupils and have their confidence. The personality of the teacher and the attitude of the parents is the most helpful factor. If both meet the problems of life frankly and try to help children in a friendly and sympathetic manner, the emotional problems of young pupil will be better solved.

4. Should the teacher have himself psycho-anlysed in order that he may better understand the whole process in the interest of his pupils? Even if the teacher's normality is conceived, he is not yet out of the wood. Everyone is abnormal in one way or the other, according to Freud. Thus the teacher can practise rough and ready self-analysis without the least need of having turned himself into a 'case'.

5. Children learn by imitation. Therefore, the behaviour of the persons around them should be free from all abnormalities. This is possible if there are no problems of adjustment and the unconscious is free from all repressions. A neurotic teacher or a neurotic parent creates many problems

for children in the class or at home. Such a teacher is inconsistent in his behaviour and hinders the moral development of children. Such a teacher or a parent may have temper tantrums, dislike for certain students, dislike for other teachers and he may disregard moral and social code. The knowledge of the unconscious will help such an individual to mend his ways and thus attain mental health.

6. Repression should be avoided. The teachers and parents should realize that if a child is checked to behave in a particular way, he may not behave in that way, but this impulse may become a part of the unconscious. Repression is not a solution of the problem, it is creating problems for the future. The repressed desires come to the surface more vigorously and in a disguised form and thus the individual is unable to deal with them at the conscious level. Thus for normal development of the children their impulses should be recognised and outlet provided for them in the form of co-curricular activities.

Inferiority Complex

An early disciple of Freud broke away and set up a rival school called 'Individual Psychology'. Alfred Adler disagrees with Freud's emphasis on sex and his distinction between the conscious and the unconscious. For Adler the basic urge is striving for superiority or self-assertion. In normal individuals this is adjusted to reality and integrated with social drives, thus leading to reasonable satisfaction through achievements. In childhood the urge to superiority is thwarted in many directions because of child's weakness and helpness and the omnipotence of his parents. This situation may be aggravated by the presence of actual physical defects, by imagined defects, by excessive parental severity or by other factors. In such circumstances the individual acquires an inferiority complex. Thus when the basic urge for superiority is thwarted as frequently happens, the person feel inferior and an inferiority complex results. A genuine inferiority complex implies a repressed idea of some real defect (or of some imagined weakness, which the person's strong self-assertiveness will not allow him to recognise.

The development of inferiority complex depends on:

(a) inferiority feeling because of some physical or intellectual deficiency; and

(b) a strong self-assertive impulse that prevents the individual from reconciling himself to a position of inferiority: he cannot bear the thought of it.

The *feeling of inferiority*. It may be due to either of the following causes:

(1) Physical Defect. Adler remarked that feelings of inferiority often developed in persons having a physical handicap. Lame, undersized, ugly or deformed, very thin or very fat children may feel inferior and attempt to compensate for their defects. Actually the inferiority felling does not arise from the defect itself but from the unfortunate comparison with normal persons. If everyone were crippled, none would feel inferior. Thus physical factors influence personality only because social factors make them important.

(2) Intellectual Defect. Physically the child may be quite fit and normal but he may be dull-headed. He is weak in studies and is ridiculed by teachers and taunted by students. He feels inferior in the class.

(3) Social Inferiority. There are various grades in our society. We do not have a classless and casteless society. Some are considered as high born and others as low born. These low-born have to experience social inequality every now and then. Slaves and the untouchables were looked down upon by others. Even in mid-twenties we find strong racial discrimination in South Africa. Those who are socially inferior come to have inferiority feeling in them.

Now this inferiority feeling does not always lead to inferiority complex. An individual may be physically or intellectually deficient, yet he may not feel it so much. He may have accepted it for good and may no longer be troubled on that account. In the case of such an individual inferiority feeling will not lead to inferiority complex in him. But when the defect in the individual proves a standing trouble for him then inferiority feeling develops into inferiority complex.

How does this complex satisfy itself? How does it express itself? It will express itself in exaggerated talk, walk and laugh, loud manners, loud colours, all mannerisms, habit of criticising others, always, always looking to the bad points of others and ignoring their good point, telling psychological lies, eagerness to find one's name and photo-in-print, wearing gaudy clothes, etc. Thus this complex gives rise to paver-compensation.

Negative behaviour of the following kind may also be caused by this complex:

(1) Retirement from Society. An individual suffering from this complex may not like to attend meetings and functions and to face people. He would like to lead a solitary life.

(2) Self-pity. He indulges in self-pity for inviting sympathy of other people. He usually says "Who am I? I am nobody. I am the most unfortunate person". In this way he wants to get the sympathy of other So much so that for getting this sympathy he would contract some physical ailments as well, so that the people may come to him and enquire about his health and this will give him importance.

9

Child Behaviour and Treatment

A child is said to be an abnormal child when he deviates from the normal standard of behaviour. He experiences difficulties to make proper adjustment to the environment. He is also called a 'delinquent' as he falls away from the accepted standard of social behaviour. 'Problem Child' is the other name assigned to such a child. He is called a 'problem child' because his behaviour is a problem for the school, for the home, for the society and even for himself.

A line of demarcation, though not a distinct one, can be drawn between the 'delinquent child' and a 'problem child'. The 'problem child' may be said to be at the first stage in maladjustment and a 'delinquent child' at the second. If proper care is not taken to handle the 'problem child' he may become a 'delinquent child'.'

According to the accepted meaning of the term, a person is said to be adjusted when he is in harmony with a reasonably adequate environment; he is relatively happy, efficient and has a proper degree of social feeling. The person equipped with a sound mind and body is prepared to cope successfully with the problems with which he is confronted and is consequently likely to be in good mental health. He possesses the qualities that will assist him to adjust himself with other people.

By maladjustment we mean the degree of disharmony between the individual and the environment.

According to *Herbert*, "A person is not in harmony with his work if it is too hard or too easy. If it is too hard, or if the student has too little capacity excessive failure is experienced; if it is too easy or if the student has too high ability for his task, the work is dull and deadening."

CAUSES OF BEHAVIOUR PROBLEMS

(I) Heredity Factors

(a) Physical Conditions. There are many diseases which are inherited. T.B., epilepsy etc. are generally inherited. If parents suffer from these diseases, their children also suffer from these diseases. They are unable to adjust themselves to the accepted pattern of behaviour.

(b) Intellectual Factors. H is not uncommon to find children of low I. Q. whose parents too have low I. Q. Such children have a weak will and can be taken in very easily.

(c) Temperament Conditions. Unstable temperament of children may be ascribed to unstable temperament of their parents. They are easily provoked and are likely to misbehave.

Some psychologists hold that criminal parents produce delinquent children. They quote some studies based on various famous and notorious families. There is a classic example of the Juke family. As the ancestors of the family were notorious, hence most of the offspring happened to be delinquents, criminals and maladjusted. But recent research shows that delinquency is not an inherited trait although emotional traits and setup are inherited to some extent. But how those emotions are to be trained and exploited, depends upon environment and education.

(II) Environmental Factors

Among the environmental causes we may discuss: *(i)* Home Environment *(ii)* School Environment.

(i) Home Environment

1. ***The Rejected Child.*** The unwanted and the neglected child does not grow as a normal child. A child robbed of all love, sympathy, affection and appreciation always find himself insecure and may develop hatred for the family and even for the society.

2. ***Defective Discipline.*** Too strict or too lenient parents having different standards of discipline have an unhealthy influence on their children. Over protection of the child reduces his ability to meet the hard tasks of life. On the other hand, a rigid discipline deprives the child of independent thinking and may develop in him revolting tendencies.

3. ***Vicious Home Atmosphere.*** Constant quarrels between the father and the mother and hostile attitude of the step-parents have unhealthy effects on the life of the child. There is every likelihood of the child Becoming immoral if one is immoral at home: criminal parents are likely to produce criminal children. All these factors hinder the natural development of the child. Shortage of accommodation and the sexual indulgence of the parents in the presence of young children lead to unhealthy sex practice.

(ii) School Environment. If the school discipline is too strict and if it is undemocratic, children will develop an inward aversion for the school. The defective methods of teaching, unsympathetic attitude of the teachers, lack of security, lack of recreational facilities, detective time table, defective curriculum etc. may develop hatred for the school.

(III) Insecurity at School

He feels insecurity due to many reasons. The child tries other avenues for self-expression and these may lead him to form delinquent behaviour.

Lack of Aptitude

A child may not acquire the ability to learn a particular subject. His performance in it may remain poor He may lose his interest in it fully. Teacher will punish him for not doing home task in the subject and he may become maladjusted in school environment due to his incapacities.

Remedies

1. Pupil-Teacher Contacts. The modern educator believes in the victim "prevention is better than cure". As the child enters the school he should be observed closely and if any sign of delinquency is detected, it should be checked very promptly. The teacher should always be mentally alert to develop mental alertness in the pupils. He should be sympathetic, pains-taking, appreciative and trusting. He should study the child carefully in and outside the school. He should try to learn him thoroughly. He should try to find out his home conditions as thoroughly as possible. The teacher should be impartial and unprejudiced. He should try to develop in him a strong self-regarding sentiment.

2. Congenial Home and School Environment

(a) Mental disorders are created due to unfavorably home and school environments. If the child has become delinquent due to uncongenial home conditions, the teacher should guide the parents to adopt suitable methods of upbringing. Growth of the child's home environment cannot be improved, he may be shifted to a school having hostel facilities.

(b) The child must be saved from the unhealthy influence of his companions in or outside the school. If it is felt that the atmosphere of a particular school is not conductive the proper growth of the child, it is always desirable to withdraw the child from such school and put him in some other school.

(c) Sometimes the environment of the locality in which the home is suited is not congenial. The guidance counsellor in that case should suggest the parents of the child to shift their residence.

3. Freedom and Self-Discipline. There are two great enemies of mental health; *(a)* Feeling of insecurity, and *(b)* feeling of inferiority. These two demons can be killed by a knowledge of mental hygiene. Unnecessary rules and regulations greatly upset the mental equilibrium of the child. A child who is given an atmosphere of freedom, develops initiative, courage, satisfaction and confidence. There is mental retardation due to severe punishment. Our philosophy of discipline must undergo a drastic change. The teacher should not be regarded as a policeman by the child. Hobbes writes, "The fool cannot be mended by flogging and he who flogs is the greatest fool."

A. S. Neil says, "We could abolish canning by an Act of Parliament, but no Act of Parliament can abolish the fear of a teacher or a system." Hence the right approach would be to give sufficient freedom to the child.

4. Intellectual and Social Life of the School.

(a) Pupils must be given ample scope for self-expression. The class should not be teacher monopolised. Children must be provided opportunities to think and act independently. Methods of teaching should be adopted according to the individual needs of children. Activity methods *e.g.* Play way, Project method, Oalton' Plan etc., should be encouraged.

Audio-visual aids develop interest in the lesson. Weak pupils must be given individual attention.

(b) Students must be taught how to use leisure hours most profitably and satisfyingly. Recreational activities would be very helpful.

(c) Creative activities must be introduced in school. They help to provide outles for the increased fund of energy in children. These activities are very much helpful in sublimating instincts.

(d) The child should never be given an idea that he is a misfit, worthless and good-far-nothing. If the child fails repeatedly, he is haunted by such feelings. Our approach to promotions and non-promotions requires a radical change. The system should not be too much examination-ridden.

5. Medical Examination. Children should be frequently medically examined and remedial measures should be adopted to safeguard the health of the child. Sometimes mental disorders are created due to defective physique.

6. Special Institutions. Some of the delinquents will require special treatment. They should be sent to child guidance clinical. A great care should be taken in such cases that the child does not lose his self-respect and hot mix up with hardened delinquents. The parents have a special responsibility and under all circumstances their attitude should be of sympathy and not of hatred. In every town there should be welfare councils to guide the parents and the teachers about the handling of such children.

Symptoms of Behaviour Problems

(i) The students may be out of step with the group.

(ii) The pupil may manifest inconsistent changes in his behaviour.

(iii) The pupil may unfold anti-social learnings.

(iv) The pupil may reveal frequent nervousness.

(v) The pupil may failing the examination continuously.

(vi) The pupil may project emotional disturbance through such overt acts as thumb-sucking, nail-biting, whistling, blank-staring, head-scratching, etc.

(vii) The pupil may feel extremely shy or timid.

(viii) The pupil may show continued lack of interest and enthusiasm in the school work.

(ix) The pupil may remain listless and absent-minded in the class.

(x) The pupil may show perpetual laziness, tiredness or bore dom.

Types of Behaviour Problems

1. Truancy running away from home and school
2. Stealing
3. Cheating
4. Aggressiveness and bullying
5. Lying

1. **Truancy.** A child is said to be truant if he has the wandering mania and avoids school. Such a child leaves for school at the proper hour but remains absent. Burt thinks that such children can be tempted to commit delinquent acts.

   A child plays truancy because he does not find an atmosphere of security and interest in the school. A school is said to be the "lengthened arm of the family or an extension of home. If the teacher is unsympathetic and does not show affection to the child, he will fail to inspire confidence in him. The child feels distressed and tries to seize every possible opportunity to remain away from the school. The individuality of the child should be respected. He should not be treated like dumd-driven cattle. His sense of pride should not be injured. Emerson has rightly stated, "The secret of education lies in respecting the child." He wants to be heard. His opinion should not be brushed aside simply because he is a child.

The child may not be interested in certain subjects. This may be due to the defective methods of teaching or the poor personality of the teacher or lack of aptitude on the part of the child for those subjects. A psychological approach is needed to locate the causes of truancy in every individual child. The teacher should endeavour to make his teaching effective by using audio-visual aids, illustrations, diagrams, etc. He should make the classrooms and his lessons very attractive which may captivate the attention of the child. Educational guidance should be provided and the child helped to select right subjects if truancy is caused due to wrong selection of subjects. The child should be assigned work according to his mental capacity.

The child may avoid school if he is afraid of some of his class-fellows. There might be bullies who trouble the child and the child feels insecure. The child must be protected from this menace. The teacher must see that the child is on no account teased and ridiculed.

2. **Stealing.** By stealing we mean taking something that does not belong to us. In the case of small children when a sense of property rights is not

developed the act of taking something that does not belong to them may not be termed as stealing. But in the case of Secondary School students the sense of property rights is sufficiently developed and such acts will be definitely termed as stealing acts. Stealing may be due to:

(i) Unfulfilled desire for possession due to bad economic conditions at home.

(ii) Low ethical and moral standards.

(iii) Unreasonable denial of privilege.

(iv) Tendency of teasing others resulting in the habit of stealing.

(v) Sex repression.

From the very beginning an attitude of respect for the ownership of some possession which belongs to others should be inculcated among children. The initial experiences of the child in taking some thing that does not belong to him should be regarded as errors but it should be impressed upon the child that such behaviours are undesirable ones. The stolen articles recovered from the child should be restored to their owners very tactfully without injuring the self-respect of the child.

As in the case of other abnormal behaviour, the attitude of the parents and the teachers should be very sympathetic. They should hate this habit and not the child. We should arrange for necessary sex education, healthy recreational and leisure time facilities. We should also fulfil their reasonable desires. A check on their company should also be kept. Judicious use of punishment may be of some help in some cases.

3. **Cheating.** Children usually cheat when goals which are beyond their reach are set before them by teachers or parents or both. Cheating is also resorted to by children during examinations and in completing other assignments. Different means should be adopted to check, as far as possible, the tendency on the part of the child to be unscrupulous. These may be enumerated as under:

   (i) Emphasising the importance of honest work;

   (ii) Making the school work so interesting that he may not feel the temptation of shirking work;

   (iii) Vigilant supervision during examination so as to eliminate the possibility of allowing him to use unfair means;

   (iv) Setting goals before him which are within his reach;

   (v) By developing in him the feelings of security and self confidence.

4. **Aggressiveness and Bullying.** Stem, is of the opinion that children suffering from neglect grow into bullies and take to teasing those children who are in the good books of the teacher. According to the psycho-analyst bullying may be due to the reactions of either ego complex or the sex complex.

   Davis states, "Bullying is almost exclusively a trait of boys and occurs with uniform frequency between the ages of 9 and 15 years. It appears without great variation of incidence in the average intelligence range among young boys. There is a tendency for it to increase in older boys with increase of intelligence quotients from 60 to 99. Beyond this level it occurs rarely."

Ample scope for self-expression should be given to children. The abilities of such children should be appreciated. Their energies should be diverted to social service activities, games and recreational activities. The need for special counselling and therapy is great if bullying is due to jealousy.

5. **Lying.** Children tell lies generally to avoid punishment or to get out of difficulties. According to Burt there are seven types of lies: *(i) Playful*—when the children tell lie during play. *(ii) Confusion*—when the children are unable to distinguish between facts and fiction. *(iii) Vanity*—when children tell lie to attract self-attention *(iv) Evenge*—when a child tells a lie to be little the importance and achievements of others. *(v) Selfish*—when the child tells a lie to conceal his wrong action. *(vi) Loyalty*—when the child tells a lie to prove the superiority of his own group over others *(vii) Pathological*—when a child tells a lie to hide certain bad sex habits.

HOW TO CONTROL BEHAVIOUR PROBLEMS?

Generally speaking, two methods are employed for the control of behaviour problems and they are: *(i)* prevention *(ii)* punishment.

Prevention. It may be repeated that anti-social conduct is the outcome of a tendency of satisfying a thwarted or checked motive. So the best way of preventing such acts is to satisfy the needs of the children in respect of their social, economic and hygiene conditions. Our attention should be directed to the betterment of their environments. Ethical training should be given from the very beginning. Adaptability, altruism and harmony should be emphasised constantly. The social influence is the best way to give the child direct teaching in practical morality. Morality cannot be taught but it is caught. So much emphasis should be laid to present examples of good moral behaviour rather than precepts. The parents should also be educated to appreciate the value of these principles.

Punishment. The 'revenge' hypothesis of punishment must be rejected. The positive and correct view of punishment in a school is to reform the child by means of punishment. The child must be made to realize that he has committed a wrong act and he should not have done so. He must feel sorry for the wrong that he has done.

DEFENCE MECHANISM

Meaning of Defence Mechanism. Adjustment mechanism is a device used by an individual to achieve satisfaction of the need indirectly. This helps in reducing tensions and assists him in maintaining self-confidence and self-respect. Within limits adjustment mechanisms are desirable and very helpful in dealing with frustration. Carried to extreme, they lead to behaviour disorders. Some common mechanisms are explained below:

1. **Compensation.** Compensation is a concept where the individual attempts to cover up his weakness in one area by exhibiting his strength in another. A student deficient in physical activities may compensate himself in showing good results in the academic field and *vice-versa*.

2. **Identification.** Identification is a concept when an individual attempts to identify himself with some successful person. To hide his own failures, a student may identify himself with his father and talk about his success.

3. **Day-dreaming.** The imagjnative fulfillment of needs is called day-dreaming. Day-dreaming provides mental relief to an individual if it is done within limits. It becomes very detrimental when it is carried to excess.

4. **Rationalization.** Rationalization means shifting of responsibility for our failures to factors outside it *i.e.* many students attribute their failure to the stiff question paper.

5. **Repression.** This means pushing one thoughts and feelings into the unconscious mind. This is very common among all of us. We try to forget what makes us feel inferior, ashamed, guilty or anxious. A child punished by the teacher tries to keep out of his consciousness all those ideas that produce anxiety.

6. **Projection.** There is a tendency to 'push out' upon another person one's own unrealised, frustrated ambitions, or attribute to another one's own faults. For example, school learners are often the victims of their parents' projection of their former hopes for higher education and higher social status.

Role of the Classroom Teacher in Pupil Adjustment

The classroom teacher plays a most strategic role in manipulating the environment to bring about an improved adjustment of pupils. Raymond N. Hatch and Buford Stefflre describe the role of the classroom teacher in providing a healthy classroom environment that would complement the adjustment process of each pupil as follows:

1. Provides a classroom climate that permits young people to feel free to express themselves and to put forth their best efforts as individuals and as members of groups.

2. Has an appreciation that deviation from acceptable behaviour is caused due to factors that stem from the school, the honie and his community.

3. Develops a youngster's self-respect and self-esteem by compliments for work well done, a smile or a word or recognition.

4. Recognises that chronic behaviour cases may be sent to specialists for diagnosis and treatment.

5. Recognises that a student who "causes no trouble" may by experiencing serious emotional conflicts.

6. Accepts that every pupil is different, and because he is different, he will achieve most if the teacher knows, understands, and plans activities in keeping with his needs.

7. Develops comprehensive records by collecting sociometric information, autobiographies and similar information-through classroom setting.

8. Participates and contributes to the effectiveness of case conferences.

9. Practises good mental health.

***

10

Psychology of Learning

Learning means the modification of behaviour of an individual. It is said to be equivalent to change, modification, development, improvement and adjustment. It is not confined to school learning, reading, writing, typing, cycling, cooking but it is a comprehensive term which leaves permanent effect on the individual. While approaching a burning match stick the child gets burnt and he withdraws. By this incident he learns to avoid not only the burning matchstick but also all burning things. Learning has been defined in many ways as follows:

According to **Walker,** "Learning is a relatively permanent change in performance that occurs as a result of experience."

According to **Jones and Simpson,** "Any change of behaviour which is result of experience and which causes people to face later situations differently may be called learning."

Woodworth, "Any activity can be called learning so far as it develops the individual (in any respect, good or bad, and makes his behaviour and experiences different from what that would otherwise have been."

Garden Murphy, "The term learning covers every modification in behaviour to meet environmental requirements".

Henry P. Smith. "Learning is the acquisition of new behaviour or the strengthening or weakening of old behaviour as the result of experience."

Pressey, Robinson and Horrocks. "Learning is an episode in which a motivated individual attempts to adapt his behaviour so as to succeed in a situation which he perceives as requiring action to attain a goal."

Kingsely and Garry. "Learning is the process by which behaviour (in the broader sense) is originated or changes through practice or training."

Nature of Learning

1. Learning is the acquisition of new behaviour.
2. Learning is the process by which an activity originates.
3. Learning is the total reaction of total situation.
4. Learning is the perceptual reorganisation of the situation.
5. Learning is goal-directed activity.
6. Learning is universal in nature. Man is rational and he learns the most.
7. Learning is the change in behaviour as a result of experience.

All Animals Learn

1. Learning is motivated by adjustment.
2. Learning is acquisition, retention and modification of experience.
3. Learning is a never ending growth. We always aspire to learn more and more.

4. Learning is process and product.
5. Learning is a life long process. It starts with birth and comes to an end when the individual dies.

Main Characteristics of Learning

Yoakman and **Simpson** have enumerated nine general characteristics of learning which we discuss below:

1. Learning is Growth. The word growth is generally associated with the body which is growing, but through the mental growth of the learner. Although it is latent yet we can perceive its growth. Through his daily activities the child grows both mentally and physically. Therefore, we say that learning is growth through experience.

2. Learning is Adjustment. Learning helps the individual to adjust himself adequately to the new situations. Children meet with new situations which demand solution. Repeated efforts are required to react to them effectively. Life is full of experiences, and each experience leaves behind some effects in the mental structure. These effects modify his behaviour.

3. Learning is Organising Experience. Learning is not mere addition of knowledge. It is not mere acquisition of facts and skills through drill and repetition. It is the reorganisation of experience.

4. Learning is Purposeful. All true learning is based on purpose. Purpose plays a big part in learning. According to **Ryburn**, "This purpose is always connected with the use of some instinctive power, with the use of the energy with which we are endowed with birth." We do not learn anything and everything that comes in our way, in a haphazard manner. All schools activities should be purposeful so that the child should feel real urge for learning.

5. Learning is Intelligent. Meaningless efforts do not produce permanent result. Any work done mechanically is without any soul. When a child learns something unintelligently, he is likely to forget it very soon. He does not assimilate but simply commits to memory. Only efforts made intelligently have lasting effects.

6. Learning is Active. Learning does not take place without a purpose and self-activity. In the teaching-learning process, the activity of the learner counts more than the activity of the teacher. The principle of learning by doing is the sole principle and has been recommended by all modern educationists. It is the basis of all progressive methods of education such as the Dalton, the Project, the Montessory and the Basic.

7. Learning is both Individual and Social. Learning is more than an individual activity. It is a social activity also. Individual mind is affected by the group mind consciously as well as unconsciously as individual is influenced by his friends, relatives, classmates, parents etc., and learns their ideas, feelings and actions. Social agencies like the family, church, film and gangs of playmates have a tremendous influence on the child and are always moulding and remoulding him.

8. True Learning Affects the Conduct of the Learner. There is a change in the mental structure of the learner after every experience. By **Colvin** learning has been described as the "modification of the reactions of an organism through experience."

9. Learning is a Product of the Environment. Environment plays an important part in the growth and development of the individual. Environment should be healthy and rich in educative possibilities.

Factors Affecting Learning

Learning is influenced by various conditions of life and school. Our attempts should be to create such conditions as are conductive to effective learning and which help students to make the most satisfactory adjustment to life. The following factors influence learning:

1. Hereditary Factors. Neither we can change nor increase hereditary endowment. Of course, we can use it and develop it. This differs in different individuals. Some are very rich in the matters of hereditary endowments while others are very poor. The native intelligence is different in individuals. Children vary also in particular abilities. The intelligent children can establish and see relationship very easily and more quickly. Our ability to learn and the rate of learning are conditioned by our heredity. Maximum use should be made of the hereditary endowment.

Attempts should be made to see to it that children get opportunities to use and develop their hereditary endowment.

2. Physical Conditions of Children. The physical conditions of children also affect learning. Bodily weakness, chronic illness, malnutrition, fatigue and bad health are a great hindrance in learning. The home conditions—bad ventilation, unhygienic living, bad light, overcrowding etc., affect the rate of learning and the general response of the child. Sometimes children have to walk long distances to and from the school and this also influences learning.

Physical conditions of the classroom are the other determining factors.

It may also be remembered that learning is affected by the physical teachers—their health, voice and speech.

3. Goals Set before the Pupils. A definite goal should be set before each child according to the standard expected of him. Immediate goals should be set before small children and distant goals for older ones. It must be remembered that the goals should be very clear and the children must understand these goals.

4. Stimulation. Best learning takes place when the teacher is successful in arousing the interest of the students. "The guidance of the teacher is mainly a matter of giving the right kind of stimulus to help him to learn the right things in the right way", write Ryburn.

5. Guidance and Instruction. Suitable guidance should be given to the students in selecting the best response to their environment. Demonstration is very helpful to teach various skills.

6. Association of Things. Thorndike points out that things which we want to go together should be put together as a part of one process. Then it becomes easier to make the students understand their connection.

7. Result of a Total Situation. Learning is affected by the whole situation. It is not always possible to estimate the result of one individual factor. Learning is fruitful and permanent if the total situation is related to life.

8. Emotional Conditions. Children should be praised when they show good results. This gives them encouragement to show all the more better results and they develop confidence, hope, self-reliance and self-respect. Sympathetic attitude on the part of the teachers gives stimulus and a sense of security to the students. We should discard our habit of fault-finding. This develops fear and feelings of insecurity and of inferiority.

THEORIES OF LEARNING

Psychologists differ at the nature of learning process. Accordingly they have propounded different theories.

Some of the important theories of learning are as follows:

1. Learning by trial and error.
2. Learning by insight.

3. Learning by imitation and observation.

4. Learning by conditioning.

1. Learning by Trial and Error

The chief exponent of this theory was Thorndike. He make many experiments on rats and cats. He concluded that an individual makes many random efforts to reach a goal. Most of his efforts go useless in his aim. By further trial and error he goes on eliminating useless movements and synthesising useful ones. At last he reaches the aim. In further trials he need not repeat the useless movements. He will perform the activity quite easily in further attempt as he learnt to perform the real needed movements after eliminating the useful ones. His typical experience in his connection is given below:

The Cat Experiment. He shut-up hungry cat in a big cage. An attractive piece of food was placed outside the cage. The cat looked at the piece and tried to get at it. It extended its paws through the bars of the cage but the piece was far away. It tried every part of the cage but all its efforts failed. It thrust its nose through the bars but all in vain. There was a latch inside the cage. While it was making random movements its paw struck against the latch. The door of the cage opened. Next week the experiment was repeated. The cat made some random movements again but was successful in opening the door sooner than before. In the third or fourth trial there was no random movement. The cat pushed against the latch and went ouside. It learnt the method of opening the door by trial and error.

The experiment sums up the following stages in the process of learning:

(1) *Drive.* In the present experiment it was hunger and was intensified with the sight of the food.

(2) *Goal.* To get the food by getting out the box.

(3) *Block.* The cat was confined in the box with a closed door.

(4) *Random Movements.* The cat, persistently, tried to get out of the box.

(5) *Chance Success.* As a result of this striving and random movement the cat, by chance, succeeded in opening the door.

(6) *Selection (of proper movement).* Gradually, the cat recognised the correct manipulation of latch. It selected the proper way of manipulating the latch out of its random movements.

(7) *Fixation.* At last, the cat learned the proper way of opening the door by eliminating all the incorrect responses and fixing the only right responses.

Educational Utility. In solving problems of mathematics in the school and those of life in the world we do follow this method in many cases. There is a tendency in animal as well as in men to find out the solutions of difficult problems by trial and error method but the whole behaviour of man is not based on this sort of learning. Skills like walking, talking, running, swimming, cycling, reading and writing can be well explained by this theory. Pupils should remember the motto of 'practice makes a man perfect,' 'work hard' 'try, try again'.

2. Learning by Insight

Kohler and **Koffka**, were the chief exponents of this theory. They stressed on the totality of the process of learning. They took the process of learning as a synthetic activity which brings forth complete solutions of problems. They referred to the sudden appearance of solutions in many cases. Insight means penetration into the nature of things to find out the solution of a problem without necessary trial and error.

Experiment 1

In one of his experiments **Kohler** shut up his chimpanzee, Sultan by name, in a big cage. Out placed a banana at a considerable distance of the cage. Close the cage there were put two sticks—one of them a long one and the other a bit shorter. The shorter stick could be screwed into the long one. The long stick could not reach the banana but if the other one was screwed into it, the banana could be touched. Sultan tried to get at the banana. He tried the longer stick but it did not reach the fruit. The other was still smaller. He sat down and began to play with the sticks. But he was still brooding over the matter. Suddenly an idea flashed to him. He thrust the smaller sticks into the hole of the longer one and thus managed to get at the banana with the help of the combined sticks.

Experiment 2

In another experiment the chimpanzee was shut up in a room with unscalable walls. A banana was hanging with the ceiling. The animal was hungry. He jumped at the fruit but it was too high. He left the efforts and sat down. There was a box lying in the corner of the room. The animal began to play with the box. He then suddenly got up and pushed the box to the centre of the room below the banana, jumped from it and got the fruit.

Kohler says that learning is a question of perception and not mere motion-activity or mere trial and error. He insists that this sort of learning is very useful in difficult and complicated institutions.

In fact, man does not always learn through trial and error. He often learns through insight. Anyhow learning by insight is much superior to learning by trial and error and we should encourage the children in this process.

Educational Implications

(a) Learning by insight leads to transfer of training.

(b) It saves time and energy because it is quick, efficient and permanent.

(c) It can be used while teaching lessons because the teacher can proceed from whole to part.

(d) The teacher can arouse the motivation of pupils psychologically in the classroom.

3. Learning by Limitation and Observation

We find that children learn much by mere imitation. They observe doing various things. They then try to intimate the same activities and learn many things in this way. Even in school the children learn reading and writing and many other processes by imitation, and most of our behaviour is imitated.

Thorndike put some cats in a cage and studied their behaviour as regards the process of imitation. He came to the conclusion that cats do no imitate. Therefore, he does not give value to this theory. But the apes of Kohler imitated. In fact animals differ in this tendency. There is no doubt in it that man learns a lot by initation.

4. Learning by Conditioning

By conditioning we modify the behaviour of an individual in such a way that the response originally connected with a particular stimulus comes to be aroused by a different stimulus. The classical experiment of Pavlov will make the process of conditioning clear.

Pavlov was Russian psychologist. In one of his experiments he fitted a tube in the lower jaw of a dog. The dog was kept hungry and was offered food at a fixed time. Simultaneously with this act of offering the food to him, a bell was rung. It was natural that the dog secreted saliva when he saw the food. The saliva went into the tube and it was measured. The experiment went on for some days. After that the bell was rung one day but no food accompanied it. The dog secreted the saliva even then. It was observed that the saliva went on coming in the same quantity with the ringing of the bell for some days. The actual stimulus to bring forth the response, *i.e.*, the secretion of saliva, was the sight of the food but it was conditioned in such a way that another stimulus which ordinarily had nothing to do with secretion of saliva began to stimulate it.

Educational Implications. Most of the habits are conditioned reflexes only. Similarly, some sentiments are also conditioned reflexes. The school can exploit this mechanism to a great extent. The children learn to speak with the help of this process. Direct method of learning, the use of audio-visual aids, associating various subjects with incentives are based on this theory. It may be helpful in formulating principles regarding rewards and punishments. It is also useful in the learning of languages.

All the theories explained above help in the process of learning but man does not learn through any one of the theories exclusively. The child does learn through trial and error as the cats of Thorndike did but he does not stop there. Often he benefits from the power of insight but he does not stop there too. He observes and imitates others also—insects, animals, men and inanimate physical forces. Many times different stimuli combine to develop conditioned reflexes in him. He synthesises all those modes of learning and goes on developing.

LEARNING

I.P. Pavlov (1849-1936), an eminent Russian physiologist and a noble prize winner for his work on physiology of digestion, while experimenting on the gastric secretion in dogs observed that any stimulus frequently associated with the presentation of food aroused salivation. This observation led to the famous conditioned response theory of learning. He noticed that an incidental stimulus was sufficient to bring salivation. Then his attention was diverted to the possibility of producing saliva to an unnatural stimulus.

Likes trial and error, conditioning deals with certain basic principles of learning process. It holds that the formation of SR connection, its strengthening or weakening depends upon association between two things.

Presentation of a stimulus arouses a response in every normal organism. When you see a friend you welcome him, when you see a snake you run away from it. Sight of food arouses salivation. Here friends, snake and food are natural or unconditioned stimuli and responses like welcome, running away and saliva are natural or unconditioned responses.

However, when an unnatural or conditioned stimulus is frequently associated with a natural or unconditioned stimulus, the 'O' starts showing his conditioned response to the stimulus. The conditioned response here is equal to the unconditioned responses, *i.e.,* saliva. In other words, saliva is the natural response to food. If food is associated with bell for several trials, bell alone brings out saliva. In short, due the association between the unconditioned (Food) and conditioned stimulus (Bell) the 'O' responds to the conditioned stimulus (Bells) in the same way (Saliva) as he responds to the unconditioned stimulus. This is called conditioned response learning. In case of Pavlov's dog, bell is the conditioned stimulus (CS) and Saliva is the conditioned response (CR).

Conditioning is supposed to be a process by which a response (Saliva) is attached to a stimulus (bell) different from the one which originally elicits that response. In simple words, a response is said to be conditioned when some stimulus other than the already effective one comes to arouse of modify it for the establishment of a definite stimulus response connection. A non-effective stimulus, therefore, brings an effective response due to conditioning. This pattern of behaviour is observed when learning by conditioning is complete.

The nipple in the mouth of an infant in an unconditioned stimulus and sucking is an unconditioned reflex. But when the sight of the bottle produces sucking response in the baby, it is called conditioned response. Similarly, happiness at the sight of a friend's letter, fear for the doctor, crying at the sight of water, are certain examples of conditioned responses. When an injection needle pricks the muscle of the baby he cries out of pain. Next time when only he sees the needle or the doctor, he cries with the anticipation that the needle would now prick him again. Here the pricking of the needle is the U.S. crying is the U.R., sight of the needle is the C.S. and crying is C.R. Strengthening of the SR connection therefore depends upon the association between two stimuli.

CLASSICAL CONDITIONING

The conditioning technique developed by Pavlov is famous as the classical conditioning technique. The following experiment conducted by Pavlov on a dog is known as classical conditioning experiment. Pavlov made a minor surgical operation in the cheek of the dog to measure the rate of salivation. The animal was kept in a sound-proof room. During the experiment a servant was feeding the dog. Pavlov to his great surprise noticed that one day, only the sound of the footsteps of the servant made the dog to salivate. The very incident created such an interest in Pavlov that he devoted most of his time to study the phenomenon of conditioning.

To start with the experiment, when food was placed in the mouth of the dog, it brought saliva. On other occasions, only a bell was rung, but it did not bring any salivary response from the dog.

Then Pavlov rang the bell first and after an interval of 5 seconds placed the food in the mouth of the dog. In this first trial bell alone did not bring saliva until food was not placed in its mouth. Only after the repetition of bell-food sequence for several days, when the dog could connect the bell with the food and anticipated food at the sound of bell, did it salivate to the bell only, even before seeing the food. Pavlov noticed that the dog salivated to the presentation of bell only after several trials when learning by conditioning was firmly established. From this Pavlov inferred that stimulus response connection has been established. The dog has finally learnt to respond to the C.S. This technique of establishing a response to a conditioned or artificial stimulus is called classical conditioning process. Pavlov, in course of his many experiments, demonstrated that the dog can be made to salivate to any stimulus, however, unnatural and irrelevant it may be. This discovery of Pavlov made a significant contribution to the learning theory.

Pavlov's classical conditioning can be explained by the following pattern, which Pavlov used in his experiment on dog :

1. Natural or unconditioned stimulus (U.C.S.) food. — Natural or unconditioned response (U.C.R.) Salivation
2. Conditioned stimulus (C.S.) —No salivation
3. C.S. (Bell) 5 seconds interval U.C.S. (food) —Unconditioned response U.C.R. (Saliva)

Condition 3 is repeated for several trials until an association is established between bell and food (C.S. and C.R.)

4. C.S. (Bell) —C.R. (Saliva)

In any classical conditioning experiment in the C.S., U.C.S. pattern, the C.S. should always precede the U.C.S. and the time between the two must be constant and very close in all trials. If the time gap is too large! Conditioning may not be established because lack of close temporal pairing of the C.S. and U.C.S. will not be able to establish the association between C.S. and U.C.S. While establishing the salivary response to a tone in one experiement the following observations were recorded:

No. of presentations of sound and feeding	*No. of drops of saliva in 30 seconds*
1	0
9	18
15	30
31	65
41	64
51	69

[From Munn, O.N.L. (1954) Psychology page 118, Time Sequence in Conditioning.]

In this experiment after nine presentations of the C.S. and U.S. in close proximity, conditioning was established. It is also noticed from this table that the number of drops of saliva increased with number of repetitions of the conditioning process.

The strength of conditioning can be found out in terms of saliva and in terms of latency (the time elapsing between the bell and the saliva).

Time Sequence in Conditioning

Usually is conditioning technique the C.S. precedes the U.S. by a fraction of second. Sometimes it is almost simultaneous. As a matter of fact, about 3 seconds give the best result as studies show. It is also found that if we measure the effectiveness of conditioning, the strongest conditioning occurs with shorter latency period, *i.e.*, near about 3 seconds.

The most vital point in Pavlov's classical conditioning technique is that food always follows bell irrespective of the salivation of the dog. Whether the dog salivates or not, does not matter. Food is always presented after bell with the lapse of a very short time interval.

Besides Pavlov, Bechterev, Watson and many more psycho-logists have conducted experiments on conditioning. Wever made respiratory conditioning to belt. Pavlov and his associates have observed certain important phenomena in conditioning which are discussed below.

Stimulus Generalisation

It is a tendency for the CR to be aroused by a similar stimulus other than the stimulus aroused in training. Generalisation in conditioning occurs to a certain class of stimuli rather than to a specific stimulus. Pavlov noticed that when a C.S.C.R. bond has been established by conditioning, a stimulus which is similar to the C.S., can produce the same response and he called this stimulus generalisation. The more similar the new stimulus, the greater is the probability for generalisation and *vice-versa*. If the dog is conditioned to salivate to tone, it will salivate to any type of tone like electric bell, worship bell, college bell, buzzer, ding dong bell and other sounds.

Watson in an experiment on the development of fear in children has demonstrated stimulus generalisation. Albert, a small child, used to play with a rabbit without showing any fear. Watson produce a loud sound whenever the child started playing with the rabbit. After a number of trials, the child started showing fear towards the rabbit, associating rabbit with the occurrence of loud sound. Then the child showed fear in gerenal towards while furcoat, bunch of cotton and to all other stimuli having similarity with white rabbit. Stimulus generalization in conditioning happens usually more in childhood particularly when the child has not developed the capacity of differentiate between two stimuli. This is why, during infancy the baby considers every women to be his mother. This tendency of generalization Pavlov attributed to a spread of effects from the region stimulated to other parts of the organism.

Stimulus Differentiation

Differentiation develops out of generalisation. Though in the beginning mostly generalisation in conditioning is found, the organism can be conditioned to make a response only to a specific stimulus by appropriated conditioning procedures.

Suppose you want to positively condition a dog to a tone of 400 cycles and negatively condition to 800 or 1200 cycles. You present the reinforcement only after 400 cycles tone and do not present reinforcement when the other tones are presented. If this is done for several trials the dog will learn to discriminate between these tones eventually. In this case the animal is positively conditioned to 400 cycles and negatively conditioned to 800 and 1200 cycles. Since it is not given any reinforcement at 800 or 1200 tones, these are not reinforced.

Children gradually learn to differentiate one stimulus for another in their own environment. In the early period they consider any woman as their mother. But gradually, as they grow up, they differentiate their mother from other woman. The woman who fondles, nurses, feeds and takes every care of the child and sleeps with him is considered as his mother.

Discrimination in conditioning has certain utilities in learning. Though usually stimulus generalization facilitates learning making, it is easy and quick, sometimes it also inhibits learning, creates confusions misunderstanding and many emotional problems. Like Albert, if one is afraid of any stimulus which has some similarity with white rabbit, he will have many adjustment problems. Differentiation at this point can prove useful. It can overcome the interfering and inhibitory effect of stimulus generalization. At the same time, if the differentiation is pushed too far, it leads to experimental neuroses. Munn, therefore, remarks "Sometimes as the difference is reinforced and unreinforced, stimulation becomes too small for the animal to discriminate, a nervous breakdown occurs."

Experimental Extinction

Once a C.R. is set-up, if one goes on repeating it without giving reinforcement, it tends to be extinguished. Sometimes people ask, how can one eliminate a conditioned response once it is established? The answer to this is experimental extinction. The process by which a C.R. can be weakened and finally eliminated is called the process of experimental extinction. It is a process by which a well established C.R. is eradicated by repeating the C.S. without the application of reinforcement. Take the case of Pavlov's dog. After the dog has learnt to salivate to the sound of the bell, it will continue to salivate to the bell for a certain period, although food is not given after bell. However, after some such trials when the dog will see that no food is coming after bell, the connection between bell and food will grow weaker, the flow of saliva will decrease. At last, the dog will not salivate to the bell at all.

Similarly, in a study of "The Eradication of a tactile conditioned reflex of man the shoulder region of the subject was conditioned so that is elicited a galvanic skin reflex. Vibration of this region was then repeated without presentation of shock. There was a gradual weakening of response and finally complete elimination".

Internal Inhibition

After the establishment of a C.R. if the reinforcement is not provided check to salivate becomes stronger and stronger. So much so that it becomes inter-natural in nature.

Internal inhibition is a kind of negative learning not to salivate and can be applied to Ebbinghaus's curve of forgetting. But when the inhibition becomes weaker it leads to spontaneous recovery like reminiscence in forgetting. The idea of Ebbinghaus's curve of forgetting was applied to the concept of internal inhibition. It was said that this check or block was something which is acquired, *i.e.*, learning not to salivate. The negative learning not to forget is also forgotton to the same extent. However, this extinction is only a temporary suspension of response because of an internal set.

Spontaneous Recovery

Pavlov was of opinion that complete or permanent extinction of a C.R. is not possible. When the experimentally extinguished response reappears again after a period, it is called spontaneous recovery. This concept can be compared with reminiscence in forgetting. In this process even without the presentation of food, bell produces a few drops of saliva. Pavlov noticed that once the flow of saliva was completely extinguished, after about 30 minutes of rest interval the dog again salivated to the C.S. without U.S. But if again no reinforcement is provided after the C.S., spontaneous recovery will grow weaker and weaker and would at last fail to reappear.

Higher Order Conditioning

In course of his experiments on dog, Pavlov found that once conditioning was firmly established, for further conditioning, he could use the conditioned stimulus as unconditioned stimulus. When the dog is conditioned to salivate to Bell, Pavlov used this Bell (instead of food) as a U.S. for establishing further conditioning. Pavlov was of opinion that a conditioned stimulus can be used in much the same way as an unconditioned stimulus. He stated that more elaborate forms of behaviour can be developed by the process of chain of conditioned response.

First order or original conditioning

Food	—	Salivation
Bell	—	?
Bell	—	Salivation

Second order conditioning

Bell	—	Salivation
Light	—	?
Light	—	Salivation

Third order conditioning

Light	—	Salivation
Colour	—	?
Colour	—	Salivation

The arousal of the same response, *i.e.*, saliva to light by frequently associating it with bell but without presenting the food is called second order conditioning, as it could conditions a second neutral stimulus.

Though Pavlov claimed that a third order conditioning can be possible in the same way he could not proceed after the second order in case animals. However, with human beings, all sorts of complex learning can be possible by the process of higher order conditioning, he asserted.

Negative Conditioning/Unconditioning

Otherwise known as backward conditioning or negative adaptation it is learning not to make a response. The 'O' by the technique of backward conditioning can be made not to show a response to a neutral stimulus. Thus, instead of U.S. (Food) following the C.S. (Bell), C.S. will follow the U.S., *i.e.*, reverse to the pattern of classical conditioning technique, food (U.S.) will be given first and Bell (C.S.) will be presented next with an interval of 5 to 6 seconds between each presentation. As the 'O' will get the reward first it will not have any motivation or need to make a response (to salivate). So the C.R. would not be strengthened. If at all there will be any salivation, it will be marginal.

Many of our bad habits like nail biting, bed wetting, moving the leg all the while, various ticks and mannerisms, thumb sucking, smoking, alcoholism, breast feeding in case of older children, irrelevant fears can be removed, withdrawn by negative conditioning. Various habit patterns can be broken by this procedure. Thus, negative conditioning has valuable implications in practical life.

Whenever the rat proceeds for food, if it get electric shock, it will avoid food. A child who is punished while entering into a river will avoid the river in future. Mann reports that is sexually mature male rat is given electric shock everytime is approaches a female rat, it soon avoids female rats. When cockroaches are given electric shock for running into the dark, they learn to go to the lighted place instead of approaching for darkness. Tigers of Sunderban (West Bengal) over the last decade have killed at least 650 persons officially and the unofficial record is about 1000. The forest department worried over the increase in human deaths introduced something which was new in India, the use of electrified dummies. These dummies which look extremely life-like have been placed at a few corners of the sanctuary. Officials explain that when the tiger attacks the dummies, it gets electric shock and this persuades it from further attacks on humans. The projects officials claim atleast an 80% reduction in the death rate due to this method of withdrawal conditioning.

When alcoholics are given to take alcohol containing a drug which produces violent vomiting, they develop aversion for alcohol. Similarly, for babies who do not give up breast feeding, quinine is smeared on the nipples and then only they develop aversion for breast feeding. Negative conditioning is, therefore, known as aversive conditioning.

Withdrawal Conditioning

Becheterev, another Russian physiologist and a follower of Pavlov, taking animal and human subjects, found that when the 'O' gets a painful stimulation in a part of his body, it withdraws from it. Withdrawal may take place from electric shock, beating or any painful stimulation. Bell or light is presented before shock. After some trials by seeing the light or hearing the sound of the bell the 'O' withdraws that specific part of the body where shock is anticipated.

Experimental Neuroses

In recent times, the phenomena of neuroses has been studied by the process of generalisation and differentiation. If differentiation is pushed too far the 'O' fails to discriminate between two stimuli, becomes completely non-adoptive and is unable to salivate to any stimulus due to conflict. Consequently, nervous break down occurs. The animal suddenly becomes wild. It resents the situation.

An experiment on circle and ellipse can be referred to demonstrate experimental neuroses. When the circle and ellipse became very much similar, the animal unable to discriminate became wild. Physiological changes in respiration, heart beat, blood circulation etc., took place. It showed abnormal symptoms and behaviour disorders.

In experimental neuroses there is a clash between positive and negative forces to or not to salivate. Anxiety neuroses is produced experimentally by this method.

Implications of Conditioning in Practical Life

The contribution of Pavlov to the psychology of learning can be said to be equally important like Freud's as Pavlov as advanced certain concepts like generalisation, differentiation, withdrawal conditionings, unconditioning and experimental neuroses which have tremendous significance in life. In fact, Pavlov's discovery was so powerful that it became completely Pavlovian.

Conditioning works in every sphere of life. Bulk of learning in animals and children develops due to conditioning, language development and different habits, take place because of conditioning. Therefore, it became a key technique not only for physiology, but also for psychology, mental hygiene and therapy. Watson, therefore, remarked that the whole system oif behaviourism he has worked out in terms of habit.

When Watson found that habit is not as simple as he thought, he realized the role of conditioning in habit development. Thus, he remarked, "I had worked the thing out in terms of habit formation. It was the enormous contribution Pavlov has made and how easily the conditioned response could be looked upon as the unit of what we had been calling as habit. I certainly form that point on gave the master his due credit."

Observation of animal and human behaviour led Pavlov and Watson to believe that all our habit patterns, behaviours, attitudes, likes and dislikes, values, etc., can be attributed to conditioning. Conditioning also works as a technique for behaviour modification, elimination of behaviour problems. It is also very significant in emotional learning. Watson and

Rayner (1920) believed that it is the only way by which emotions can be acquired. "Since fear or anxiety is a common symptom of mental disturbance we are led correctly to anticipate that classical conditioning figures in the development of such disorders".

Thus, the sort of dream which Pavlov had, came true to a large extent. Due to the practical implications of conditioning in life it has occupied a very prominent position in the learning psychology even today.occupied a very prominent position in the learning psychology even today.

LAWS OF LEARNING

Thorndike formulated laws of learning. Laws of learning are divided under two parts:

(1) Primary law, (2) Secondary law.

Primary law of learning

Law of Readiness Law of Exercise Law of Effect

1. Law of Readiness. Readiness means a preparation for action. It is a kind of 'action tendency' aroused through preparatory adjustments, sets and attitudes. The fuifilment of this tendency is satisfying and its non-fulfilment is annoying. Thorndike employed physiological terms in describing this law.

Learning is a matter of interest. The learner must be made ready to learn. When a person feels ready to learn, he learns more effectively and with greater satisfaction than when not ready. There are some motives, desire or purpose without which no learning is possible. So, for learning the learner must be mentally ready.

Educational Implications. This law can be effective in the following ways:

(*a*) To arouse the interest and attention of the students by asking suitable questions.

(*b*) This law is useful in arousing curiosity of the students. Curiosity is indispensable for learning.

Motivation is an important factor for learning. It is also based on the principle of readiness. If the learner is properly motivated he will be ready for the work and apply his energies vigorously.

2. Law of Exercise. This law is known as law of practice or law of use and disuse. If any activity is exercised we come to have efficiency in doing it. If it is not repeated we soon forget it. It means repetition of an activity strengthens the nerve connections and on the other hand disuse weakens the bond. In short it can be said that law of exercise as a whole emphasises the need of repetition practice and drill work in the process of learning. Children learn spellings and pronounciation according to this law.

Educational Implications. In educational field this law can be effective in the following ways:

It Leads to Formation of Habits. If good acts are repeated again and again then they become habit. So it is the duty of the teacher to see that children are given a great deal of practice in good activities.

By Practice Handwriting can be improved. Bad handwriting can be improved by practice. For this the teacher can ask the students to do regular practice.

Correct Pronunciation. It has to be learnt by practice and incorrect pronunciation can be unlearnt only by avoiding its repetition.

Bad Habits can be Eradicated. According to Dunlop Bata theory of learning, if the children are made to practice consciously, then they automatically tend to leave their bad habits. For example if a child is in the habit of thumb-sucking or nil-biting (chewing) then he should be asked by the teacher not to repeat this habit consciously. The underlying idea is that he will become conscious of this mistake and avoid the same in future.

The element of forgetfulness can be delayed or avoided because by practice the activities become deep rooted. So forgetting can be avoided to some extent.

Mathematics is dependent wholly on practice. Arithmatical tables, formulas and definitions can be learnt only with the help of practice.

Skills like music, painting, typing shorthand, athletics etc., can be developed to the maximum with the help of this law.

3. Law of Effect. Thorndike has defined this law as—"When a modifiable connection between a situation and response is made and is accompanied by a satisfying state of affairs, that connection's strength is increased, but when made and accompanied by an annoying state of affairs its strength is decreased."

It is also called as the Law of Pleasure and Pain or Law of Satisfaction and Annoyance. The word effect means the effective result of the activity. The child has to perform a number of activities. Every activity has its effect. Some activities end in pleasure and others end in pain. The activities which are associated with pleasure or satisfaction tend to be repeated again and again and the learning becomes more effective. Activities which are assoicated with pain, punishment or annoyance are not repeated and their strength is decreased. The entire system of rewards and punishments is based on this law.

Educational Implications. The educational utility of this law is as follows:

Theory of reward and punishment is based on this law. Reward should be given for desirable behaviour and punishment should be associated with undesirable behaviour.

This law is helpful in forming and developing the desirable sentiments in the pupils. Positive sentiments should be associated with satisfying state of affairs.

Problem Behaviour and Delinquent Behaviour can be improved by associating it with annoying state of affairs (punishment).

Formation of Good Habits. Good habits can be formed in children by associating them with reward, satisfaction or praise. Undesirable habits can be eradicated by associating them with punishment, dissatisfaction and blame.

Memory is also connected with the law of effect. Pleasant things are generally remembered better than unpleasant things.

Interest is directly related to this law. Interest causes satisfaction and satisfaction promotes learning and better learning gives higher satisfaction. In the selection of subjects, books, hobbies games and curricular activities pupils prefer which is interesting to them.

Control of Emotions. With its help, the teacher can control the emotions of anger and jealousy of the students.

Some times it appears that a punishment is more effective than reward. Strong punishment brings about a desired attitude towards learning.

It is also found that it is human tendency to remember certain highly unpleasant incidents better than pleasant incidents.

Secondary Laws of Learning

Secondary laws of learning are as follows:

Law of Multiple Response. This law implies that when an individual is confronted with a new situation he responds in a variety of ways before arriving at correct response.

Law of Analogy. An individual responds to a new situation on the basis of the responses made by him in similar situations in the past. He makes responses by comparison or analogy.

Law of Partial Activity. According to this law the learner has the capacity to select the important from the irrelevant element in order to determine appropriate responses.

Law of Associative Shifting. This law is also known as the conditioned response. A response may be shifted from one situation to another which is presented at the same time. In other words any response which is possible can be linked with any stimulus.

Law of Sets and Attitudes. Learning is guided by a total attitude or 'set' of the organism. The learner performs the task properly if he has developed a healthy attitude towards the task.

Law of Recency. It means that whatever is recently learnt by the child is retained by him. The law may be defined as 'recent acts are lasting'. Hence students should revise their courses just before the examination.

Law of Intensity of Stimulus. To this law, if a stimulus is strong the response will be strong and *vice a versa*. Examinations present an intense stimulus to study and hence bear a positive effect on learning.

Law of Primacy. Learning that takes place in the beginning is the best and lasting. It is a normal saying that 'First impression is the Last impression'. It implies that pupils should make the right start and should be serious from the first day. Teacher should impress his pupils from the first day of teaching. It seems the experiences that are acquired by the child at the primary stage have lasting effect.

Law of Belongingness. This law shows that if a response belongs to a situation, the learning will be more effective. Connection between stimulus and response is natural. The teacher should create natural atmosphere in the classroom and appeal to the natural tendencies of the child.

Factors or Variables of Learning

Maturation. Learning depends upon maturation. If the individual is matured to learn a particular activity, he will learn effectively. If the individual is no mature, learning will not be effective.

Readiness. If the learner is ready to learn a particular activity he will learn better and quickly.

Attention and Interest. If the learner is motivated to learn a particular task he will take more interest in the task with full attention and hence will learn that task better.

Capacity. The greater the capacity for learning a person has, the better will be the learning.

Memory. A learner who has good momory will learn quickly and effectively.

Mental Health. A child who is mentally healthy *i.e.,* free from frustrations, conflicts, anxieties and worries will learn better.

Motivation. Motives like reward, completion, level of aspiration, success and punishment etc., are powerful incentives to the learner for better learning.

Perception and Sensation. Perception and sensation are the basis of all cognitive learning. The stronger the power of perception, the greater the amount of learning.

Fatigue. Fatigue causes boredom and indolence and hence has negative effect on learning.

Food and Drugs. Food also affect learning. Poor diet, alchoholic drugs, tobacco and addictive items adversely affect learning.

Will. Will to learn is an important factor of learning, and it arouses, sustains and regulates the pattern of activity, and leads to better attention, better motivation and hence better learning.

Practice. 'Practice makes a man perfect' is a well known proverb. Learning is more efficient when practice is distributed at intervals over a period of time when it is considered in one period as in cramming.

Timely Testing. Occasional and periodical testing motivates the pupils to be regular in their studies. If the pupils are regular in studies they can learn better. Moreover through tests the learner knows his exact achievement, his accomplishment and there is little scope for under estimation.

Time of Learning. Experiments have shown that there are significant variations in learning efficiency during different hours of the day. It has been established that morning and evening hours are the best hours for study. During the day there is decline in the mental capacity due to noise.

Guidance. Guided learning is always better than unguided learning, Guidance saves times and energy of the learner, eliminates wastage and stagnation. But too much guidance should be avoided so that student may not learn the habit of remaining dependant upon teachers.

Vigorous Application. Slow learning is seldom efficient. Learning vigorously is a great asset and it pays much. The students should be taught to work whole heartedly. They must put their heart and soul while learning something.

Knowledge of Result. Knowledge of result particularly the specific knowlege of progress of the learner improves his performance, motivates him for greater learning and serves as an incentive towards increased effort.

Pleasantness of Task. Generally pleasant tasks are learnt quickly than the unpleasant tasks.

KOHLER'S INSIGHT LEARNING THEORY

According to German Getalt psychology Kohlers learning is insight. Insight is a important constituent in the solution of problems and is found in the higher class of animals and human beings. It is the best method among the methods of learning.

According to Kohler a person can deduce the solution by insight if he perceives the situation as a whole. Kohler, prepared some simple problems for experiments with dogs, hens, monkeys and chimpanzees. In an experiment a hungry animal was released from the house while some food was placed behind the fence adjoining the wall. Both the dog and the hen trotted around in the vicinity of the wall but as soon as they found the way out they made their exist and reached the food. This perception of the change in the meaning of the wall in insight. Bofore the insight the wall was an insuperable obstacle, but after insight it was not longer an obstacle but an object necessitating of new relations, the discovery of new patterns and the formation of new organisations.

The most famous experiments conducted by Kohler in relation to insight were those that were carried out on chimpanzees. Some bananas were placed outside the cage of a chimp called Sultan, who was then given two sticks so cinstucted that they could be fitted together. Sultan tried to pull the bananas with the sticks, an effort which he kept up for an hour, but he got tired of the attempt and gave it up for playing. While playing he brought the two ends together and suddenly he had an idea which resulted in his fitting the smaller stick in the hole of the bigger one. He then used the two together to draw the banana inward. The two sticks disintegrated but he fitted them together again. He then pulled in everything within reach as if he were trying out his discovery. The next day he took far less time to fit the two together. It is a peculiarity of insight that once the solution is learnt, it is not forgotten though its memory may become hazy with the passage of time.

The above experiments make it quite obvious that learning by insight has certain characteristics of its own. They are briefly as follows:

1. Insight is sudden.
2. Insight alters perception.
3. Old objects appears in new patterns and organisation by virtue of insight.
4. Insight is relative to the intellectual level. The higher species of animals including human beings have more insight than the members of lower species.
5. In insight understanding is more useful than dexterity of hands.
6. In Woodworth's opinion, insight is sometimes hindsight and at others it is foresight. The quote him, 'Foresight is seeing the way to the goal before taking it our perceiving the uselessness of a certain lead without trying it and hind-sight is observing that a lead is good or bad after trying it. When the whole situation is clear and above board, there is a good chance for foresight, but when important characteristics of the situation have to be discovered by exploration and manipulation, hindsight is the best we can expect.

7. Some psychologists ray that learning by insight is associative learning. Insight appears suddenly after the manipulation of thought or objects for a small thought significant length of time.

8. Previous experience is of assistance in sight, though its excess does not necessarily increase insight because organised perception too is an essential factor in learning.

9. If the pieces essential for the solution of the puzzle and present together when perceived, insight comes about earlier.

10. Maturity also affects insight as evidenced by the smoother working of insight in older age than in adolescence.

The above mentioned characteristics of learning through insight apply both the human and animal learning. The solitary difference is the fact that a human being by virtue of his superior capacities of experiencing and understanding; observes relation between various objects quickly and sees the patterns concealed in them with alacrity. He is assisted in this by language. As a matter of fact insight occurs only when the learner perceives the related link hidden in the activity. The learning curve is altered suddenly due to insight. Insight is impossible in an extremely unfamiliar problem, because familiarity is very necessary for insight. A student of literature will have no insight in any scientific problem because he does not know even the a b c of science. When the subject of study becomes a part of life, insight becomes easier. History can be made alive by exhibitions, Geography by travelling and Arithmetic by shop accounts. Fimiliarity is also important besides the theoretical study.

One example of human learning by insight will suffice. A student of Arithmetic tries hard to solve a difficult problem of Arithmetic. He tries many methods but fails to secure a solution. He gives up and lays it aside or goes to sleep. After some time suddenly or when he is awakened the solution suggests itself and he notes it down in his note-book. When he is confronted with similar problems in the future, he will have no difficulty in solving them. The insight method is superior to imitation or conditioned response because both the later methods take more time. It is superior to trial and error in the following respects:

1. Trial and error emphasises the acquisition of motor skill but in insight mental effort is stressed upon.
2. The person keeps an eye on the goal in trial and error and all activity is goal directed, but in insight it is the unconscious mind which exerts the most while the conscious activities are either very few or aimless.
3. While insight depends upon perception, trial and error depends upon sensory motor coordination.
4. Every new problem has to be tackled from the very beginning if the trial and error method is used. On the other hand, both generalisation and differentiation are present in insight, which adds to the possibilities of transfer of learning and the use of old insight in the solution of novel problems.

Students will be permanently helped by the use of the insight method of learning in place of the trial and error method in their study and other daily activities. They will also be above to conserve their energy. Suppose that a person has to arrange furniture in a room. An average person will determine the position of the table by using the trial and error method and shifting the table from place to place. An intelligent person will take up a position from where the whole room in visible, and imagine all the possible positions of the pieces of furniture in an imagined framework of the room and then place the respective pieces accordingly. But this does not mean that trial and error method is not meant for the intelligent. But no means is this so. In many noval situations progress is not possible without it.

THORNDIKE'S TRIAL AND ERROR THEORY OF LEARNING

Trial and Error Theory of Learning. For nearly half a century, one learning theory dominated all others in the U.S.A. despite many attacks on it and the rise of its many rivals. It is the theory of E.L. Thorndike (1874-1949). This theory was given by him in 1898, in his book the *'Animal Intelligence'*.

The basis of learning accepted by Thorndike in his earliest writings was association between sense impressions and impulses to action. Such an association comes to be known as a 'bond' or a 'connection'. Because it is these bonds or connections which become strengthened or weakened in making and breaking of habits. Thorndike's system sometimes has been called a 'bond' psychology or simply 'connectionism'. As such it is the original S—R Psychology of learning.

To quote **K.P. Pandey**—Thorndike's theory of learning is based on the following three elements:

(a) The Stimulus element which involves an environmental event.

(b) The response element which indicates a behavioural act.

(c) The formation of a connection or bond which implies that every stimulus is linked with some kind of response and thus makes for the building block or structure of behaviour. **Pandey** in his book *"Advanced Educational Psychology for Teachers"* further states that the *formation of a bond* (S-R bond) is the key expression in describing the learning theory of Thorndike. When an oganism is said to have learned something, it is essentially the formation of a connection or bond between a stimulus and a response.

Connectionism has two phases:

First phase was before 1930.

Second phase was after 1930 because Thorndike made important changes later on the basis of experiments. We shall examine this theory as follows:

There are four characteristic features of Trial and Error Learning :

1. There is some sort of a motive that arouses or sustains the activity. This motive may appear in the form of need, a problem or a goal. Essentially the equilibrium of the organism is disturbed and this impels the organism to react to the situation in an effort that comes to terms with it.
2. Several different kinds of responses are made.
3. Finally there is a progressive integration and establishment of the reaction by which the goal is achieved.
4. There is progressive elimination of superfluous unsuccessful or wrong form of activity.

The essential point in trial and error is the second point—the process by which the correct response is identified through trying various responses until a solution which permits the attainment of goal is achieved.

The Puzzle Box Experiment. Thorndike studies the character of Trial and Error learning in a number of experiments on cats. A favourite device was his puzzle box used years ago by him for his studies of animal learning.

In one of the experiments a hungry cat was placed in the box and the door was closed. A fish was placed outside the box. The cat was given 100 trials, ten each morning and each afternoon for five days. The cat was fed at the end of each experimental period and then was given nothing more to eat until after the next session. In after opening the door in any trial by jumping or by chance, he went in immediately to the food, he was allowed a small bite. A complete record was made of the cat's behaviour during each trial.

It may be mentioned that besides these cat's experiments which became so common and cheap, it has trained some classical experiments performed by Ebbinghaus on memory and by Brain and Harter on Telegraphy. But these experiments of Thorndike are different from Ebbinghaus experiments w.r.t. two points and those points are that of : *(i)* Motivation, *(ii)* of Reward and punishment. He aid that the world cannot ignore reward and punishment and motivational factors.

As early as 1913, Thorndike wrote, "Both theory and practice need emphatic and frequent reminders that man's learning is fundamentally the action of laws of readiness, exercise and effect. He is first of all an associative mechanism working to avoid what disturbs the life processes of the neurons. If we begin by fabricating imaginary powers and the faculties or if we avoid thought by loose and empty terms or if we stay lost in wonder at extraordinary versatility and inventiveness of the higher forms of learning, we shall never understand man's progress or control of his education."

Criticism. A serious limitation of this theory is its lack of understanding. Thorndike did not consider understanding important. He merely assumed that it would follow as a natural result of well organised learning. He believed that insightful learning, though it did occur, was infrequent.

Educational Implications of Trial and Error Theory

1. Effect of Motivation. It is the most important factor in all learning. Motivate the child.

2. Exercise Patience. Learning by Trial and Error theory is always gradual. The teacher must exercise patience with the child if the child does not show any progress immediately in any learning situation.

3. Make Learning Meaningful. Effect of belonging to a thing should be exploited.

4. Place of Exercise. Exercise has its own place in education and learning. Repeat, give a sufficient drill in some tests.

5. We must learn basis things needed for it in any learning.

6. This theory has drawn our attention to the principle of learning by doing. You will learn only when you do a thing.

S-R BOND THEORY OF THORNDIKE

One of the most accredited among all the current theories on the law of learning is the one presented by Thorndike, in America. Talking of its importance Tolman says, "The psychology of animal learning, not to mention that of child learning has been and still is primarily a matter of agreeing or disagreeing with Thorndike or trying in minor ways to improve up him. Gestalt psychologists, conditioned reflex psychologists, sign gestalt psychologists, all of us here in America seem to have taken Thorndike, overtly or covertly, as our starting point."

Thorndike first presented his theory in his book *'Animal Learning'* published in 1968. The clearest form of his theory is seen in the three volumed treatise *'Educational Psychology'*.

His theory may be understood in a systematic way with the help of three major laws which are as follows:

1. Law of Readiness.

2. Law of Effect.

3. Law of Exercise.

Writing on the subject of the importance of his laws in the action of learning Thorndike says, "Both theory and practice need emphatic and frequent reminders that man's learning is frequently the action of the laws of readiness, exercise and effect." Accordingly, in Thorndike's opinion, man's learning takes place according of these laws.

He drew a learning curve for men and animals and concluded from it that usually the methods employed are similar in both classes of creatures. Until 1930, Thorndike laid particular emphasis on these three laws.

Law of Readiness

The law of readiness describes those situations in which the person who learns either invites the object of his learning or rejects it. Readiness include all those preparatory adjustments which immediately precede the action. Reminding the learning of his past experience mental preparation for the understanding of new things, diverting his attention towards the subject to be learned, the altering of the environment to suit the learning, are all included in learning. This readiness creates a desire for learning and turns the learners's mental attitudes towards the suject to be learned.

In Thorndike's the view law of readiness is active in three following conditions:

1. When a conducting unit is prepared to go into action, its work is quite satisfactory because nothing is done to alter its working.

2. When a conduction unit is forced to act while it is not prepared to do so its behaviour is of a nature calculated to excite anger.
3. The inactivity of a conduction unit which is ready to behave, may be unsatisfactory and any reaction may arise is connection with that deficiency.

Law of Effect

The meaning of the law of effect is the effect of learning in answer to question as the success or failure of learning has very significant bearing on the law now under study. Success brings with it satisfaction and along with it a strengthening of the relation of the facts. Failure increases dissatisfaction and the absence of the relation amount the facts weakness them. Thus, we may compare success to a reward or failure to a punishment and desire to repeat success or avoid failure or the inevitable antecedants.

In 1932, Thorndike propounded a new theory on the basis of his experiments about the law of effect, and this he entitled "Spread of effect." This novel theory postulates that by the activity of learning adjustments are not left unaffected. For example, the son of a businessman is ahead of his class in arithmetic because he has already learnt some accountancy in connection with sales in the shop.

In 1935, Thorndike made some modification in the law of effect, based on experimental findings. He now said the influence of reward or punishment is not equivalent and neither it is paradoxical. The effect of reward is for more influential than that of punishment, the strengthening of associations due to reward is not paralleled by the demoralisation caused by dissatisfaction as possible in order that he may learn with success . Encourage the child when he does some thing and congratulate him besides rewarding him with object of desires in order to bring desirable spirit in his learning.

Law of Exercise

The second law, of any consequence in human and animal learning is the law of exercise, which is based on the laws of use and disuse. The repeated application of an activity fixes it firmly in the mind while on the other hand no psychological reference is intended. The relation is weekened through continuous disuse. Whenever there is an appropriate situation, the activity which is firmly entrenched might take place. This law, taking a cue from this universal experience, emphasises repetition in the activity of learning. Repetitive application of the activity results in the formulation of a habit in the muscles and the nerve fibres of the brain so that there is a facility in its execution in time of need. The element of understanding in repetition was not adequately stressed in Thorndike's law of readiness. For example, it is a rule that if repetition in the memorising of a poem is complemented by an attempt to understand and mutual relate the different stanzas, the learning may be affected with ease. Not so with Thorndike, who considered the mechanical repetition of learning individually sufficient. This type of memorising becomes rote learning highly undesirable thing, and the forgetting of one line resuls in the forgetting of the rest while the recollection of the important makes a clear understanding of the subject-matter and constant renewal quite as important an constant repetition. Thus, Thorndike's mechanical repetition came in for a lot of criticism and he reached by effecting modifications.

Importance of the Major Law

These major laws enunciated by Thorndike are of great practical importance. Very few of us realise the effect which reward, encouragement, praise etc., have on learning. These theories are of importance not only in the teaching of others but also in personal activity to be learned should be created in the learner, be it oneself or some other, because the learning will be greatly expedited. And the meaningful practice of the learnt activity will help its retention in no small measure.

Subordinate Laws

Other five subordinate laws were also mentioned by Thorndike in relation to the three major ones studied above. Though a methodical explaination of true laws as given by Thorndike his later expositions sometimes contain their description while at other occasions they are lacking in it. He does not consider these subordinate laws to be of equal importance with the three major ones mentioned above. These five subordinate laws are:

1. Multiple Response. The first subordinate law is called varied reaction. A person seeks to solve a novel problem placed in front of his in accordance with his instincts and learned behaviour, because his search in conditioned by these two. There are many multiform and diversified responses in behaviour which guide a person in attaining success and makes learning possible. The learner reaches the solution by the variation in the response.

If the activities are not multiform the person would never get the correct solution. The theory of learning by trial and error if founded on multipurpose response and diversified reactions. If a person adopts a particular method of approach but does not change it in case of failure and gives up his attempts or if nothing new suggests, that person will never learn anything.

2. Set or Attitude. This is the second law of learning. Learning is conditioned by the attitude and set of the creature. The response of a person in a specific situation is dependent upon his permanent adjustment in a particular culture. On seeing a figure or idol a Hindu child will bow his head but a Muslim will not pay any respect. Both these responses are affected simultaneously by current tendencies. In an extraordinary situation, the worshipper may even throw the status. The set or attitude decides not only the response of the person but also the object from which he will derive satisfaction or classification. A first class student cries on scoring 50 per cent marks, while a third class student feels delighted with the same score. The reaction of a student on scoring certain number of marks depends upon the set, attitude and the tendency present in him at the time.

3. Prepotency of Elements. The fourth subordinate law of learning is the prepotency of elements. Every problem has some fundamental proponent element. The learner gets greater success if he bases his response on those elements, though this depends on the insight and capability of the learner. This kind of capacity is of great help in though learning. The insight, into a mathematical problems, of a student of this particular subject cannot be equalled by that of a student of languages into the same problem because the student of mathematics will grasp its fundmentals with consummate ease.

4. Associative Shifting. This is the first and last law of learning. The title quite obviously indicates that the position of the response of the learner shifts. This shifting is done in respect of the basic stimulus or some related associative stimulus. To take an example, a dog starts salivating when he sees food, and approaches the bearer with his tail wagging. The result of constant repetition of this phenomenon is that dog wags his tail on the mere perception of the man and the shape of dish. Thus, the response originally directed to the food is now aimed at the man and the dish because both these objects are associates of the main stimulus, the food. Thus, an associative shifting in the response is observable.

5. Response by Analogy. This is the third law of learning and is called the law of assimilation. A person will respond in a manner similar to the one in which he has behaved previously if he finds that similarities between the previous situation and the new situations are none too numerous, the response will be similar of that in the first.

All the law subsidiary and main, presented by Thorndike are important in learning, both for the teacher and the student. They are applied comprehensively in education though all the psychologists are not agreed upon the truth and usefulness usually attributed to them.

The above described laws of learning are not intended to convey the impression that Thorndike's attention was confined only to the laws. Actually, Thorndike paid even greater attention to the practical aspect education and made attempt to absolve the difficulties to the teachers and taught alike. Thus, Thorndike attended to the specific aspects of learning and did not rest content with a general description of the activity. He has mentioned many factors which may assist in learning but which are not implied in and cannot be derived from his laws of learning. For example, he has stressed the following five things which assist in the progress of learning:

(i) Interest in the work,

(ii) Interest in improvement,

(iii) Significance,

(iv) Problem Attitude,

(v) Attentiveness.

To these five. Thorndike added two which in his opinion, are not indisputable. These are absence of irrelevant emotion and absence if worry. In this way, he encouraged practical experience and measurements. He himself conducted experiments throughout his life and made continuous progress in his theory. He is fundamentally a behaviourist, not withstanding his acceptance of the effect of introspection of human being and he frequently used subjective words. He encouraged the psychological revolution in the field of education and emphasised the study of elements according to specific situation.

❋❋❋

11

Individual Differences

No two pupils are alike. The differ from each other in hundred and one respects. They differ in age, sex, hereditray potential, intelligence, achievement, interests, aptitudes, needs—physical, social, emotional and developmental. If there are forty pupils in a class there are forty problems to solve, if the teacher wants to be effective. For example, one child may listen to the teacher's words of advice, the other may not be at all hearing them: one may be a hard worker, the other may be lazy and lethargic: one may do the home work quickly, the other may not submit it even after repeated warnings: one may be intelligent, the other may be mentally retarded.

Causes. Each child is a unique individual and differs from every other and presents individual problems. Individual differences among children are related to their developmental state at any time. The developmental state refers on the one hand to the level of maturation and on the other to the resultant of the process of growth and effects of experiences. The causes of individual differences are:

1. ***Difference in Growth Rate.*** Some children grow rapidly and some grow slowly. Some grow mentally at a faster rate, some at a very slow rate. Some grow physically and mature early; some grow late. The different parts of the organism grow at different rates. Each child has his own growth rate. The result

is the variety of ages that a child possesses. The different ages that a child has at one time may be a chronological age, a mental age, an educational age, a social age, a dental age, a grip age, an organismic age and so on.

2. ***Interaction of Heredity and Environment.*** A large number of individual differences are caused by the intereactive process of heredity and environment. To each child heredity provides a potential and the dynamic forces of environment act upon that a potential in a different way. Let us illustrate how the interactive forces of heredity and environment produce differences in individuals. We may have for the sake of illustration one trait (intelligence) and at one end of the diagram we place the rod measuring the rate of mental matuirty (I.Q.).

3. ***Difference in Socio-Economic Backgrounds.*** Some of the differences are caused by differences in socio-economic backgrounds. These differences are seen in pupils' reaction patterns. Differences in socio-economic backgrounds may lead to differences in diet, cultural opportunities, ideals, attitudes and adjustive actions or in family behaviour habits.

There are three children of the same parentage X or Y each. The hereditray potential for these children A.B.C or for P.Q.R is the same being represented by the equality of height of the cones. But as environmental factors influence members' sets differently, the hereditary potential is realised in defferent amounts or degrees. With least stimulating environments only a part of the potential is realised (A, P) and with very stimulating environments we have full realisation of the potential (C,R) The differences between the six children are due to interaction of hereditary potential and the environment.

Physiological Differences. The layman and the scientist both realise and recognise that differences exist among individuals in the innate ability to learn. A certain, a mongoloid or a microcephalic does not learn with the facility of a normal individual. It is a fact though it may not be obvious that among the pupils who appear to be normal, there are also enormous differences in degrees of ability.

The basic physiological differences may be, for example, due to visual difficulty or hearing difficulty or other sensory disability or glandular dysfunction or dietary deficiency. A child who appears to be normal may be having any or some of these difficulties with the consequent impariment of learning. For example, visual difficulty which is evidenced by rubbing the eyes, learning forward to see the board, tilting the head, hearing difficulty which is displayed by turning one side of the head towards the source of sound, asking that questions be repeated, and other sensory difficulties like speech defects, inattention and listlessness cause individual differences in learning.

Teachers must recognise that some of the individual differences arise because of basic physiological differences. They must recognise that these differences exist and demand that teachers should not force all children to learn at uniform rate. When children begin to show indifference, failure, boredom inattention, tantrums, they indicate through these symptoms that teachers are expecting too much or too little from them.

INDIVIDUAL DIFFERENCES AND EDUCATION

1. Curriculum. In school, the curriculum should be modified to suit the needs of the dull children. Failure to achieve this adversely affects the development of all three kinds of children. Whereas the backward students start playing truant from school the brilliant children find the studies inadequate and turn their intellect to more perverses.

2. Limited Size of the Class. Keeping in mind the individual differences of the students, it is advisable that if they are to be taught properly, a class should not include more than 20 students. With 50 or more students it is impossible to teach them, keeping in mind their specific requirements.

3. Method of Education. It is never advisable or efficacious to use the same method of education in the case of all children. It should be varied to suit and conform to their individual differences and mental requirements.

4. Educational Guidance. Knowing the personal differences between his students the teacher can render them signal service by guiding them in their educational career. It is the teacher who can tell them the subjects they must choose to pursue in their higher studies if they are not to do violence to their natures.

5. Vocational Guidance. Different professions require some specific physical, mental and personality traits of the individual. Hence, knowing their peculiar mental make up and their tendencies the teacher can guide the students in the vocation that they should adopt.

6. Contribution of School, Family and Community in Education. Knowledge of differences among children determines that education in school is not completely sufficient since many differences are due to the family and community. Hence, according to modren educational psychologists, to attain the objective of all round development of individuals, prescribed by modren education, the co-operation of school, family, community and the religious institutins is sought.

7. Individual Training. Having knowledge of individual differences, now many methods of individual training have been devised. In America, the Dalton Plan, Project Method, Winnetka Method, Contract Plan and Activity Programme

Methods have been devised for individual training. A brief resume of the various methods is given below:

(a) ***Dalton Plan.*** In this, children are not taught in class-rooms. They are given subjects that suit their interests and they are given a project that covers a period of 15 days to a month. Such treatment leads to the development of naturality, independence, co-operation and sociability etc.

(b) ***Activity Programme.*** In this method, keeping in mind the interests of the students, activities are prescribed in order to define the curriculum. These activities are based on democratic principles. This helps to develop democratic notion in the children.

(c) ***Winnetka System.*** In this method, the student on his own tries to attain a cretain definite objective and the teacher offers very little assistance. Later on, through some tests, the extent to which the student has attained his goal is descovered.

(d) ***Project Method.*** In this the children are required to do work of every day requirements, such as cooking. stitching, furniture making, etc. And in the process of this work, they are taught novel things.

(e) ***Contract Plan.*** In this, similar to the Dalton method, the subjects of study are determined and similar to the Winnetka method the student's progress is meassured through tests. In this manner it is a synthesis of the Dalton and Winnetka method.

It is evident from the above description that modern education makes proper arrangements for a child's education, keeping in view his peculiar nature and special abilities. In a democratic society every individual has the right to achieve a definite level of development. Hence, even more essential it is that individual differences be kept in mind while educating people of democratic countries.

TYPES OF INDIVIDUAL DIFFERENCES

1. Average Intelligence. The following brief description may serve to make individual differences a simple concept that can easily be grasped. Individuals are seen differing in considerable measure in respect of their general intelligence. It is not possible to send to schools children with an intelligence quotient of below 50. Children with intelligence quotients between 50 and 70 can learn only the very simplest tasks. Even the small schools trouble children whose intelligence quotient varies between 70 and 80. Children between 75 and 90 I.Q., are considered morons and they have considerable difficulty in progressing along with other children in their learning. Generally, 40 to 60 per cent of the children in schools have I.Q.s. varying between 95 and 105, being the children with average intelligence who form the basis for the formulation of the syllabus and curriculum as well as the method of teaching. Children who are either above or below this level of intelligences require special educational methods and conditions. Children with intelligence quotients varying between 115 and 120 are considered brilliant or intelligent.

2. Alacrity in Learning. Difference in the quickness or alacrity in learning is visible not only in children of different ages but also among children in the same age group. This difference is dependent upon their maturity and educational background. Differences in the alacrity of learning result in benefits accruing from formal education.

3. Special Abilities. During the junior high school as well as the college stage, the individual's differences in respect of special abilities, in addition to the general intelligence, are also important since special professions and specialised fields of vocation all need certain specific abilities. Abilities of this kind are concerned with mental, artistic, personality or motor ability.

4. Motor Ability. The individual's movements of the hand and feet and other physical abilities are seen to be very individual, as they do not resemble another's to any great extent. Till the individual attains adulthood, his manual dexterity, rate of muscular movement and resistance to fatigue develops continually. In this manner, the same individual in different ages and different individuals in the same age group manifest considerable differences in manual dexterity.

5. Differences of Background. In school the differences that the children exhibit are the outcome of their different families and their communities. Attitudes towards education and authority differ in each family, culture and class. Some of these attitudes are favourable while others are unfavourable to education. In either condition, the differences of attitudes results in differences among children. Besides these attitudes, the child's emotional, social, aesthetic and moral development is influenced by his family and the neighbourhood.

6. Mental Age. Children of differing ages as well as children of the same age show differences in their respective mental ages. Generally speaking, all students studying in the same class differ according to their mental ages. It has been observed that in the age of 6, differences in mental age range up to 5 years. Mental age and education are intimately related. The child's level of education is determined according to his mental age.

7. Sex Differences. Makneimer and Terman discovered the following differences between men and women, on the basis of some studies:

(a) Women have greater skill in memory while man have greater motor ability.

(b) Female handwriting is superior while men excel in mathematical logic.

(c) Women are better then men in mirror drawing. Faults of speech etc., in men were found to be three times of such faults in women.

(d) Possessing greater linguistic ability women are superior to men in languages, similitudes, word building, compositions and use of long sentences etc. On the other hand, men are superior in physics and chemistry.

(e) Women show greater skill in making sensory distinctions of taste, pain, smell, etc., while men show greater reaction and consciousness of size-weight illusion.

(f) Women are more susceptible to suggestion while there are three times as many colour-blind men as there are women.

(g) Young girls take interest in stories of love, fairy tales, stories of the school and home and day-dreaming and show various levels in their play. On the other hand, boys take interest in stories of bravery, science, war and scouting, stories of games and sports, scouts stories and games of occupation and skill.

8. Nationality. Many studies have led to the couclusion that individuals of different nations differ in respect of nature, physical and mental traits, interest and personality, etc. Such a difference is only natural since their cultural and geographic environment is distinctive.

9. Differences Relating of Learning. In respect of learning, children manifest such differences as past experience and learning, ability in the use of various kinds of apparatus, rate of learning, interest in learning, etc.

10. Difference of Interests. As has been pointed out, the difference in sex leads to a difference in interests. Similarly, factors such as family background, level of development, differences of nationality and race, etc., cause difference of interests.

11. Difference in Respect of Development. Difference in development is in evidence not only in individuals of different age groups but also between individuals of the same age.

12. Economic Situation. Economic differences are seen causing differences in the children's interests, tendencies and character, etc.

13. Personality. Differences in respect of personality have led psychologists to much study, and on the basis of this study individuals have been classified into many groups.

Concerning these classifications of the human personality, it should be remembered that although one specific person may exhibit the main broad characteristics of one class of personality, he cannot be said to belong to only that class of personality as the differences between various personalities are so subtle and minute that it is not scientifi :ally feasible to divide them into classes.

Teacher's Advantage in Knowing Individual Differences

The objective of modren education is the complete development of the child. In this connection, the teacher has the following advantage to derive from a knowledge of individual differences:

1. This can help him to form the proper attitude towards the brilliant and the dull-witted students. It is only

too evident that very good results cannot be expected from dull-witted or medicore students.

2. Any effort to bring all or a majority of the students in the class to the same level is futile since some 50 or odd percentage of them will in variably remain below this level.

3. Improvements in atmosphere, method of teaching, and the apparatus of education cannot lead to the satisfactory teaching of all students since their individual ability to learn differs widely.

4. Knowing the presence of individual differences the teacher is not perturbed at the failure of some of his students since such failure are only to be expected from below-average students.

5. The teacher does not come to expect successes that are impossible. Individual difference makes it clear that all aspects of the personality are mutually related and to develop any one aspect it is essential that all the aspects be developed.

INDIVIDUAL DIFFERENCES IN INTELLIGENCE

Individual differences in intelligence are of three types—*(i)* individual differences in the unselected, homogeneous group, *(ii)* individual differences between groups (*e.g.*, between age levels, sexes, nations, races), *(iii)* differences within an individual. The educational significance of within-group differences is that we have to provide differing, stimulating environment to the gifted and the mentally retarded. The educational significance of between-group differences is to deal with them adequately wherever they exist. The nature of differences within the individual is to improve those qualities he is most gifted with.

Individual Differences Within a Group. For the sake of convenience we may hypothetically divide a group into slow learners, normal learners, mentally superior, bright, and dull and remember that:

1. The bright and dull achieve less under unfavourable conditions.
2. The mentally superior may succeed in their learning ability as far as interests and available educational facilities take them.
3. The normal learner may achieve good success in schools if favourable conditions are provided.
4. The slow learner will reach his limit of educability sooner than the normal or superior one. But if he is given the most favourable environmental background and learning conditions, he is enabled to learn more at his pace of learning.

Teachers and educators will have to remember that individuals evidently develop only the portion of their potential that is required by the environment. We should not let potential at any age to suffer underdevelopment as much as we can in our schools. We should understand that we are not succeeding in our schools because we are not doing out best to check under achievement. Children do achieve less than what their mental ability warrants them to achieve and it is a challenge to every teacher teaching in schools.

The Slow Learner. The I.Q., of slow learners is in most cases below 90 but there are slow learners in the range 90-110 and it is necessary for the teacher to deal properly with them because they tend to profit little from academic work done in the school and show comparative retardation in academic achievement. Recent studies show that such learners, though they reach their limits of educability sooner than the superior, are capable of learning more at their own pace if more favourable environment is provided.

Slow learners with repeated explanations, varied approaches and concrete explanations come up with absurd answers. Explanations, drills and demonstrations seem to have little effect on them. They require about three to four times as many experiences to consolidate learning as the bright or normal pupils do. Even with extra time and repetitions they reach the limit of their ability, buy they do learn in accordance with their mental age. It takes more time, more repetitions, more drill, more demonstrations and can become assets rather than liabilities in the society. The following are the suggestions to deal with them:

1. More repetition of facts in different contexts and drill on fundamentals.
2. To make learning concrete, more illustrations, demonstra-tions, examples, experiences to be given.
3. School work to be related with the occupations the learners will take up as adults.
4. Traits of punctuality, neatness and health to be emphasized.
5. Illustrations to be simple and specific, examples to be given from daily life.
6. Very little criticism or sarcastic remarks to be given.
7. Effective motivation in the form of immediate rewards, short-term goals, praise, ecouragement.
8. Promotion to be given on chronological age rather than on achievement. Grading to be done according to personality growth.
9. More schooling, more hours of school work and more years.

The present school system does schooling for the average and neglects the slow as well as the rapid learner. The bright ones are forced back and slow learners are dragged or left behind by declaring them as failures. The slow learner is the individual who is neglected because the teacher can do noting for him. He is ignored totally. But if the school wants, it can do something for him. We have, therefore, emphasized on more repetition, more illustration, more effective motivation, on no censure or blame and on cent per cent promotion so that social or emotional maladjustment may not arise.

Rapid Learners. Many words have been used to designate what we call rapid learners. The gifted. the genius, the talented and the creative are some of the terms used in psychology to designate those who stand at the top level or at one extreme end of the normal curve for intelligence. Gifted is a frequent designation and a certain specific I.Q. range has been alloted to those who are known as gifted people. Scores on intelligence testing ranging from 130 to 140 have been used to identify them. Others scores on special abilities or achievement have been used in conjunction. We have not used the word gifted purposefully here. The word gifted has greater relationship with the natural endowment which we call talent as in gift of the gab. It indicates talent, musical or artistic or of leadership and as such it is not connected with intelligence. The word 'genius' is also not appropriate so far as pupil-population is concerned, because here it is a bit meaningless term.

The class-room teacher has more to do a with rapid learner, that is, a pupil who finds school work rather easy, who is excellent in all school subjects, who loses interest in things in which his agemates are intensely interested, who is superior in character and personality traits as judged by tests or by teacher observers.

Suggestions of deal with a rapid learner we propose :

1. Enrichment of instructional programme: an abundant supply of books, laboratory equipment, illustrative

material for he may select the one needed according to his personal aims.

2. School work to give a liberal background for later professional preparation.
3. Enrichment of daily life experiences and readings to expand and clarify them.
4. Emphasis on development of personality and character traits.
5. More of verbal descriptions and generalisation, less of repetition, study beyond that required for average or slow learner.
6. Skipping of grades commensurate with social and emotional development.
7. Emphasis on well-rounded development and expansion of interests.
8. More permissiveness, freedom and challenge than more prescription of work.

The gifted or the rapid learner is a challenge to the school because he sometimes asks questions which are annoying to the average teacher. If he does not get answers to these questions he becomes bored and his energies turn to undesirable acts. Some educators therefore suggest that educational programme for these pupils should be enriched. We have emphasized the development of character and personality in the fast learners because when success comes with little effort in competition with persons who possess less mental ability, the fast learner is apt to develop egoistic tendencies. Skipping over may be adopted with caution, for it may create problems of social adjustment. Since we want the gifted person to lead the average ones, he should proceed with them and not away from them.

11

Socialization and Its Role

The social development of the child like other aspects of development, proceeds from the interaction of the organism with his environment. Although the readiness of the organism is the first requisite to social interaction, children must still learn to be socially responsive and interactive. The wide differences among children and adolescents contribute significantly to the range of social behaviour in any school-age group. These differences flourish under the influence of democratic practices. The teacher, to be effective with pupils, must recognize these differences if she is to guide each individual in his growth and learning according to his unique abilities and traits.

Biological Nature of Man

All humans belong to one biological family although several distinct races exist. The differences among the races such as blood type, rate of maturation, and psychological needs are not important physiologically. Although we may observe important differences among school-age pupils, far more important are the similarities among them appearing even during infancy.

All normal infants whine when they are hungry and depend upon others for food. No race differences are discernible in maturational pattern, brain pattern, or in the time when puberty or adolescence is reached. Upon this common inheritance of brain structure, man has developed a consciousness of self, social customs, an advanced culture, and a complex civilization. However, the average person does not always recognize this commonality of man. It is certainly present in the findings of scientific studies and in the normal precepts of religious teachings, which emphasize the brotherhood of man.

Nature of the Group

The nature of man leads to the formation of groups, a type of human relationship most useful for study. Group activities play an important role in the lives of boys and girls because through such activities are many of their needs satisfied.

We can distinguish two kinds of human relationships, primary and secondary. Primary relationships are the deeply involved ties the individual forms with his family. In former agrarian societies, most of the individual's relationships were primary. The people with whom the child lived, played, attended school, went to church, and visited were his kinfolk, his neighbors, and others he knew intimately.

Secondary relationships are those in which people are brought together in a common activity, their interest in each other are limited largely to the activity they are involved in as a group. Because populations in the United States are more mobile than ever before, secondary groups have become important, and their study will prove useful to us.

Since the nature of man leads to the formation of groups, the child must learn to adjust to varying secondary groups largely in terms of what each member of the group expects or demands of him. Certain forms of behaviour may be tolerated or even expected in one group situation, while unacceptable in others. The problem of learning to adjust to groups with different expectations and demands makes growing up difficult for the child.

Roles and Social Behaviour. In describing the social development of the child, the sociological concept of status and role are helpful. Status refers to the place an individual occupies in a particular system at a particular time. Closely related to one's status are the different roles one must learn. Society judges an individual's behaviour in terms of the appropriateness of his role behaviour. Role refers to the sum total of the cultural patterns associated with a particular status. Such factors as age, sex, and family relations determine the individual's status, since each status is associated with a role, the individual's behaviour is learned on the basis of his statuses. The individual's behaviour is also judged by society's expectations of what that behaviour should be. In modern society an elementary-school child is expected to behave respectfully to an adult, merely because he is younger and less experienced. Children and adolescents who are disrespectful of their teachers fail to play their roles properly. Boys are expected to be somewhat more unruly or aggressive than girls; if they are not, parents tend to worry about them. On the other hand, overactive, aggressive girls are regarded as tom—boys and their behaviour tends to be discouraged.

From infancy throughout life, the individual learns to play certain roles. Parents, teachers, other adults, and children tend to judge the growing person according to his success in mastering these roles. When the child or adolescent successfully plays the role expected of him, his behaviour is reinforced. When he does not meet the role expectancies, his behaviour is discouraged. These experiences have an important bearing on the child's development of a self-concept. In the home the child may be the center of attention; he may dominate others, and may form an idea of himself as the center of most activities. In his social relations outside the home, however, he may find himself avoided and rejected by other children.

Thus, he withdraws from group activities and assumes a different role from that in the home.

A child develops social roles in activities outside the home by the way he interacts with other children. If he wins leadership and prestige roles and plays them successfully, his confidence is enhanced and leadership characteristics are developed. The experience of participating in group activities and being evaluated by others have a powerful influence on his developing self-concept, the social roles he plays, and the aspirational level he develops.

As children develop physically, mentally, emotionally, and socially they are faced with the task of adjusting their behaviour; old roles are modified or abandoned, and new ones must be mastered. Much of the child's self-concept stems from his success in mastering appropriate role behaviour.

Sex Identification. An important factor in the development of the child's self-concept is his ability to identify with his sex. A boy must learn to think of himself as a male if his behaviour is to be appropriate. Similarly, a girl must see herself as a female if she is to assume her appropriate sex-roles. Thus must children identify with their own sex long before they enter school. Katcher investigated the ability of four-, five-, and six-year-old children to discriminate sex differences. He used a series of colored pictures, which permitted the children to determine sex by their hair style, clothing, breasts, and genital organs. He found that errors in discrimination decreased with age and that there were no significant differences between the ability of boys and girls to discriminate sex differences. Interestingly, he found that clothing, hair style, genitals, and breasts, in that order, made for ease in identification. This study tends to illustrate that young children often respond to sex symbols in identifying sex.

An independent study by Pauls and Smith also indicated that children tend to learn both their own sex roles and what parents expect of them at an early age. An investigation by Rabban explored the influence of social class upon the identification with one's sex role among nursery and lower-elementary-school children. Diverse groups of children differentiated by occupational and community characteristics were studied. Pairs of toys were validated for use as cultural media invested with sex-appropriateness. The results show that boys are more clearly aware of sex-appropriate behaviour than girls in both middle-class and working-class groups. Also, boys and girls of the working-class group are earlier aware of sex-role pattern than are boys and girls of the middleclass group. Concerning age differences Rabban concludes:

(a) Three-year-old boys and girls of both groups show incomplete recognition of sex differences and as a group are unaware of any appropriateness of sex-typed objects.

(b) The fourth and fifth years are periods of growth in clarification of sex role for working class boys, while the sixth year is particularly significant for middle class boys.

(c) Working class girls accept the sex-appropriate patterns by six years of age, but middle class girls do not fully acquiesce to the definition of appropriate sex-patterning even by the eighth year, when all other groups have accepted the social expectations.

Consciousness of Group Membership. Very early in the child's life, group membership begins to function. Favourable attitudes are established toward certain groups while unfavorable attitudes are established toward other groups. It has been pointed out that small children are largely free of prejudices. Certainly no child inherits the prejudices of his parents through the germ plasm. Two questions may be considered about prejudice toward other groups among children and adolescents: When does prejudice toward other groups appear? How is this prejudice acquired?

A study reported by Radke-Yarrow sheds some light on the first question. Using a questionnaire, she obtained responses from adults about the beginning of their prejudice toward certain minority groups. She concludes, from studying their responses, that during early childhood (seven and eight-year-olds in her study), they begin to feel the minority status of these groups. Increasingly, with advancing age, children begin to see their affiliation with one group, while a gap gradually develops between them and certain other groups.

Prejudice toward other groups is learned and is not different from other learnings. It is perhaps more complex and more subtle than much of the learnings involving motor skills and understanding. It seems likely that much prejudice has its roots in stereotyped concepts regarding the role and status of different sub-groups. Prejudice frequently reflects basic personality characteristics, illustrating further the unity of character and personality. This was observed in the findings of one study in which children who were most fearful, least confident and secure, and more suspicious of others displayed the greatest intolerance toward Negroes and Jews.

Awareness of Race. Several studies have indicated that children in America become aware of racial differences at a relatively early age. Stevenson and Stewart used tests to determine children's ability to discriminate physical differences between Negroes and whites. The tests also elicited attitudes toward race. A group of 125 white and 100 Negro children between three and seven years of age were tested. They found a rapid increase with age in the ability to discriminate among the children of both races. White children tended to develop discrimination at a younger age than Negroes, and Negroes tended to assign negative roles to Negro children more frequently than whites assigned such roles to white children. It seems likely that these findings reflect differences in past learning and experiences of the two groups of children.

Cooperative Behaviour. Most of the play of two and three-year-old children is parallel play, with few indications of true cooperation. With increased maturity cooperative play appears, especially when the child has had opportunities to be with older children. Cooperative group activity is rarely understood before the child is six or seven years old. Of course, there is more cooperation among friendly groups than among those less friendly.

As children grow, cooperativeness and the ability to play together without supervision increases. Leadership characteristics are evident even among kindergarten children, the roles of leader and follower varying with the situation. Cooperative behaviour improves as the child advances through the elementary-school grades. The nature and extent of cooperativeness at a given age will depend on the maturation and experiences of the child, and the social climate of the particular situation.

Competition *versus* Cooperation. The relative influence of a competitive and a cooperative social climate upon the behaviour and performance of children was studied by Stendler, Damrin, and Haines. The children's behaviour in painting a classroom mural was compared when they worked for a prize and when they worked cooperatively to create a mural, which if judged satisfactory, would bring a prize to each member of the group. It was observed that during cooperative activity, there was relatively more friendly behaviour, more mutual help, and more sharing of ideas and materials. On the other hand, during the competitive activity, there was relatively more unfriendly behaviour, obstruction of the work of others, and general refusal to share materials.

Although many teachers and adults believe that competitiveness is part of man's hereditary nature, it is important for us to recognize that research findings fail to support this belief. Those who have visited among the Eskimos or Australian aborigines are often amazed at their lack of competitiveness. Mead has pointed out that members of certain tribes in New Guinea are strikingly non-competitive in their relations with each other. It is interesting to note that in the study by Leuba rivalry was found among all children born in the United States, where competition is part of the social structure from the first year of life. No signs of rivalry were observed in the foreign-born children's performance. Furthermore, it has been noted that a child might be highly competitive in one group and quite cooperative in another, depending largely upon the demands and structural composition of the particular group.

It appears likely that the tendency for children to compete or cooperate arises not only from their learning and experiences, but is also intimately related to their self-concept, attitudes, and needs. The child who has unsatisfied needs for love and affection will likely be less able to cooperate than the child who is secure. The parent and teacher should focus attention upon the individual—John or Sally—rather than compare him with others.

Importance of Peers. At no time is the peer group so important to the individual as during the teen years. The peer group provides the teen-ager with a sense of belongingness at a time when conflicting loyalties, identifications, and values make him unsure of himself. Within the peer group the adolescent can acquire the status often denied him in the adult world—a status, which is predictable and based upon values he can understand, and expectations he can fulfill.

The peer group enables the teen-ager to gain social recognition through his personal qualities and achievements, something he cannot get through most formal educational programs. Dating patterns, athletic contests, and other activities build a clear-cut sex role into the self-concept of the adolescent. The boys assert maleness in athletics and the girls compete for prestige through dating and other social activities. In these ways the peer group, far more than the formal school program or even the home, defends the individual through the security of group membership against the uncertainties of adolescence.

Attaining a Satisfactory Role. It has already been suggested that peer activities furnish teen-agers opportunities to attain a better understanding of their sex role. This is a very important developmental task adolescents face. The insecure or rejected adolescent finds social development a most unpleasant undertaking, and may tryout various adjustment methods in an effort to solve his problems. Studies of adolescents have revealed several important facts about their relation to their peers:

1. The adolescent desires the approval of his peers.
2. The importance of peer approval increases as the individual reaches and grows into adolescence.
3. Good peer relations during pre-adolescence are perhaps the best assurance available for good peer relations during adolescence and post adolescence.
4. Pre-adolescents and adolescents like to imitate their peers or those slightly older than themselves.
5. Early adolescence is accompanied by the formation of cliques. These cliques play an important part in satisfying certain needs of adolescents.

Peers *versus* the Home. Because teen-agers frequently find in their peer groups the sympathy and understanding they cannot find at home, peer involvement becomes an extremely important socializing force. The greater the cohesion and solidarity of the peer group, the greater the extent to which it will take over the role of the family in the socialization of growing boys and girls.

The family and the peer group expect conformity to their ways of behaving. If the teenager departs very far from expected ways of behaving, he is likely to be punished, one-way or another. In the family group he will most likely be scolded; in the peer group he may be left out or expelled from the group. In a situation known to one of the writers, a teen-age girl was isolated from her peers because of her firm attachment to the religious teachings of her parents and church-teachings, which prevented her from studying or attending movies on the Sabbath. She was described by her peers as "narrow" and "fanatic," and was virtually without friends among her age-mates. This was an extreme case; ordinarily the group achieves conformity to its ways by effectively creating a climate of opinion, which gently coerces the teenager into acceptance of the group's ideas and ways of behaving.

Unless the parent's standards have become his own, the peer group's definition of situations becomes more important to the teenager than those of his parents. He is playing the role for the teen group—by the teen-group's standards; thus, success and failure is judged by teen standards rather than by the standards of parents, teachers, or other adult leaders. This means that parents today have only 12 to 14 years in which to give the child experiences in making decisions about personal and social development.

Involvement in Community Activities

The growing child lives and learns in his total environment. His behaviour patterns and personality development cannot be understood apart from the cultural background in which he lives and learns. As he grows into and through adolescence, his social world broadens. The family group furnishes the major environmental stimulation during the early years. During the pre-adolescent years the play groups and gangs furnish considerable stimulation. With further growth the social environment broadens so as to include many secondary groups, with the larger cultural pattern of the community exerting an ever increasing influence.

Formation of Groups and Gangs. Teenage boys and girls are particularly interested in forming groups, societies, gangs, and clubs. These appear most frequently among heterogeneous groups, such as those found in the large modern high school. Scientific investigations show that as a rule the members of a gang are likely to be of about the same level of intelligence. They usually come from within a limited geographical area and are very apt to be neighborhood affairs. Individuals are affected by the behaviour patterns of the gang, and tend to influence the formation of behaviour patterns in others by their activities. The group is generally quite similar in its desires, likes, and dislikes; there is considerable social uniformity in its attitudes and ideals. Loyalty to different members of the group reaches a high pitch and may even surpass the loyalty established earlier to such ideals as honesty and truthfulness. It is at this point, in particular, that the teachings at school, in the church, and elsewhere should function.

The structure and behaviour of a gang is molded in part through its accommodation to the life of its members. The groups in ghettos, in suburbia, along a business street, in the small town, or in an industrial village vary in their interests and activities not only according to the social pattern of their respective localities, but also according to the layout of the buildings, streets, alleys, recreational facilities, and the general topography of their environments. These conditioning factors within which the children and adolescents live and develop furnish a setting within which gang behaviour operates. So marked is the influence of such factors as bodies of water, hills, and plant life in determining the location and character of activities, that in some cities delinquent gangs have been classified on this basis.

It is well for teachers and other adult leaders to realize that gangs represent the spontaneous effort of boys and girls to create a society for themselves where none exists adequate to their needs. They derive from such associative experiences satisfactions they do not get under the conditions the adult society imposes—the thrill and zest of participation in activities involving a common interest. The gang functions with reference to these conditions in two ways: it offers a substitute for what society fails to give; and it provides relief from suppression and unsuccessful activities. It fills a gap and affords an escape. The formation and behaviour patterns of gangs furnish a good basis for judging the effectiveness of community and institutional, educational, social, and recreational programs for children and adolescents.

Social-class Influences. Many factors in the socio-economic class group a child belongs to affect his emotional and social development. Some of these factors can be called cultural, since no clear line can be drawn between socioeconomic and cultural influences. Habits of cleanliness, good manners, and tidiness are much more difficult to acquire in a home where ignorance reigns and sanitation is largely unknown. In homes where good manners are of little consequence and financial conditions make it impossible for children to participate in activities with other children of the community, social and emotional development are likely to be retarded. Children in more favorable socio-economic circumstances are encouraged to be tidy, to display good manners, and to attend school regularly. These differences leave their imprint on the child's emotional and social development.

Social-class influences are reflected in parents attitudes toward school and in their expectations of their children's educational and social development. This is clearly revealed in a study reported by Stendler. Interviews were held with mothers of first-grade children prior to the child's entrance to the first grade and after he had been in school approximately two months and had received his first report card. An analysis of the results of these interviews showed significant social-class differences. A child's chance of attending pre-school decreases as one goes down the social ladder. Parental expectations for their children also become less ambitious as one goes down the social scale, although half of the lower class mothers expressed a desire for their children to finish high school. This contrasts quite sharply with the percentage of lower class children who actually finished high school at the time this study was made. Upper class children were more often taught the alphabet, nursery rhymes, and writing or reading before entering the first grade. Also, middle and upper class parents showed greater concern over school attendance and report cards. Evidence shows that such anxieties and concerns affect the growth and behaviour of children and adolescents.

Social-class influences become more pronounced when the child enters junior-high school. These influences may be observed in the cliques children form, the social activities they pursue, and even in the curriculum pattern. The intra and inter-dating patterns of teen-agers closely parallel the clique patterns. In one study of sixteen-year-olds the population was divided into five social-economic classes. A study of dating patterns showed that 61 per cent of the dating was between boys and girls of the same class; 35 per cent between boys and girls of adjacent classes; and 4 per cent between boys and girls separated by an intervening class. There was no dating between members of the polar (extreme) classes. The schools must be cognizant of this condition, if they are to develop an effective social and recreational program. Socialization is made easier when there is increased social solidarity, although this does not lead to a better understanding between individuals from different socio-economic groups.

Membership in Minority Groups. As individuals become affiliated with different groups in school and elsewhere in the community, they may develop conflicting loyalties. This is especially true for members of minority groups, since the larger and more inclusive community organizations and agencies are likely to foster ideals and attitudes dominated by the majority element. For children and adolescents from minority groups, adjustment is difficult because it is fraught with more opportunities for conflicts. For example, the attitudes, beliefs, and behaviour patterns of teen-agers of Greek-born parents, living in a family culture that is largely Greek but located in a third-generation German neighbourhood, would be in conflict with those of other children in the community. Unless the minority group, through family and church, furnish an idealistic and functional program for adolescents, serious conflicts are likely to appear.

Discrimination and hostility directed toward minorities is a major concern of the church, school, and other social institutions. Studies of the formation of attitudes toward racial and religious groups illustrate the principles of learning presented. These studies also reveal some of the unsolved problems of our society. The nature and cause of prejudices will vary with different groups. Prejudices are likely to be found in some degree in most communities throughout the United States. A child growing up in a town where considerable prejudice exists against him as a minority group member, will feel the effects of this prejudice with injurious consequences for his self-concept as well as his concept of others.

Children who are members of the majority group tend to take on the prejudices of the majority group. Frequently teachers and other adult leaders share many of these prejudices. Those who do not are likely to run into difficulty with the members of the community. In discussing a controversial problem, a teacher will feel safe only when he assumes the prejudices of the power—structure of the community. Thus pupils sometimes have their prejudices reinforced by the institutions of the community, including the schools and churches. Some evidence suggests, however, that education contributes to the development of favorable attitudes toward minority groups.

Leisure Activities and Socio-economic Status. A number of studies have shown that different socio-economic groups in the United States have different cultures, although these cultures share a common culture including language, political attitudes, interest in sports, food habits, and the like. Thus, one will find groups of teenagers culturally alike in some ways and culturally different in other ways. An interesting question relating to the interests of adolescents is, What is upward social mobility?

An outstanding feature of the activities of upper-class children and youth is their relative exclusiveness. They attend summer camps where the cost would exclude the major portion of children. They travel to resort areas and stay at hotels patronized by a select group. Often they attend school where only boys and girls from homes like theirs are to be found. They are in many ways protected from the rough edges of life which children from the lower class constantly stumble against. However, they frequently lack the close association with their parents, characteristic of the life of lower-class children.

While the activities of upper-class children and adolescents tend to be exclusive, those of the middle class may best be described as selective. Middle-class children and adolescents are required, because of financial considerations, to use public facilities. They are usually found in the public schools, the public parks, and other public areas. However, a selective process is continuously operating among middle-class children and their parents. The parents try to choose the parks, the playground areas, and the forms of entertainment on the basis of middle-class culture and values. Middle-class parents, especially in modern suburbia, tend to be more discriminating and put greater pressure upon their children to achieve and move ahead socially than do lower-class parents. In suburbia success is usually defined as "moving ahead," failure, as not moving ahead. Parental anxieties and pressures are very great among middle-class families, creating many difficult problems for teen-agers unable to fulfill parental expectations.

The activities of lower-class children and adolescents are generally confined to the areas around which they live. They pursue those activities available to them in nearby playgrounds and sand lots. Welfare services are usually welcomed. Unprotected from the difficulties of life, the boys especially engage in athletic competition and depend upon physical strength and stamina. There is frequently little parental supervision, and usually, few parental barriers to their growth in responsibility.

These differences, although not rigid, are important. The socialization of many lower-class children frequently presents a difficult problem, especially when teachers fail to recognize the nature of parental and peer pressures. The problem of the school is not to attempt to stamp out the influences of the early background experiences; but to enrich these experiences with a variety of worthwhile cultural experiences. This is done by creating a favorable climate for learning and continuously reinforcing the learnings at school.

✱✱✱

Index